How To Enjoy The *Boring* Parts Of The Bible

How To Enjoy The *Boring* Parts Of The Bible

Philip Rosenbaum

Wolgemuth & Hyatt, Publishers, Inc.
Brentwood, Tennessee

The mission of Wolgemuth & Hyatt, Publishers, Inc. is to publish and distribute books that lead individuals toward:

- A personal faith in the one true God: Father, Son, and Holy Spirit;
- A lifestyle of practical discipleship; and
- A worldview that is consistent with the historic, Christian faith.

Moreover, the Company endeavors to accomplish this mission at a reasonable profit and in a manner which glorifies God and serves His Kingdom.

Published April 1991. First Edition.
Printed in the United States of America.
97 96 95 94 93 92 91   8 7 6 5 4 3 2 1

Wolgemuth & Hyatt, Publishers, Inc.
1749 Mallory Lane, Suite 110
Brentwood, Tennessee 37027

Library of Congress Cataloging-in-Publication Data

Rosenbaum, Philip.
How to enjoy the boring parts of the Bible / Philip Rosenbaum.—1st ed.
p. cm.
Includes bibliographical references and indexes.
ISBN 1-56121-067-6
1. Bible—Appreciation. 2. Bible—Study. I. Title.
BS538.5.R67 1991
220'.07—dc20   91-7711
CIP

Dedicated to
Pastor Kent Bennett
of Shenandoah County, Virginia,
who first recognized my gift and
encouraged me to use it.

The first thing
for people to be taught
is to enjoy great things greatly.

AUGUSTINE BIRRELL,
"John Milton," *Obiter Dicta,* 1887

CONTENTS

PREFACE

Have you ever tried to read the Bible through?

Many people think they should, but have never done so. Some have tried and failed; others have never tried. Yet nearly all of them have some idea, however vague, of vast and barren regions stretching to the horizon, filled with the bleaching skeletons of average Christians. These are the boring parts of the Bible, desert lands most feared by those who know least about them.

Some people *have* read the Bible through, but the prospect of doing it again does not fill them with joy. They remember the boring parts, but not fondly or well. At best, they think of them as things to be endured, like difficult subjects in school or dreaded vegetables on the dinner table. If we tell them we have found treasure in the dry places of the Old Testament, they are likely to reply, "Can any good thing come out of Leviticus?" The answer: "Come and see."

For the way to Christ passes through the boring parts of the Bible. "Do not think that I came to destroy the Law or the Prophets. I did not come to destroy but to fulfill" (Matthew 5:17). We cannot fully understand the work of Christ unless we know the Law and the Prophets He came to fulfill. How shall we know them if we always skip the boring parts?

This is a guidebook to that much-avoided desert, the boring parts of the Bible. It will help you to know the desert, to learn how to live in it, to enjoy its beauty, and to find its treasures. For believe it or not, there are treasures better than gold or oil waiting to be discovered in these man-forsaken regions. Won't you come and see?

ACKNOWLEDGMENTS

And what do you have that you did not receive?

(1 Corinthians 4:7)

The Rev. James B. Jordan read the manuscript of this book and made many helpful suggestions. He also assisted me in finding a publisher.

Jay P. Green, Sr., introduced me to the world of Hebrew and Greek reference works and to many fine commentaries and for his permission to quote from the Interlinear Bible.

Jerry B. Jenkins, Carole Sanderson Streeter, and Nina Mason Bergman encouraged me to write this book.

From George Scarola I learned much about the importance of paying attention to detail.

From the late Dick Dabney I learned by example not to fear writing about myself.

Vernon Lyle Johnson showed me that The New American Bible employs different verse numbers in a few of the boring parts.

Bob Case generously allowed me the use of his laser printer.

I am grateful for the use of the libraries at Golden Gate Baptist Theological Seminary in Mill Valley, San Francisco Theological Seminary in San Anselmo, and the Graduate Theological Union in Berkeley.

INTRODUCTION

Is it wrong to call parts of the Bible boring? Some godly people may think, "Even if there are boring parts in Scripture, it is disrespectful to say so. It is true that Elisha was bald, but it was wrong to call him a baldhead.[1] Likewise, it is wrong to call any part of God's Word boring." I believe motivation is the decisive issue here. The youths who called Elisha "baldhead" meant to mock him (and they were punished for that sin). If, in honoring and defending the Word of God, we admit that parts of it are boring, I trust that no disrespect is involved. Those who honored Elisha did not think it necessary to provide him with a toupee.

Another potential difficulty is that by calling parts of the Bible boring, we shall only strengthen some people in their resolve never to read them. "I don't read anything boring," they may say, "and I certainly won't read the boring parts of the Bible." These lovers of excitement should consider the testimony of the Apostle Paul, "All Scripture is given by inspiration of God, and is profitable for doctrine, for reproof, for correction, for instruction in righteousness, that the man of God may be complete, thoroughly equipped for every good work" (2 Timothy 3:16).

If we fail to read the Scriptures which equip us for good works, simply because some of them are not exciting, aren't we likely to cease from those good works as soon as they bore us? He has little experience in the Christian life who thinks that God will never require him to do something dull or monotonous. For example, bringing up children takes first place in the list of good works for women (1 Timothy 5:10). Is there no tedium in mothering? "Is there no balm in Gilead?"[2]

Some people dismiss the boring parts as irrelevant sections of the Old Testament. I wonder how they account for the beginning of the New Testament, for the first twelve verses of Matthew are taken directly from Old Testament genealogies. Evidently God values every portion of His Word, even as Christ values every member of His body. In 1 Corinthians 12, Paul spends many verses emphasizing the importance of each member of the body of Christ. Then he adds, "Those members of the body which seem to be *weaker* are necessary. And those members of the body which we think to be less honorable, on these we bestow greater honor" (vv. 22–23).

One purpose of this book is to bestow greater honor on certain parts of the Bible which have long been without honor. If we can enjoy ourselves in the process, so much the better.

Some may be tempted to say, "In the good old days, no one would have dared to call the Word of God 'boring.'" If only they will review Ecclesiastes 7:10,[3] I will be happy to admit that they are right. For the word *boring* did not come into common usage in our language until recently.[4] Now, of course, in the age of Madison Avenue, it is invoked by every child and used by millions of adults. As the hymn says, "New occasions teach new duties."[5] When new accusations arise against the Word of God, it is necessary to answer those which cannot safely be ignored. May God grant you profit and pleasure from this answer!

PART 1

INTO THE DESERT

1

BREAD IN THE DESERT

It's easy for most of us to admit that there are dull sections of the Bible. The question is, what to do with them?

Let's look at a Scripture verse that can help us to appreciate the boring parts: "Man shall not live by bread alone, but by every word that proceeds from the mouth of God" (Matthew 4:4). If a Christian were to take this statement at face value, he would not despise or ignore a single inspired word of God. Much less would he ignore whole chapters and books of the Bible. Rather, he would honor and respect the entire written revelation, as did his Lord and Savior. Christ always displayed profound reverence for the Scriptures,[1] and He spent His life fulfilling them, no matter how obscure or irrelevant they seemed to others.

"Ah!" you may say, "Matthew 4:4 obligates me to read the boring parts, not to delight in them. You can increase my guilt, no doubt, but where's the joy you promised?" This brings us to the crux of the matter. God has said that we are to *live* by every word of God. Now, what is God's idea of life? Did He say it is "solitary, poor, nasty, brutish, and short"?[2] Did He say it is "a tale told by an idiot, full of sound and fury, signifying nothing"?[3] No. He said that He created life, that He is the Lord of life, that He has life in Himself. This life, which He desires to share with us, is eternal, abundant, and triumphant. Therefore, to live is to be like God, to share in His life and His joy forever. And we are to live by every word of God, including the boring parts of the Bible.

Does it seem ridiculous to say that the boring parts are essential to our spiritual health? Consider Deuteronomy 8:3 (the passage Christ is quoting in Matthew 4:4). It tells us that God gave the Jews manna to teach them that every utterance (or every thing) from the mouth of God is as essential to us as bread. What has modern man learned about the staff of life? After a generation of infatuation with white bread, we have discovered that whole grain bread is good for us. The body needs the indigestible fiber of the whole grain to function at its best. Of course, no one eats only fiber or bran, but avoiding them completely leads to poor nutrition. So it is with the boring parts, which are (I trust you will agree!) the least digestible portions of Scripture.

"So what are you saying? That a Christian must eat bran muffins for breakfast and read the begats while he's at it? Is that your idea of the 'abundant life'?"

Well, not quite. What I am saying is that we need to care for our souls as well as our bodies, and that God designed the food for our souls as carefully as He designed the food for our bodies. If you like white bread, fine; just make sure that somehow you get some fiber in your diet. If you prefer the exciting parts of the Bible, that's fine too, as long as you sprinkle some boring parts into your reading. Your body will be healthier if it gets a little fiber every day, and your spiritual life will be more robust as you take in the boring parts. Many people who were raised on white bread are satisfied now with bread from whole grains. Who knows? In time you could acquire a taste for the whole Bible.

Two Views of Scripture

Let's look at it another way. Some people complain about the Bible. They say it is too long, hard to understand, boring, poorly organized, and even contradictory. Their view of Scripture is like the world view of the Roman poet and philosopher Lucretius:

> The universe was certainly not created for us by divine power: it is so full of imperfections. In the first place, of all that is covered by the wide sweep of the sky, part has been greedily seized by mountains and the woodland haunts of wild beasts. Part is usurped by crags and desolate bogs and the sea that holds far asunder the shores of the lands. Almost two-thirds are withheld from mankind by torrid heat and perennial deposits of frost.[4]

How different this is from the biblical view of the world: "Then God saw everything that He had made, and indeed it was very good" (Genesis 1:31)!

Praise the Lord from the earth,
You great sea creatures and all the depths;
Fire and hail, snow and clouds;
Stormy wind, fulfilling His word;
Mountains and all hills;
Fruitful trees and all cedars;
Beasts and all cattle;
Creeping things and flying fowl;
Kings of the earth and all peoples;
Princes and all judges of the earth;
Both young men and maidens;
Old men and children.
Let them praise the name of the Lord.
(Psalm 148:7–13)

Is your view of Scripture more like Lucretius' view of Creation—or God's?[5] For you to rejoice in the Bible as the psalmist rejoices in the earth, you must find a way to love the boring parts.

It's not so hard to do. If a city dweller can learn to love the desert, you can learn to love Leviticus, for the central metaphor of this book is that the boring parts are the desert places of the Bible. They are not, I hasten to add, an endless expanse of lifeless sand dunes, but a desert of sagebrush and cactus flowers, eagles and armadillos, sandstone cliffs and natural arches, petrified trees and disappearing rivers—in short, a desert like much of the American West.[6] There are many things we need to learn about this desert, for to know the boring parts is to love them. But before we get the lay of the land, let's take a closer look at our opening Scripture.

The Benefits of Desert Life

Where were Moses and Jesus when they said, "Man shall not live by bread alone, but by every word that proceeds from the mouth of God"? They were both in the desert. Moses tells the people in Deuteronomy 8:3 that God led them through the desert to humble them and to test them, to know what was in their hearts. The people, as you may remember, had some trouble passing this test, but God did not make the test easier. He did not lower His standards. He waited until the people were ready to follow His lead. Then He brought them into the Promised Land, and none of their enemies were able to stand before them.

Many Christians, as they come out of Egypt, hope to helicopter from the Red Sea to New Jerusalem. They want nothing to do with the

Law, the desert, or the Amalekites. They want the abundant Christian life, and they want it now. However, they are not the first people to seek a short cut to the Promised Land. The original group did not prosper;[7] and their modern successors, it seems to me, are not overwhelming the enemy. God's ways are surer than our ways, and they are usually slower as well. He brings us into the desert of the boring parts to know what is in our hearts and to prepare us for what's ahead. If we rebel and set out on our own, whom should we blame when trouble comes upon us?

Jesus quoted Deuteronomy 8:3 in order to resist the devil. With that verse He overcame the temptation to forsake the leading of the Holy Spirit. If you have been led by the Spirit into the wilderness of the boring parts, no doubt the tempter has come to you, saying, "If you are a child of God, turn from these stony parts to something nourishing, like Mark or Philippians. Don't be an idiot; it could take you forty days to reach the book of Joshua.[8] What a waste of time you could be using for the Lord! Take my advice, and get out of the desert. You deserve a break today." The trouble is, if we take his advice, we lose the blessings the Lord has prepared for readers of the boring parts.

The people whom God brought out of the desert were tough, alert, not easily distracted, and able to overcome every tactic of their foes. They were able to build a new nation for God. If we could learn, in every area of the Christian life, to follow the Spirit instead of the serpent, to wait on the Lord no matter how long, to finish each task no matter how hard, we also would be victorious in the cause of Christ. Reading the boring parts with clenched teeth will not make us like Caleb and Joshua. However, accepting all of God's Word as good, and honoring (and even reading!) every part of it, is a very useful step toward the kind of Christian character that is not tossed about by every wind of doctrine.

Some years ago, my wife and I met an intelligent, well-educated couple in church. One evening over dinner they confided to us something that troubled them. Someone had told them, "Jesus might have been a cripple." When I said that dozens of Scriptures refute that notion, they seemed surprised. Not being familiar with the boring parts, or not knowing how to use them, they did not realize that God requires perfection in each atoning sacrifice. The Passover lamb, the sin offerings, and the sacrifices on the Day of Atonement all had to be without blemish.[9] No animal could be offered to the Lord that had any noticeable defect.[10] Moses said that a man, though otherwise qualified to be a priest, "shall not go near the veil or approach the altar, because he has a defect."[11] How then could Christ our Passover, Christ our great High Priest, be deformed? The Messiah had to be without blemish, both morally and physically. In other words, He had to be perfect, as God is perfect, in order to satisfy God's judgment on our sin. This is, of course, a doctrine to be found in the New Testament, but it may be more fully understood and applied by those who know their boring parts.

Counting the Cost

Are you willing to consider this revolutionary doctrine, living by every word of God? Jesus said we should count the cost before taking up the cross. Let us count the boring chapters of the Bible. Believe me, there aren't many areas of the Christian life where you can so accurately determine the price before taking the plunge!

My definition of the boring parts is a rather restricted one. I exclude any passage that either relates action or stimulates the modern reader to useful meditation. Therefore, I do not consider either the stories or the secular laws of the Old Testament as genuine boring parts. The stories have human or historical interest for us. The civil and criminal laws of the Jews we can compare to modern codes of law, thereby gaining an insight into their culture and way of life (not to mention our own). We may not be thrilled by all these laws and stories, but we should be able to relate to them in some capacity.

It is much harder for us to relate to lists of names, to descriptions of objects and buildings and portions of land, and to laws and rituals of Old Testament worship. These are what I call the boring parts of the Bible. Most of them are found between the giving of the Ten Commandments in Exodus 20 and the journeying of the Jews in Numbers 10. In other words, the end of Exodus, the book of Leviticus, and the beginning of Numbers constitute the great desert of the boring parts. (The only other extended boring parts are found in 1 Chronicles and Ezekiel.)

I trust that no one who finds life interesting would consider Genesis or the first half of Exodus dull. Thus, most readers can reach the great desert without too much difficulty. After passing through that forbidding region, there are certainly some boring chapters to be encountered, but they are interspersed among some of the most exciting stories in the Bible. In Numbers 10–36 we find, for example, the sending of the spies, the rebellion of Korah, and the misadventures of Balaam.

I do not include the book of Deuteronomy among the authentic boring parts because it consists of sermons and exhortations which Moses gave to the children of Israel. A sermon is, or should be, a word which the hearer can absorb and digest. Whether a sermon requires more or less rumination from us, it must be digestible in order to be edifying.

Having always found that Moses' sermons meet this standard, how shall I call them boring? (To tell the whole truth, Deuteronomy has long been one of my favorite books of the Bible.)

The book of Joshua is predominantly boring from chapters twelve through twenty-one, but there are several interesting passages to be found there. In fact, I cannot find two consecutive chapters in Joshua without something stimulating in them. If we ignore chapters twelve through twenty-one, we shall have to live without Caleb's amazing conquest, the story of Caleb and Achsah, the daughters of Zelophehad, the survival of the Canaanites, the second sending-out of scouts, and the cities of refuge. Our strength is certainly small if we cannot tolerate even one boring chapter at a time in order to gain such treasures!

From this bird's-eye view of the boring parts, we can see that the desert is not endless and that it contains many delightful oases. If our rate of travel is three chapters per day, I believe there is only one place (Leviticus 1–7) where we will have to pass two days and two nights without any visible water. I count nine other places where we must spend a day and a night in arid country, but only four of these are in the great desert.[12] The other five are located far off in 1 Chronicles and Ezekiel.[13] It seems to me that any seasoned traveller, spending only two consecutive nights without water in a year-long journey, would have little reason to complain. The prospect of passing through dry lands on nine other days scattered singly through the year would hardly daunt him. In other words, an ordinary pilgrim with a little motivation, a little grit, and a little preparation can feel confident about accomplishing this journey.

What enabled so many American families to make the arduous journey to California and Oregon in the days before the railroad? No doubt the more adventurous souls looked forward to the pure physical challenge of crossing the country, but most of the settlers simply wanted a better and richer life for themselves and their children. To obtain it, they were willing to endure hardship for a season. (You will be happy to hear that only a tiny percentage of them turned back or perished on the trails.) In the same way, a few of those who tackle the boring parts are simply looking for a challenge or a road less travelled. Most of them are ordinary Bible readers who are responding to the Lord's command to live by every word of God. They do not want to pass through the desert just to be able to say they did it, but they are willing to be led by the Spirit of God, and they are attracted by the promise of a deeper and richer Christian life. It is for them, to help them accomplish their journey with joy, that this book is written.

2

FINDING WATER IN THE DESERT

It's easy to emphasize the differences between our day and the times when the Bible was written. You can't meet a woman at a well in a culture where every home has running water, and you can't feed the five thousand if you're preaching to them by satellite. That was then, we start thinking, this is now. That was the age of miracles; this is the age of technology. We can't expect primitive miracles like getting water from a rock, because we have modern miracles like swimming pools and fire hydrants. We can't live off the promises of God in suburbia the way the Jews did in the wilderness. You can't have Big Macs and manna too. Yet modern life has deserts which Moses never dreamed of, and modern Christians need God's supernatural help in order to pass through them. We must confine our remarks to the desert of the boring parts, but the principles which apply there are valid in other areas of life as well.

For most of us, the passage of time has only made the boring parts more forbidding and impassable. You may have running water and all the latest conveniences, but chances are the boring parts seem a lot drier to you than they did to the people who followed Moses. You don't need to pray to get a drink of water, but you do need to pray if you're going to get fulfillment from Leviticus and Numbers. That's where the promises of God come in. The Lord has made many promises concerning the desert, and we can apply them to the desert of the boring parts.

> When the poor and needy seek water, and there is none,
> And their tongues fail for thirst,

I, the Lord, will hear them;
I, the God of Israel, will not forsake them.
I will open rivers in desolate heights,
And fountains in the midst of the valleys;
I will make the wilderness a pool of water,
And the dry land springs of water.
I will plant in the wilderness the cedar and the acacia tree,
The myrtle and the oil tree;
I will set in the desert the cypress tree and the pine
And the box tree together,
That they may see and know,
And consider and understand together,
That the hand of the Lord has done this,
And the Holy One of Israel has created it.
(Isaiah 41:17–20)

Could this happen to you in the desert of the boring parts? Yes, it could. And when it does, you'll see the promises of God are as living and powerful today as ever they were at Sinai or Mount Carmel.

Grow in Wisdom

There are three basic strategies for finding water in the desert. Before we discuss them, however, we need to talk about wisdom. For the object of this book is not to make you learned in the trivia of the boring parts. Rather it is to help you grow in wisdom and grace. The boring parts are a unique means which God has provided for our spiritual growth. Let us not misuse them.

It's easy to become proud of one's knowledge of the Bible, whether it be little or great. God gives us the bread of His Word to nourish our souls, but pride turns it to stone. The word-made-stone can feed a stony heart, but not a hungry soul. If we desire spiritual growth, to grow in godly wisdom rather than worldly knowledge, we must understand how a man gets wisdom. The first thing, of course, is to ask for it, as Solomon did.[1] James gives us excellent advice on how to do this: we must "ask in faith, with no doubting," believing that God "gives to all liberally and without reproach" (1:5–8). If you find it hard to believe that God will give you wisdom, confess your unbelief and ask Him to help you overcome it. Once you have asked, you have only to obey and be patient, for "the fear of the Lord is the beginning of wisdom" (Psalm 111:10).

The first chapter of Daniel shows us how the fear of God leads to wisdom. Daniel and his three friends were carried off to Babylon with other promising young Jews before the destruction of Jerusalem. Anyone could see that the way to advancement for these young prisoners was when in Babylon, do as the Babylonians do. Was not even Jeremiah saying that the exiled Jews should settle down, prosper, and pray for the land of their captivity? Many a worldly young man was only too ready to take this advice without heeding the rest of God's Word. Since Daniel and his friends are singled out for their devotion to the dietary laws of the Jews, we can reasonably assume that the rest of their company disobeyed those laws. (We're not the first of God's people to ignore the boring parts!) While these four were faithful even in what they ate, the others were probably studying hard and scrambling for advancement. It is worth noting that the Bible says not a word about Daniel and his friends studying or going to class. Presumably they did, but that was not the source of their wisdom. "As for these four young men, *God gave* them knowledge and skill in all literature and wisdom; and Daniel had understanding in all visions and dreams" (Daniel 1:17, emphasis added). When they stood before King Nebuchadnezzar, none of their peers could compare with them. So the godly were chosen to serve the king, and we hear no more of their worldly companions.

If you want to get wisdom from the boring parts, you need to be faithful to God in the little things in life. What has Daniel's story got to do with the boring parts of the Bible? Plenty. Wisdom is still the gift of God today, and God still gives it to those who obey Him as Daniel did. Where do you have an opportunity to be faithful to God and different from the world, or different from believers who are following the world? That's the situation in which to prepare your heart for the gift of wisdom. Obeying God in those little things (which are big in His sight) will do more to enhance your studies than reading this book. For it's the gift of wisdom that really opens the Bible to us and makes it exciting. Without that gift, our best efforts amount to little.

We must guard against turning God's good news into condemnation. How easy it is to conclude, "If wisdom comes through obedience like Daniel's, I can forget about wisdom. Woe is me, for my sins are ever before me!" Which of us cannot say this? Perhaps that is why James tells us that God gives "liberally and without reproach" to all who ask him for wisdom. Yes, you have weaknesses and you have sins, and you need to fight the good fight against them. But remember that God knows how to emphasize what is positive in the lives of sinners who turn to

Him. When an unruly child asks his father to help him learn obedience, even a foolish parent will try to encourage him. How much more, then, will your Father in heaven encourage you to seek wisdom! (If you still have doubts on this score, I suggest you meditate on Psalm 130.)

Is it your goal to grow in wisdom as you study the boring parts? Then take heed to obey God in the little things in life. By doing so, you will surely benefit from the three strategies outlined below.

Strategy 1: Travel Light and Travel Fast

This strategy is mostly for beginners and the faint of heart, but once in a while everybody needs to use it. Those who travel light and travel fast speed across the arid sections and linger at the oases. In doing so they come to know and delight in the many stimulating stories scattered among the boring parts. People who never enter the desert will never discover the budding of Aaron's rod or Caleb's conquest of the gigantic children of Anak.[2] The knowledge of these and many other wonderful events is the first fruit harvested by new readers of the boring parts. You will find it refreshing as the waters of Elim and abundant as the grapes of Eshcol. You may not always think the oases worth the trek through the arid lands around them, but I promise you that often you will.

"Well then," you may be tempted to retort, "why not just fly into the oases and see the desert from the air? Why trudge every inch of the way, as if we were still living in the age of the camel and the oxcart?" One of the joys of coming to an oasis is that you arrive there tired and thirsty. You can't really know the place if you hop out of an air-conditioned tour bus, take a few snapshots, and zoom away to the nearest golf resort. But even if you think that kind of travel is the real thing, there are other factors to consider.

Unless you read every word of God, you are sure to miss some of the exciting parts. No book in the world can guide you to every interesting verse and allow you to skip every boring one. Even if someone guides you to Jabez (two interesting verses among nine boring chapters in 1 Chronicles), you will miss the conquest of Gedor and the defeat of the Amalekites at the end of the same chapter.[3] There are just too many places where stimulating verses are dropped into the boring parts, as precious gems are scattered here and there in the crust of the earth. You won't find diamonds in a sand trap, and you won't find all of God's gems unless you are willing to walk through the desert and look for them.

Have you ever had the experience of seeing a fine painting on its stretcher and then seeing it again in a beautiful frame? The difference can be truly astonishing. Paintings aren't framed just for their protection; they are framed to enhance their beauty. That's why skilled craftsmen spent many, many hours carving frames appropriate for the works of the old masters, and that's why those frames are highly valued by connoisseurs today. The boring parts are (among other things) an elaborate frame for the stories they surround. He who would see all the beauty in the stories must see them in the frames God made to go with them.

There's not much to learn about traveling light and traveling fast. You just put your brain on automatic pilot and scan the boring sections, reading the words but not really digesting them. The trick is staying awake enough to notice when things become interesting. Your technique will improve with practice, and some days you'll do better than others, but even on a bad day you're likely to find something to quench your thirst for excitement. Numbers 9–36 (mostly exciting) and Joshua 12–24 (mostly boring) are excellent places to practice this strategy, for there you will find mingled things tedious and surprising.

Even accomplished students of the boring parts may have days when they should employ this strategy.[4] We all have our limits, and we all have our own least favorite Scriptures. It's better to travel light and travel fast for a time than to pass out from thirst in the sections that are hardest for you. God will be pleased if you delve into His Word a little more each time you go through it. He has a lifetime of surprises in store for you, even in the sections that seem driest to you now. Don't try to grasp it all in one reading. Eat and drink what you can and go your way. There will be more food for thought the next time you pass by.

Strategy 2: Travel Slow and Dig Deep

If you really want to know the desert, you can't rush through it. You have to take your time. But how can you camp out in a place with no water? You either have to bring your water with you, or bring the equipment which will enable you to find it. Since there's a limit to how much you can carry, you must find water if you plan to stay long. The people under Moses often obtained water by supernatural methods, but sometimes they had to dig for it.[5] This strategy deals with digging, the natural way of finding water in the desert.

Whether you use a pick and shovel or a modern drilling rig, you need tools to find water. Are there tools for finding water in the boring parts? Yes, there are. In fact, so many wonderful tools are available to us, the problem is not so much obtaining them as learning how to use them properly.[6] Reference Bibles, commentaries, dictionaries, concordances, archeology books—there are libraries full of tools which can enhance our study. The secret to using them properly is first to believe that there is water to be found. After that we have to be prepared for a little sweat and labor. Then it isn't hard to discover which methods work best for us.

"All Scripture is given by inspiration of God, and is profitable" to us (2 Timothy 3:16). Translated into our desert metaphor, this means that there is water to be found in all the boring parts. God has already provided the water you need for your journey across Leviticus and Numbers. To prove it, you must step out in faith. If your faith is weak, ask Him to help your unbelief, but don't let fear keep you from the desert. (The way of faith always seems risky—unless your faith is perfect). Use the boring parts to build your faith. Use them to learn that God is good and that He cares for you. Believe me, life has greater trials in store for you than reading the begats. The trust you gain in the desert of the boring parts will serve you well in time to come.

Today, everyone is trying to make learning easy and fun. (Have you noticed that the more we do that, the less our children seem to know?) God has a different idea about learning, at least in the boring parts of the Bible. He hasn't spent a lot of time trying to make them stimulating, has He? Almost no one finds them enjoyable without laboring at it. Since this kind of learning requires work, the trick is learning to enjoy the work. If you have never enjoyed intense labor (whether mental or physical), it's unlikely that this strategy will do much for you. But if you have ever felt satisfied after splitting your firewood, finishing your taxes, or cooking a fine meal, you can learn to enjoy digging in the dry sections of Scripture.

Bible Study Tools

There are many ways to use Bible study tools. Some of them provide perspective and background on different sections of Scripture. Others help us to find biblical passages relevant to the one at hand. Hebrew and Greek reference works give us insight into the original languages.

The simplest method, which combines all the others, is looking in a good commentary to see what other godly people have gleaned from the Word. Not everyone approves of this method. Some Christians say that you shouldn't use commentaries, that the Holy Spirit will tell you all about the Scriptures without the help of man. Such thinking is fine with me as long as it's consistent. If you never need a cookbook, a telephone directory, or an owner's manual, then I think you can do very well without a commentary. But if you are not self-sufficient in the things of this world, perhaps you would do well to consult the collective wisdom of the Church of Christ. On the other hand, there are some very real dangers inherent in the use of commentaries. Satan doesn't spend a lot of time perverting the Yellow Pages, but he hates the Word of God with a passion. Nothing pleases him more than a commentary which turns the truth into a lie, or distorts it beyond recognition. And even the best commentators fall short of perfection. Therefore, it is probably better not to use a commentary at all than to use one blindly and without discernment.

I had read the Bible through two times before I ever looked in a commentary. Since then, I have often been blessed by the wisdom of godly expositors (not to mention the others). Therefore I encourage you to spend time discerning what is good in the commentaries available to you, but not before you become acquainted with the Word of God. Beware of putting your trust in man, for it is your responsibility to "test the spirits, whether they are of God" and to "know the spirit of truth and the spirit of error."[7]

Reference or study Bibles can be helpful guides through the boring parts. They put things in perspective, refer us to other relevant Scriptures, and provide explanatory notes. All of this is good if it is done right. I caution you, however, that explanatory notes in a Bible are only the commentary of man placed next to the Scriptures of God for your convenience. Beware of giving the notes credence simply because they are in your Bible. And beware of notes which consistently use the Scriptures to expound systems of theology, especially concerning the end times. A good commentator will let you know where Christians disagree, helping you to choose wisely among contending theories and theologies. There is rarely room for this in a study Bible, so some editors present their position as if it were God's. I encourage you to let God speak for Himself.

I think we can learn a useful lesson here from the history of our English Bible. The first man to translate the Hebrew and Greek Scriptures into English was William Tyndale (ca. 1492–1536). He was persecuted by the English clergy, who said, in effect, that if God had wanted us to have an English Bible, He would never have given us the Vulgate. So Tyndale went to Germany, where he started printing the New Testament with a lengthy prologue and notes, some of them taken from Luther's works. Most of Tyndale's notes were simply informative (and milder than Luther's), but a couple of them were quite polemical. Before the printer finished typesetting Matthew, the authorities of Cologne forbade further work on the book. Tyndale fled to Worms, where he issued the first printed New Testament in English, in a smaller edition without a prologue or explanatory notes.[8] Though I greatly admire Tyndale, I see the hand of God in his troubles, ensuring that the first English copies of His Word, like the stones of His altar,[9] were not polluted by the hand of man.

I highly recommend the use of concordances in your study of the Bible. First and foremost, they will help you find Bible verses you can vaguely remember, but whose location you may have forgotten. They also aid in the study of particular words and topics which may interest you. More advanced concordances help you investigate the usage and meaning of the Greek and Hebrew words which underlie our English translations. (See appendix: Suggestions for Further Study, for more detail.)

Bible dictionaries enable you to turn quickly to concise information on almost any biblical subject. For example, if you are confused about the differences between the altar of sacrifice and the altar of incense, a Bible dictionary is the first place to look. However, dictionary articles are necessarily brief; they are inadequate for studying a subject in depth.

The Plot Thickens

It is very important, in writing a guidebook to the boring parts, not to make the guidebook itself boring. I, for one, will soon find this catalog of Bible study tools wearisome, unless I interject some examples. I had read the Bible for years before I learned, to my great surprise, that when Jesus asked Peter three times "Do you love me?" He used a different Greek word for love the third time. In fact he switched to the same word Peter was using in his answers.[10] This explains, at least in part, why Peter was grieved the third time and why John repeats the wording of only the third question. Some commentaries point this out, as do some study Bibles. You could also discover it through the use of word-study books or an interlinear New Testament. But you could read the English text forever without knowing the whole story.

Perhaps you will be better convinced by an example from the boring parts themselves. Though the catalog of David's mighty men in 2 Samuel 23 is interesting at first, the last sixteen verses are simply obscure names (vv. 24–39). The careful student of Scripture will notice in verse 34 that Eliam is "the son of Ahithophel the Gilonite," the infamous counselor of Absalom. But unless you use Bible study tools, how will you remember that in 2 Samuel 11:3, Bathsheba is called Bathsheba, *the daughter of Eliam,* the wife of Uriah the Hittite? How different the whole story looks once we know that Ahithophel may well have been Bathsheba's grandfather! How the plot thickens!

Here's an example from the very heart of the boring parts. In Numbers 4 we are told at some length how the Jews wrapped up the sacred furniture and utensils when they journeyed. All the precious things were wrapped in blue cloth, except two. The showbread (with certain utensils) was covered with a scarlet cloth, and the altar was covered with purple (vv. 7–8, 13). Perhaps you know that the veil of the temple was blue and purple and scarlet, but that does not explain why the bread and the altar were wrapped in colors different from the others.[11] Careful use of a concordance reveals one other time in Scripture where purple and scarlet are mysteriously linked—in the robe that Jesus wore before Pilate. When Christ, the Bread of Life, was ready to be sacrificed for us on the great altar of God, He was wrapped by others in scarlet and purple. (Matthew tells us the robe was scarlet; Mark and John say it was purple.[12] Most commentators either ignore this apparent discrepancy in the gospels or are puzzled by it.) I do not pretend to understand the symbolism perfectly, but I believe Numbers 4 provides our best commentary on the color of His robe.

More About Tools

Now to return to our catalog.

Topical Bibles can facilitate your studies by locating for you all (or most of) the Scriptures related to your subject of interest. After you have looked up the two altars in a Bible dictionary, you might want to search the Scriptures to learn more about them. The easiest way to find the relevant passages is to refer to a topical Bible. Once again, a word of caution is necessary. All reference works are written by men, not God. They may distort some things, and they cannot possibly lead you to all that the Spirit of God desires to reveal to you in the Word. A skillful digger values and cares for his tools, but he also knows their limits.

I highly recommend the perusal of books and articles on biblical archeology. You can get a smattering of archeological knowledge from Bible dictionaries, but you need more than that. Why? Archeology provides wonderful evidence on both the trustworthiness of the Scriptures and the foolishness of the men who doubt them. You won't be thrilled by Numbers 33, which lists the camping places of the Jews, just because you have read your archeology, but you will *know* that you are reading an accurate, historical list, one that will be important to scholars as long as the earth turns. Such assurance is invaluable. Even if you don't love the details about who dug what up where, you will be blessed by seeing the Word of God confirmed in the most surprising ways. (Christians with perfect faith will not be surprised, but the rest of us can use the encouragement.)

What more shall I say? For the time would fail me to tell of word-study books, Greek and Hebrew dictionaries and concordances, the Interlinear Bible, computer programs, and many other useful tools. If you would know more, see appendix, Suggestions for Further Reading, where I go into these matters in more detail.

The Quest for Books

I consider it imperative to say a few words about buying books. It's easy to spend a small fortune on reference works. Stick to the bare essentials until you know what you need. I encourage you to visit the library at your church or your local Christian school, college, or seminary before you go to the bookstore. (Most colleges and seminaries allow public use of their libraries.) Study a couple of topics in depth at the library and you will quickly discover which tools are right for you. Then it's time to think about buying.

Good Christian used bookstores are very hard to find.[13] The religion section in an average used bookstore, if it has anything you want, may ask more for it than a discounter who sells it new. But for out-of-print books and those happy moments when they have what you want at a bargain price, the used bookstore is a delight.

New bookstores enable you to see and know a book before you buy it. This becomes significant if you hate returning imperfect books or wrong orders to discounters through the mail. If you are not familiar with the variety of tools available, an experienced salesperson may be able to help you. Your pastor, priest, or learned Christian friend may also have good advice on books. However, you would do well to ponder this riddle: What do Christian reference works and love have in common? Answer: In both we are surprised by the taste of our friends. Take the time to discover what's right for you.

If you know what you want, some discount mail-order catalogs offer real bargains. You have to wait for your books and you have to pay shipping costs, but the savings can be considerable. Beware of ordering books you've never seen just because they sound great in the catalog.

Cursed be he who goes into his local bookstore to browse—and then orders by mail from a discount catalog. This did not Abraham. (He went to the library and did his research there.)

Strategy 3: The Lord Will Provide

Though I freely admit that *The Lord Will Provide* is my favorite strategy, please remember that one good method does not exclude another. Rather, all three work together for good in ways beyond our understanding. You may be traveling light and fast over an arid page, when something catches your eye, and for the first time you understand it. Or God may reveal some treasure to you in a moment of inspiration, but leave you to dig it up on your own. Another time, when you are bleary-eyed and half buried in books, He'll suddenly bless you with spiritual truth. His ways are not like our ways. Use all three strategies—and expect a blessing.

When Moses led the children of Israel through the wilderness, most of their food and much of their water was provided by supernatural means. What's more, their clothes did not wear out in forty years![14] They left Egypt in haste at the command of the Lord, and He supplied all their needs. He did not, however, supply all the garlic, melons, and slave drivers they longed for. He provided what they needed to draw close to Him, to prepare themselves for freedom.

These things were written for our example. We may venture out into the desert of the boring parts, trusting in God to supply all our needs, simply because we are obeying His command. Has He not told us to live by every word of God? So what if you don't have a seminary degree and reading knowledge of Hebrew? (Neither do I.) So what if you're unprepared? You are just like the Jews who left Egypt in haste. They bound up their kneading bowls in their clothes, put them on their shoulders, took the Egyptians' silver and gold, and went out into the wilderness. They had no time to prepare; they just went. Their task was simple: to trust in the Lord with all their heart, and lean not on their own understandings (Proverbs 3:5). As long as they did that, it was well with them. God never failed them, and He will never fail you. The *only* thing you need to make this strategy work is faith in God. Everything else is excess baggage.

Try to be content with what He gives you, even if it's not much at first. The Lord does not like it when we complain. (Are you overjoyed when your kids complain?) I suppose that if you get stuck in the desert you can cry out to God, plead His promises, tell Him your burden is too great, and suggest that His reputation among the heathen will suffer if you perish. But the truth is, I don't remember having done any of that. All I did was read my Bible. I don't really know why I started to read the whole Bible. I just did. Due more to ignorance than faith, I was blessed not to heed evil reports about the Word of God.[15] The rest of this book is my personal testimony that when we step out into the desert with even a drop of faith, God will certainly give us the things we need.

Someone has said that an ounce of a man's own wit is worth a ton of other people's. Well, an ounce of your own personal inspiration from the Scriptures is worth a ton of knowledge derived from commentaries. The amazing thing is that God is able to give you tons of your own inspiration.[16] It is true that we all have different gifts and different abilities, and that some of us will find more in the boring parts than others. Yet each of us needs to have our own testimony, our own first-hand experience that the Word of God is living and powerful. If from reading what I've written you gain a ton of knowledge, my hope is that it will do you good. But when you yourself get water out of some rock in the boring parts, this book will have served its purpose.

> Now to Him who is able to do exceedingly abundantly above all that we ask or think, according to the power that works in us, to Him be glory in the Church by Christ Jesus throughout all ages, world without end. Amen. (Ephesians 3:20–21)

PART 2

THE MAJOR BORING PARTS

3

NUMBERS 7

I consider Numbers 7 to be the most boring chapter in the Bible. It is certainly one of the longest chapters. Very long and very boring—sounds formidable, doesn't it? The editors of some modern Bibles have seen fit to abridge it drastically or remove it entirely. Yet I can honestly say that for me it is one of the most moving parts of Scripture. I can't say "one of the most exciting" (for then it would not be boring), but one of the most stirring, one of the most awe-inspiring. It took me years to come to a proper appreciation of it. Nothing would give me more pleasure than to shorten that time for others.

How is this chapter different from other chapters? Of its eighty-nine verses, sixty are devoted to twelve *exactly identical* lists of things offered to the Lord at the dedication of the altar.[1] The twelve tribes made twelve identical offerings, and *each thing* offered by each tribe is written out in full. Nothing is abridged or summarized. Furthermore, twelve additional verses are used to tell us which leader of which tribe offered on which day—none of which is very exciting. (The names of the leaders are listed twice already in the first two chapters of Numbers, so that information is not new to us.) Wait! We're not done yet! Five more verses list the total amounts offered by the twelve leaders. To sum up, seventy-seven verses are superlatively boring, and it is with these that we are primarily concerned. (Of the other twelve verses, 1–11 are nothing to write home about, but since they relate action, they do not fulfill our criteria for boring parts of the Bible. Verse 89 is unique; it will be discussed later in this chapter.)

The Goliath of the Boring Parts

I admit that to make Numbers 7 interesting is a challenge. What could be interesting about twelve identical lists? But challenges cause us to grow, calling forth all our resources of soul and spirit. If we can get water out of this rock, nothing shall be impossible for us. Is Numbers 7 the Goliath of the boring parts? Well, then, once we deal with their champion, the rest of them should be easy to enjoy. David didn't start with the baggage boy of the Philistines. He went right to the top. With equal confidence in God's goodness and guidance, let us seek to do the same.

Why Would God Do This?

The first question that comes to mind is, "Why would God do this?" Why would He waste so much precious space (and so much of our precious time) on something so repetitive and obscure? If we believe that He is fully as intelligent as modern Bible editors, it follows that He also could have abridged this chapter. For some reason He chose not to. What could it be?

Additional suspense (if any were needed) comes with an awareness of the special place Numbers 7 occupies in the desert of the boring parts. Most of the boring parts are located between Exodus 20 and Numbers 7. Between those chapters there is very little action to refresh the weary traveller.[2] After Numbers 7, the boring parts diminish quickly. The rest of Numbers alternates between well-known stories (the rebellions, the twelve spies, Balaam and his donkey) and sections that are dull but less memorably so. As for Deuteronomy, I hope you remember why I do not include it among the authentic boring parts.[3] After Deuteronomy we have to travel all the way to 1 Chronicles and the end of Ezekiel to find long sections that are dreadfully boring.

Numbers 7 is the capital of the kingdom of boredom. It can only be approached by passing through the great desert. Few travellers ever reach it, and, of those who do, none consider trying to overthrow the fortress. They slink by, glad to be past the place, and they do not look back. Like the gate to Dante's inferno, its portal reads, "Abandon hope, all ye that enter here."

Numbers 7 appears impregnable, but with God all things are possible. True, it is useless to beat our heads against the walls—the twelve lists—for they cannot be destroyed. Yet where force is futile, a little strategy may make us more than conquerors. Our object is to capture the fortress intact and transform it into a monument to the glory of God.

We shall do so by returning to our original question: Why would God make such a place? How could anyone ever profit by its existence? There are two main answers to this question. The first is practical; the second is glorious.

On the practical level, Numbers 7 shows us that all the children of God are equal in their Father's eyes. The size, the wealth, even the virtue of the twelve tribes make no difference: each offering is the same. It is one thing for God to say, "You are all equal." It is quite another to demonstrate it by a visual lesson lasting twelve days. Considering the frictions which were to develop among the tribes, it was essential for them to understand their equality in the divine covenant. These things "were written for our learning" (Romans 15:4). Surely the same lesson needs to be understood by modern Christians, whether as individuals, families, or churches. Or are the days past when one group of God's people might say to another, "You have no part in the Lord"?[4]

Glory and Transcendence

This practical lesson is easy to understand, but it suggests other questions: Why would God teach this here? Why wait a whole year after coming out of Egypt to demonstrate something so basic? Is there something special about the altar that makes it necessary to perform the twelve offerings at its dedication? These questions bring us to the glory and transcendence of Numbers 7. For there is something special about this altar.

There were two altars in the time of Moses, one for incense and one for animal sacrifices. The altar of incense was made of wood covered with gold. It stood before the veil in the Holy Place, where the priest burned incense on it every day. This altar of gold, as it is sometimes called, was a very important part of the tabernacle furnishings. The atoning blood was placed on its horns in several important Mosaic rituals, most notably on the Day of Atonement. However, no offering was appointed for the altar of incense.[5]

The altar of burnt offering was made of wood covered with bronze. It stood in the courtyard outside the tabernacle, where burnt offerings were offered upon it daily to the Lord. It was also used for most of the other animal sacrifices, including the sin offerings in Leviticus 4. This altar had a less exalted position than the altar of incense. It stood outside the tabernacle, it contained no precious metal, and it could be approached by the common people.[6] Since it had meat, fat, and blood burned on it every day, it could hardly be sweet smelling and spotless.

Yet, when God established the law of Moses, it was the only sacred object to receive an offering of dedication. That offering takes up the seventy-seven boring verses of Numbers 7.

Only the altar is dedicated, and its offering takes up more space in the Hebrew Bible than the song of Moses or the song of David. Numbers 7 is as long as God's great declaration to Job of His power and might (Job 38–41). You'd think we could figure out from the length of the offering that something important is going on! But do we? To what shall I liken this? It's as if God designed a huge granite monument to get our attention, built it in the middle of our busiest highway—and the result? We pass by it, complaining, "That thing sure gets in the way here. Doesn't God know we have important things to be doing?" Then we move the highway, so we won't have to slow down as we go by. If we can't take a hint in seventy-seven verses, could it be that there's something wrong with our hearing?

The language of Moses pays another special honor to this altar. Twice, the Lord calls it most holy[7] using a Hebrew expression which means *holiness of holinesses*. The ark, the tabernacle, the candlestick, the golden altar—none of these is twice singled out as most holy. The phrase is used twenty-four times in the five books of Moses, and more than half of them refer to the bronze altar and the things offered on it. Why would God describe the bloody (and probably smelly) altar with the same words He used for the Holy of Holies, a place too sacred for even the priests to approach? Why would He call it and its offerings "most holy" more often than He uses that expression for all other sacred objects and offerings combined?

A passage in Joshua shows us that the Jews understood the special significance of the bronze altar. After much of the land was conquered, Joshua allowed the tribes of Reuben, Gad, and (half of) Manasseh to return to their lands on the other side of the Jordan:

> And when they came to the region of the Jordan which is in the land of Canaan, the children of Reuben, the children of Gad, and half the tribe of Manasseh built an altar there by the Jordan—a great, impressive altar. (Joshua 22:10)

The Jews almost came to civil war over this second altar, until they found out it was only a symbol—a symbol of the right of Reuben, Gad, and Manasseh to use the one true altar. Why did they build a replica of the bronze altar? Why didn't they build an ark, a tabernacle, or an altar of incense? They showed by their actions that they understood the altar of sacrifice to be the most essential object in their worship of the Lord.

This altar, then, was distinguished in significant ways from all the other sacred things of the Jews. It received the only offering of dedication, it was twice called most holy, and it alone became the object of contention among the tribes. What made it so different? Surely there is something mysterious about the altar of sacrifice. That is not hard to see. What is hard to see is that the clue we need to solve the mystery is given to us in Numbers 7.

Numbers 7:89

The offering of dedication comes on the reader without warning. No explanation is given about what the offering means or why only the bronze altar is so dedicated. After the twelve days of offering are finished, we are told only this:

> Now when Moses went into the tabernacle of meeting to speak with Him, he heard the voice of One speaking to him from above the mercy seat that was on the ark of the Testimony, from between the two cherubim; thus He spoke to him. (Numbers 7:89)

I believe this verse is highly significant—one of the most crucial verses in the law of Moses. It provides the key by which we shall convert this citadel of boredom into a house of praise.

Numbers 7:89 fulfills the Lord's promise to Moses, a promise He made when He first gave the plan for the ark and the tabernacle:

> You shall put the mercy seat on top of the ark, and in the ark you shall put the Testimony that I will give you. And there I will meet with you, and I will speak with you from above the mercy seat, from between the two cherubim which *are* on the ark of the Testimony. . . .(Exodus 25:21–22)

In Leviticus 16:2, the Lord repeated this promise, saying, "I will appear in the cloud above the mercy seat." Notice that in both Exodus and Leviticus the promise is still in the future.[8] But in Numbers 7:89 the promise is fulfilled. For the first time we are told specifically of God speaking to Moses from the mercy seat. It is a definite action in time,[9] and it comes immediately after the long and boring offering of dedication. Is there a connection between the dedication and the fulfillment of the promise? And if so, what is it?

In chapters eight, nine, and ten of Hebrews we learn that:

> The law, having a shadow of the good things to come, and not the very image of the things . . . [could never] make those who approach perfect.

> . . . But Christ came as High Priest of the good things to come, with the greater and more perfect tabernacle not made with hands, that is, not of this creation. (Hebrews 10:1; 9:11)

The writer of Hebrews refers to the holy places made with hands as *copies* or *representations* of the true holy places. In other words, the tabernacle worship used symbols to describe the way to God in Christ, for the true way was not yet clearly revealed. We can understand Christ's ministry better by considering the Old Testament worship, and we cannot understand the Mosaic rituals unless we look to Christ. To understand the symbolic significance of Numbers 7:89, we must look at the eternal things it shows us with shadows.

The mercy seat was the place where atonement was made for the sins of the people.[10] There Moses heard God speaking. So the place of atonement and the place of closest communion with God were one and the same. In Moses' time, the people could not approach the mercy seat; they were cut off from intimate communion with God. However, they could come near the altar of burnt-offering, and there they (through the priests) offered their sacrifices. In Numbers 7, the offerings are presented at the altar, but the response to the offerings is a Voice speaking from the mercy seat. Men dedicate the place of sacrifice, and God responds by taking up His promised residence in their midst. He comes among them when they give costly gifts at the altar.

The Altar and the Cross

What is the New Testament equivalent of the altar? What is the New Testament place of sacrifice? Isn't it the cross?[11] On the cross, the atoning sacrifice was offered up to God. In Numbers 7, the altar and the mercy seat are connected by events, but they are still separate places. In Christ the veil is taken away, and the place of sacrifice and the place of atonement become one. Christ is both Lamb and High Priest, and His altar (on which He offers Himself) is the cross. When the leaders of Israel offered for the dedication of the altar, ultimately they were dedicating the cross. The peculiar honor they paid to the first altar was God's way of providing in advance the honor due the altar of a better covenant. For when the Lord of glory was sacrificed for our sakes, men despised both the altar and the Sacrifice.

How carefully the altar of burnt offering was shaped, anointed, and cared for! How differently the cross of Christ was made! Roman slaves may have provided the rough-hewn crosses their masters needed at Calvary, and Christ's would have been no different from the others. Do you suppose they loved their work, as Bezaleel and Aholiab loved making the altar? Do you think those slaves were "filled with the Spirit of God, in wisdom, in understanding, in knowledge, and in all manner of workmanship, to design artistic works" (Exodus 31:3–4) when they hacked out the cross? The shadow was beautiful; the good thing to come was not. The altar that could not save was honored; the one true altar of God received no honor from men. Knowing it must be so, God provided abundant honor for the altar of His Son, and He put the bulk of it in Numbers 7.

Verse 89 is the fulfillment of the whole chapter and of all the events since Moses saw the pattern on Mount Sinai. At last all is ready; at last all is prepared. The great plan of salvation is nearly complete. We come and present our offerings of faith at the cross, we believe in Christ and Him crucified—and behold! God is in our midst, speaking with us as a man speaks to his friend! "This was the dedication offering for the altar after it was anointed. Now when Moses went into the tabernacle of meeting to speak with Him, he heard the voice of One speaking to him from above the mercy seat . . . "(Numbers 7:88–89).

What could be more fitting? What could be more glorious? For this passage is the New Testament in a nutshell. "Show Me that you believe in My sacrifice for sin, and I shall be with you. Honor Christ in faith and in deed, and I will honor you with My presence. Bring Me the things I have provided for you, and offer them according to My instructions, so that I may dwell with you forever. You shall be My people, and I shall be your God." That is the message of Numbers 7. (I hope you do not find it boring.)

When We Lust and Won't Listen

Do you see how we are like the children of Israel? God gave them manna in the wilderness, and He gives us Numbers 7 in the desert of the boring parts. Our response is just like theirs: this thing isn't what we're used to—and besides, it's boring! We don't think it is tasty or nutritious. Give us the produce of Egypt! Well, when we lust and won't listen, God gives us up to our unholy desires. Now we have commentaries that apologize for Numbers 7, Bibles that remove it, and theologies that say it doesn't matter anyway. Yes, we have what we want. But are we satisfied, and are we fit to enter the Promised Land? I have my doubts. Wouldn't it be better to trust God, to remember that He knows more than we do, and to be grateful for the things He has given us?

As there was more than one way to prepare manna,[12] there is more than one way to use Numbers 7. It shows us that sometimes God requires action from us and not words. It shows us that what He has started He is able to finish. We see that we all are equal in our Father's sight. We see, if He has given us eyes for it, the incredible planning and attention to detail that went into Old Testament worship to glorify the New Covenant in Christ's blood. We see a special honor paid to the wondrous cross. We learn that what seems boring and unnecessary to us may have significance beyond anything we can imagine. If we can apply these lessons in our own lives, how great will be our reward!

Numbers 7 in Context

It is time to look at the events which follow Numbers 7, for the chapter is even more impressive when seen in its true context.[13] What happens in the book of Numbers is not related in chronological order,[14] and there is some obscurity about the precise dates when certain things took place. However, we do know that on the first day of the first month of the second year of the Exodus, the tabernacle was set up and anointed. And that is the day mentioned at the start of Numbers 7.[15] Numbers 9 also tells us that the second Passover was celebrated on the fourteenth day of the first month. Between the first and fourteenth days of the month there are (you got it!) twelve days. Whatever the actual chronology of the different events may be, the apparent chronology is clear. The tabernacle was anointed on the first of the month; the leaders offered for twelve days; then the Passover was celebrated on the fourteenth day.[16] It is worth noticing that, while other events are related within that time frame, no days or periods of time are attached to them. There is nothing to indicate that the offering of the wagons, the arranging of the lamps, or the cleansing of the Levites took any length of time. So it is possible, and appears likely, that the dedication of the altar filled the time between anointing the tabernacle and celebrating the Passover.

Does all this seem like much ado about nothing? Consider the symbolism here.

- After great preparation the tabernacle is set up and anointed: In the fullness of time, all things necessary for God's plan of salvation are complete.

- The heads of the tribes offer precious things for the service of the altar: The believers present their bodies "a living sacrifice, holy, acceptable to God," which is their reasonable service (Romans 12:1).
- Then right away it is time to celebrate the Passover: It is the Lord's supper: He brings His spouse to His banqueting house, and His banner over her is love (Song of Solomon 2:4).
- All things are ready. We have only to bring the offerings God appoints for us, and we shall enjoy intimate communion with Him. And very soon thereafter (Numbers 10:11–13) we shall set out for the Promised Land He has prepared for us.

To see all this presented so perfectly and so graphically should fill us with wonder and encourage our faith. In the desert of this world, God has provided blessings for us beyond our comprehension. For as much as the ministry of Christ surpasses the Old Testament rituals, so much shall the glory about to be revealed in us surpass the things we know now. I, for one, am not bored by such a prospect.

4

The Begats

(Matthew 1; Luke 3; Genesis 5, 10, and 11)

The infamous begats,[1] the genealogies of the Bible, are worthy of double honor. They are the first of the boring parts, and they are the only boring parts quoted extensively in the New Testament. Perhaps that does not impress you. Perhaps to you that's like honoring the first of a hundred potatoes you have to peel, or like rejoicing over the masthead in your favorite magazine. You don't need to know the name of the subscription manager, and you don't care who was the son of Zerubbabel. But what does God think? What if He thinks the genealogical records are important? Would that impress you? You know it should!

The Genealogies of Jesus

Let's begin with the New Testament. The only boring parts in it are the genealogies of Jesus in Matthew 1:1–17 and Luke 3:23–38. How boring are they? Well, in the third verse of Matthew we find the name of Tamar. She disguised herself as a prostitute in order to become pregnant by Judah, her father-in-law. Verse 5 mentions two Gentile women, Rahab the harlot and Ruth. Verse 6 alludes to Bathsheba as "of Uriah," as if to emphasize her adultery. What kind of genealogy is this? It tells us the Messiah has Gentiles, a prostitute, and an adulteress for ancestors. Yet it never mentions Sarah, Rebecca, Leah, or any of the godly Jewish women from whom Christ descended. It's as if the Daughters of the American Revolution were to publish a genealogy of George Washington, recording every Gypsy and horse thief in his family tree while omitting every Englishman and scholar.

God's ways are not like our ways, and we learn to be grateful for that. God specializes in bringing good out of evil. He brought the Messiah to us out of a sinful family (though not from sinful seed), and He can bring the salvation of Christ to others through the likes of you and me. Whatever is irregular, preposterous, or even wicked in our lives, God can turn to good. Those who feel hopeless or inadequate ought to derive encouragement from the genealogy of Christ.

The mention of Rahab as the mother of Boaz in Matthew 1:5 is quite significant. Only here do we learn that Rahab married a prince of the tribe of Judah and that they had a son named Boaz. Yes, it was Rahab's son who was willing to marry the poor and pious daughter of Moab when his Hebrew kinsman would not. What a testimony to the love of his parents we find in the life of Boaz! With this knowledge we are prepared for Rahab's admission to the New Testament Hall of Fame in Hebrews 11:31. On the other hand, if we didn't know the mother of Boaz, would we really understand the story of Ruth? Do you see how skipping the boring parts causes us to miss things in the parts we know and love?

An Element of Glory

There are other interesting details in this genealogy, but they pale beside the main point. God started the New Testament with a genealogy because the ancestry of Jesus is a unique and essential element of His glory. Let us examine this weight of glory, for it proves both prophetically and historically that Jesus is the Christ.

How shall believers know the Messiah from impostors? In the days of Nehemiah some men "could not identify their father's house nor their lineage, whether they were of Israel. . . . These sought their listing among those who were registered by genealogy, but it was not found; therefore they were excluded from the priesthood as defiled" (Nehemiah 7:61–64).

If lack of a proper genealogy excluded a man from the priesthood of Levi, how much more shall it exclude a man from being "High Priest forever according to the order of Melchizedek"? If the priests who offered the blood of animals must be able to prove their descent from

Aaron, how much more must He who "put away sin by the sacrifice of Himself" be able to prove that He came from the loins of Abraham and David?[2]

The Scriptures make it clear that the coming Prince must be descended from David.[3] Thus, over time, the Son of David became a common Jewish title for the Messiah.[4] The Lord decided to put His Son's impeccable credentials right up front. Those credentials were important to the ancient Jews, and they are still important today. Why else would the first sentence of the New Testament read, "The book of the genealogy of Jesus Christ, the Son of David, the Son of Abraham"?

Leaving the realm of prophecy, let's look at the historical significance of these records. The Daughters of the American Revolution must be able to trace their ancestry through more than two centuries. The Daughters of the Barons of Runnymede must be able to follow theirs for nearly eight hundred years. But Matthew shows the lineage of Christ through twenty centuries, and Luke carries it back to the beginning of the world! This poor carpenter from a conquered nation could trace his descent back many times further than anyone alive today.

In the time of Christ, the Jews still knew from which of the twelve patriarchs they were descended,[5] but their records have since vanished. They are waiting for their messiah, but no future candidate for that position can possibly prove his descent from David and Abraham. The first chapter of Matthew is sufficient to destroy the claims of all pretenders to the throne of David.

Two Fathers for Joseph

Another way of estimating the importance of the genealogies of Christ is to consider the controversies they have engendered. Because Matthew and Luke give two different ancestries for Jesus and list two different fathers for Joseph, their genealogies have always been a favorite target for skeptics and disparagers of the Bible. Eusebius, writing early in the fourth century, tells us that every believer has worked out some explanation of this apparent discrepancy. He gives us what he considers the best of the many explanations current in his day, which he adopts from a third-century Christian named Africanus. It is an intricate defense, based on the supposition or tradition that Joseph's father had married the childless widow of his brother.[6] Thus, Joseph was the natural child of his father and the legal child of his deceased uncle. There were lots of explanations in the fourth century, and there are even more now. (Today, many scholars think that Matthew gives the genealogy of Joseph, while

Luke gives the genealogy of Mary.) The curious may seek out other solutions in the commentaries. I am content to know that there are plenty of answers available and that one of them is probably correct.

I love the fact that Luke is the author of the second, most disputed genealogy. For Luke is a very exact historian. Notice how he opens the chapter which ends with his genealogy of Christ:

> Now in the fifteenth year of the reign of Tiberius Caesar, Pontius Pilate being governor of Judea, Herod being tetrarch of Galilee, his brother Philip tetrarch of Iturea and the region of Trachonitis, and Lysanias tetrarch of Abilene, Annas and Caiaphas being high priests, the word of God came to John the son of Zacharias in the wilderness. (Luke 3:1–2)

It would be strange indeed to begin with such an historical account and end with a spurious or legendary genealogy. It would make as much sense as if Samuel Eliot Morison were to list Paul Bunyan and Pecos Bill among the presidents in his *Oxford History of the American People.* I, for one, am happy to assume that Luke knew more than his modern critics do, and to wait for the Lord to reveal the full meaning of His own genealogy.[7]

Old Testament Genealogies

What about the Old Testament genealogies? Surely it will be harder to glean something interesting from them. Or will it? In the very first verse of the first long genealogy we find something which seems incidental but has tremendous significance: "And Adam lived one hundred and thirty years, and begot a son in his own likeness, after his image, and named him Seth" (Genesis 5:3).

You might think I am referring to the momentous words "in his own likeness, after his image," but they are too interesting to be studied in this book. No, I am referring to the fact that we are told Adam's age at the birth of Seth. Thus begins another unique testimony which the boring parts offer to the glory of Christ.

The Sons of Adam

What has the age of Adam to do with the glory of Christ? In Genesis 4:17–22 we are given the genealogy of Cain. Notice that it provides us with *no chronological information.* Yet in Genesis 5, we are told the exact age of every ancestor of Christ—just when his son was born, the son who would continue the sacred lineage of the Messiah. The same thing happens with the genealogy of Shem in Genesis 11. Yet we are never told the ages of the fathers in the family records of Ham or Japheth. Nor are we given chronological information concerning the descendants of Ishmael or Esau. Even the family tree of Moses in Exodus 6:16–27 leaves us in the dark. The chronology of the Bible is recorded only in the genealogies which lead to Jesus Christ.

If you're still saying, "So what?," consider this. The chronology of the Bible is the only continuous chronology that exists for half the history of human civilization! Accurate secular chronologies date only from times close to the completion of the Old Testament. Scholars and archaeologists have been busy for some two centuries, trying to reconstruct the chronology of the ancient world from the buried remains of vanished cultures. How successful their current efforts are will best be judged by future generations. But one fact is clear. There is only one surviving chronology of the ancient world, and it has come to us in the genealogies of Jesus Christ.

Some cultures, notably the Chinese and Egyptian, had extensive historical records (whether or not they were accurate), but only fragments of them survive. The Jews alone were able to keep alive their own history. Two sayings are commonly attributed to Henry Ford: "History is bunk" and "You can have any color you want, as long as it's black." Because God values history more than Mr. Ford did, you can have any chronology of the world you want, as long as it's found in the genealogy of Jesus Christ.

We were moved when Alex Haley found records of his ancestors extending past slavery to Africa and freedom. How we honor him and cherish his achievement! Yet we neglect the genealogies of the one man who can trace his descent from Adam and date his family history from the beginning of the world. The former we ought to have done, without leaving the latter undone.

Calculations

The genealogies in Genesis 5 and 11 enable us to do a number of interesting calculations. For example, we discover that Methusaleh lived 243 years while Adam was still alive. Noah lived six hundred years while his grandfather Methusaleh was living, for Methusaleh died just before the Flood. (Do you think they had time to get together and swap a few yarns?) Noah's son Shem was alive all the time that Abraham lived in Ur *and* the first seventy-five years he lived in Canaan.[8] This means that Isaac was married to Rebecca before the death of Shem! It also means that whatever Adam knew could have been passed on to Abraham with only three intermediaries—Methusaleh, Noah, and Shem. In this sense Alex Haley was further down the line from Kunta Kinte, his African ancestor, than Abraham was from Adam. Is it any wonder that the Jews had special knowledge of the beginning of time?

One of the glories of the first genealogy is the history of Enoch. God often inserts wonders into the lists of the Bible, and Enoch is perhaps the greatest of them. He was a prophet, a man of faith, and one who pleased God. In a time when Christians of note are called "spiritual giants" and other absurd things, it is refreshing to see how simply God honors his servant: "Enoch walked with God." As we discover in Hebrews, he "was translated so that he did not see death." Like Christ and Elijah, this worthy man went straight to heaven untouched by the stain of death. He is an inspiration to all who seek to live godly lives in a corrupt world. He is also a preview of coming attractions for those saints who will be alive at the end of the world.[9] "Therefore comfort one another with these words" (1 Thessalonians 4:17–18).

The Sons of Noah

Genesis 10 is the genealogy of the sons of Noah. There is such a wealth of material in it that I could easily devote a whole chapter to it. I trust you will settle for a few highlights.

My father's parents were orthodox Jews from Poland. They, like other Jews from eastern Europe, were known as Ashkenazim, because they were thought to have settled among the descendants of Ashkenaz.[10] Whatever the accuracy of that tradition may be, I can tell you it is quite exciting to find in the genealogy of the patriarchs a name still in common use among one's relatives.

Jews are not the only ones who can trace their roots back to Genesis 10. Japheth had a son named Javan (10:2–5), and "Javan is by all agreed to be the father of the Grecians; hence Alexander, king of Greece, is in Daniel 8:21 called king of Javan."[11] This fits well with the statement in verse 5 that "from [the sons of Javan] the coastland peoples of the Gentiles were separated into their lands." Mizraim, the name of Ham's son in verse 6, is the Hebrew word for Egypt. Thus we learn that the Egyptians and Canaanites were both descended from Ham. In verse 14, we discover that from Mizraim's son came the infamous Philistines. When David warred against Goliath and Company, he was fulfilling God's promise of deliverance from Egypt.

Ham's grandson Nimrod (vv. 8–12) is the worldly counterpart of Enoch. As Enoch provides a pattern for spiritual men, Nimrod shows us the carnal man. Notice how busy he was, hunting, ruling, and building many cities. Like the children of Cain, who were noted for their worldly accomplishments, Nimrod left his mark in history by dint of great activity. He has ever since received long negative reviews from all the godly commentators. It seems that worldliness, like crime, pays poorly in the long run. Christians do well to be diligent in their callings, but woe to him who substitutes activity for godliness!

Some of the cities which Nimrod built, notably Nineveh and Calah, have actually been excavated by archaeologists.[12] It is beyond the scope of this book to deal with the importance of the genealogies to archaeologists, except to say that they are essential material. We must remember that the Bible is one book written for all people and for all time. A part that seems boring to us may be exciting to an archaeologist.[13] Mere awareness of archaeology does not make the genealogies interesting, but it does enable us to approach them with a sense of mystery and awe. We cease to resemble those ignorant villagers who trample on their national treasures, until science and public opinion convince them to change their ways. May we show proper respect for these ancient monuments of our Christian heritage!

The Sons of Esau

Before we pass on to 1 Chronicles and its massive genealogies, we should take notice of some shorter ones. Genesis 36 contains genealogies for Jacob's brother Esau and for Seir the Horite, whose family intermarried with Esau's. Here we find that Esau moved to Mount Seir, "a country away from the presence of his brother Jacob. For their possessions were too great for them to dwell together."[14] Verse 12 seems to show that Amalek, whose descendants were inveterate enemies to Israel, was the grandson of Esau by a Horite concubine. How sad it is when God's people find their most implacable enemies among their own relatives![15]

Verse 24 tells us of Anah, the grandson of Seir, "who found the water (or hot springs) in the wilderness as he pastured the donkeys of his father Zibeon." Imagine the young man's delight when he discovered a spa in the middle of the desert! Imagine his astonishment at the fact that we are still talking about it!

Some scholars claim that the genealogies are legendary or written for nonhistorical purposes. The wealth of historical detail, such as Anah's finding the hot springs or the battle with Midian in the field of

Moab (36:35), surely contradicts such notions. I am the first to admit that there is a lot we don't know about the genealogies and why they were written. But it will be a long time (till doomsday I suspect) before our scraps of critical knowledge will dislodge the genealogies as historical treasures in the hearts of the faithful.[16]

The Daughter of Asher

Genesis 46 records, and Numbers 26 repeats, the genealogy of Jacob's family. I pass over all of it to focus on one insignificant person, Serah the daughter of Asher. Jacob had twelve sons and one daughter, yet Serah is the only granddaughter mentioned by name.[17] Unlikely as it seems, she may have been the only granddaughter born in Canaan (among dozens of male cousins), as Jochebed the mother of Moses may have been the only granddaughter born in Egypt.[18] In any event, this Serah is mentioned in Genesis 46:17, Numbers 26:46, and 1 Chronicles 7:30. I believe she was a woman of good character, and the Lord chose to honor her with this threefold repetition of her name. However, even if she is recorded simply because Jacob's granddaughters were rare as hens' teeth, we can derive real encouragement from her appearance in the genealogies. Do you ever feel out of place, a misfit in the Church of God, a mediocrity among super-Christians?[19] Well, Serah was a woman in a patriarchal society, a girl who had only boys to play with, a non-inheritor among dozens of heirs. Yet because she was good, or simply because she was outnumbered, God remembered her. Jochebed, her only female first cousin that we know of, mothered Miriam and Aaron and Moses. She was famous for her progeny; Serah was famous for nothing at all. If Serah did anything or had any children, the Lord has hidden it from us. Yet I suggest to you that her threefold mention in the Scriptures is a better reward than cover stories in Christian magazines and interviews on Christian radio. And I believe there's a better reward than hers laid up in heaven for many an unknown servant of Christ.

5

THE RETURN OF THE BEGATS

(1 Chronicles 1–9)

First Chronicles separates the men from the boys, the marathoners from the sprinters, and the drudges from the prima donnas. It also separates many a reader from best-laid plans to read the Bible through. It is one of the major boring parts, nine consecutive chapters of genealogies and other records. These tell most of us more than we ever wanted to know about everyone from Adam to Nehemiah.

Chapter by Chapter

I shall briefly mention a few things which interest me, selecting at least one from every chapter, and trusting you to find others on your own. The more you read the whole Bible, the more familiar names will jump out at you from these venerable records.

An Overview

The first chapter repeats with little variation the genealogies found in Genesis.[1] It presents an overview of those records, which can be helpful if you desire a unified summary of the genealogies. However, because it is a summary, we have to do without some of the details. For example, Anah the son of Zibeon is mentioned again in verse 40, but not the hot springs which he discovered. Rodanim (1:7) is thought to refer to the inhabitants of the island of Rhodes.[2] Though there are two men named

Uz in this chapter (vv. 17, 42), it is not certain that either of them gave his name to the land of Job.[3]

The Good and the Evil

In the second chapter (v. 6), we find four grandsons of Judah with names identical to the four wise men thought worthy of comparison with Solomon. If these four brothers were those celebrated wise men, their fifth brother Zimri seems to have been the inevitable black sheep. Not only was he not famous for his wisdom, but he appears to be the Zabdi whose grandson Achan troubled Israel in the days of Joshua.[4] "The evil that men do lives after them, The good is oft interred with their bones;"[5] but in this family the good and the evil still live after three thousand years.

Notice in 2:35 that Sheshan, who had no sons, gave his daughter in marriage to Jarha, his Egyptian servant. I can only suppose that the name of this Gentile slave is recorded because he was a worthy man. It is thought that Zabad the son of Ahlai in the list of David's mighty men might be Zabad the great-grandson of Sheshan's daughter Ahlai and her husband Jarha.[6] If the chronicles God keeps on earth are this intricate, imagine what incredible details must be found in the Lamb's Book of Life!

The Children of Zerubbabel

Chapter 3 is a genealogy of David's descendants, and most of it is familiar to us from other parts of Scripture. However, the last four verses contain material found nowhere else in the Bible. Zerubbabel (v. 19) is the last familiar name. Governor of the Jews who returned from Babylon, he is often mentioned by the writers after the captivity.[7] Since the end of chapter 3 contains the only Old Testament genealogy of Zerubbabel, it is the only possible parallel to Matthew 1:13–16. The names being different, we cannot be sure if the genealogies in Chronicles and Matthew are related. However, we do know that the same person frequently has different names in different genealogies. And it is possible to read the confusing account in Chronicles so as to produce ten generations after Zerubbabel[8]—*the same number Matthew gives from Zerubbabel to Joseph.* (Remember that Chronicles was complete and translated into Greek before the time of Christ.) It was presumably from records like these that Matthew completed his genealogy. Until we have more knowledge, we can only wonder about Zerubbabel's descendants in Chronicles and their connection with our Savior.

More Honorable Than His Brothers

In chapter 4, we find the most unusual person in this long section of begats.

> Now Jabez was more honorable than his brothers, and his mother called his name Jabez, saying, "Because I bore him in pain." And Jabez called on the God of Israel saying, "Oh, that You would bless me indeed, and enlarge my territory, that Your hand would be with me, and that You would keep me from evil, that I may not cause pain!" So God granted him what he requested. (1 Chronicles 4:9–10)

Jabez is truly a wonder. He appears in the midst of the genealogies, yet he has no father and no son. He is more honorable than his brothers, yet we do not know who his brothers are. Presumably he is related to those descendants of Judah in whose genealogy he appears.

You could make a long and impressive list of great preachers who have devoted a sermon or a portion of commentary to Jabez. What makes him so special? I believe it is the fact that, of the hundreds of men named in these nine chapters, Jabez is the only one whose spiritual life takes precedence over his ancestry. His simple faith and prevailing prayer are a model for all who believe. He is the keystone which gives spiritual strength to this great arch of genealogy.

The sermons concerning Jabez are so many variations on one simple theme: go thou and do likewise. Matthew Henry's comment sums them all up: "The way to be truly great is to be truly good and to pray much."[9] Experienced readers of the boring parts look forward to Jabez like an oasis in the desert. They pause and refresh themselves, contemplating in his presence the sweet things of the Spirit.

The last verse of chapter 2 tells us there were "scribes who dwelt at Jabez,"

> a city which, it is likely, took its name from [Jabez]. The Jews say that he was a famous doctor and left many disciples behind him. And it should seem, by the mentioning of him so abruptly, that his name was well known when Ezra wrote this.[10]

The same verse connects the town of Jabez with the house of Rechab, upon which God placed singular honor in the days of Jeremiah. So there may be a link between our hero and that family, whose obedience caused God to promise that they "shall not lack a man to stand before Me forever."[11]

There are references to craftsmen and potters in this chapter,[12] as well as an interesting note in verse 22, "Now the records are ancient."

There is no apparent reason for this interjection.[13] I love to wonder why we find it where we do.

Though the descendants of Simeon did not "multiply as much as the children of Judah," still "their father's house increased greatly" (4:27, 38). So they went to Gedor in the days of Hezekiah and took some land from the children of Ham. Five hundred men went on to Mount Seir to defeat the remnant of the accursed Amalekites. (The vengeance of God follows hardened sinners down through the centuries, until they are destroyed.) The descendants of these five hundred Jews seem to have escaped the Babylonian captivity, for they "have dwelt there to this day" (4:27, 38–43).

Of Faith and Faithlessness

In chapter 5, we are reminded of the sin of Reuben, which cost him his birthright. Next we learn of a register made "by genealogies in the days of Jotham king of Judah" (v. 17). Then the contrasting consequences of faith and faithlessness are clearly illustrated in the history of the tribes on the other side of Jordan. When they "cried out to God in the battle, He heeded their prayer because they put their trust in Him" (v. 20). There follows a detailed list of all the riches they gained by trusting God. Yet the chapter ends with a solemn warning:

> And they were unfaithful to the God of their fathers, and played the harlot after the gods of the peoples of the land, whom God had destroyed before them. So the God of Israel stirred up the spirit of Pul king of Assyria, that is, Tiglath-Pileser king of Assyria. He carried the Reubenites, the Gadites, and the half-tribe of Manasseh into captivity. He took them to Halah, Habor, Hara, and the river of Gozan to this day. (1 Chronicles 5:25–6)

We consider a long genealogy to be some kind of family status symbol. Evidently God had a different purpose in mind when He wrote this one.

The Children of Levi

[Readers using The New American Bible (and some other Bibles) will find that their verse numbers are different from those referred to in this section.[14]] First Chronicles 6 is devoted to the tribe of Levi. In verse 10, special attention is paid to Azariah "who ministered as priest in the temple that Solomon built in Jerusalem." This may be the Azariah who withstood King Uzziah's unlawful attempt to burn incense in the holy place in 2 Chronicles 26:16–21.

Verses 31 and 32 inform us about "the service of song in the house of the Lord." The importance of this service is shown by the long genealogies given for the lead singers, Heman, Asaph, and Ethan (or Jeduthan). Each one goes all the way back to Levi, the son of Jacob. Heman, we discover, is the grandson of Samuel the prophet.[15] Though Samuel's son Joel did not follow the Lord, Joel's son Heman led the service of song in the tabernacle of David.[16] Surely the man on whom this honor was bestowed loved God with all his heart. Strange and unaccountable are the meanderings of grace in the families of men!

Verses 49–53 describe the work of the priests and give the genealogy of the high priests from Aaron through the time of Solomon. The last man named is Ahimaaz the son of Zadok. The Scriptures show him to have been a famous runner and a man of great love and sensitivity. If you know the wonderful story of his service to his king, you will linger over his name when you find it in the boring parts.[17] And should we not remember our glorious High Priest, who surpasses Ahimaaz in His power and His grace?

The rest of chapter 6 is not a genealogy but a list of cities given to the priests and Levites. If you find these verses hard to digest, ask yourself why the begats should be interrupted with this information. Perhaps it is to remind *you* that from the beginning God provided for His ministers through the gifts of His people. All the tribes gave up towns and land (as well as their tithes and sacrifices) so that the priests and Levites might live among them. Once we have ears to hear it, we can be grateful for a twenty-eight-verse reminder to provide for those who minister the Word of God to us.

Notice the mention of Beth Shemesh in verse 59. When the ark of God came back from the Philistines, the men of Beth Shemesh looked into it, and some of them were killed.[18] Was God too harsh with the residents of Beth Shemesh? We learn from our list that the town was inhabited by priests, who surely ought to have known better than to tamper with the ark of the covenant.

Does the name of Anathoth in verse 60 sound familiar? It was to one of "the priests who were in Anathoth in the land of Benjamin," that God said,

> Before I formed you in the womb I knew you;
> Before you were born I sanctified you;
> And I ordained you a prophet to the nations.

Thus the Word of God first came to Jeremiah (Jeremiah 1:1, 5).

In Trouble or in Evil

In chapter 7, we shall consider only the sad and hopeful story of Ephraim (vv. 20–27). I admit that his genealogy confuses me, and that comparing it with Numbers 26:35–37 doesn't help me much. But it seems clear that some of Ephraim's offspring were slain by rustlers from Gath, Goliath's home town. After many days of mourning, he went in to his wife and she gave birth to Beriah, which means in trouble or in evil. This Beriah had two remarkable descendants. Sheerah, "who built Lower and Upper Beth Horon and Uzzen Sheerah," must have lived in the times of Joshua. What other daughter of Israel is credited with building three towns? She must have been a very capable and active woman to receive this notice in the genealogy of her tribe. We need not think of her as one of those "who trust in their wealth . . . and call their lands after their own names," (Psalm 49:6, 11) for the people may have named Uzzen Sheerah in her honor. The other descendant of Beriah was Joshua the son of Nun.

Is your family in trouble or in evil times? God may yet bring out of it one who will do great things for His people. Yes, there is solace to be found in this sad tale of Ephraim, a story not told in other parts of the Bible.

Family Difficulties

In chapter 8, we encounter the confusing genealogy of Shaharaim (vv. 6–13).[19] There are different ideas about him and his family. Did he exile some of his relatives, whose names appear in verses 6 and 7? Or did he divorce his wives Hushim and Baara and take up with Hodesh? (As for the sixty-four-thousand-dollar question, "Was she a hussy?" charity requires us to answer in the negative.) In reality, as one scholar put it, "The allusions to the family difficulties of Shaharaim are insufficient for more detailed reconstruction."[20]

Three Items of Interest

The first verse of chapter 9 tells us that "Judah was carried away captive to Babylon because of their unfaithfulness." What follows seems to be a list of those who returned from the Babylonian captivity,[21] with special emphasis on the priests and Levites. Of the items of interest in this list, I cannot fail to mention three.

1. Verse 20 mentions Phinehas the son of Eleazar, who was high priest in the time of the judges. We are specifically told that "the

Lord was with him." This Phinehas, when he was young, was specially praised by God for stopping the Jews' fornication with women from Midian and Moab.[22] When we consider that intermarriage with pagans was the prime sin of the men who returned from Babylon, we can see why the chronicler inserted this reminder. And for those of us today who find it hard to stomach the radical action of Phinehas, it is always helpful to remember that "the Lord was with him."

2. Verse 22 says that "David and Samuel the seer had appointed [the gatekeepers] to their trusted office." Elsewhere we are told of David's role in ordering the temple worship, but I cannot find any such statement about Samuel. To me it is both interesting and reassuring to know that David drew on the wisdom and experience of Samuel when he set up that plan of worship which was to last a thousand years.[23]
3. Notice in verse 33 that the singers "were free from other duties; for they were employed in that work day and night." David and Samuel understood that the leaders of praise must attend upon the Lord without distraction. Therefore, they exempted them from menial tasks. In doing so they showed more wisdom than the whaleship officers who caused Herman Melville to complain:

> However prolonged and exhausting the chase, the harpooneer is expected to pull his oar meanwhile to the uttermost . . . (with) repeated loud and intrepid exclamations . . . (yet) I cannot bawl very heartily and work very recklessly at one and the same time. . . .
>
> To insure the greatest efficiency in the dart, the harpooneers of this world must start to their feet from out of idleness, and not from out of toil.[24]

In Memoriam

The genealogies end with a mystery. Chapter 8 is a detailed account of Benjamin's offspring, culminating in King Saul, his son Jonathan, and Jonathan's descendants. Yet there is a shorter genealogy of Benjamin in chapter 7, and another at the end of chapter 9. So Benjamin has three separate genealogies in 1 Chronicles, while Dan and Zebulun have none, and Naphtali's is limited to one verse (7:13). What gives? Why does little Benjamin garner so much, when two of his brothers have nothing and one has only a verse? No one knows for sure, though we may be able to explain the absence of Dan. His tribe is conspicuously omitted from the list of 144,000 saints in Revelation 7. Some think apostasy in the time of the judges and acquiescence in Jeroboam's idolatry are the reasons for that exclusion.[25] Yet even if that should be so, we have no idea why Zebulun should be omitted and Naphtali limited to four names.

Today, many scholars suggest that the text has been corrupted. They think that parts of 1 Chronicles were lost or distorted after the book was finished. The only evidence they offer is that we find the book confusing in some places. Therefore, they reason, the book must have been damaged or tampered with. Why is it so hard for us to admit we're confused and leave it at that? Why must we assume the Word of God is defective whenever *we* do not understand it? I believe it is better to admit our inadequacy than to invent corruptions of the sacred text which no man can prove. Some day we will know for sure why Zebulun and Dan are left out and why Naphtali has only a verse. Until then, from the speculations of man, I take refuge in ignorance. "Where ignorance is bliss, 'tis folly to be wise."[26]

When several explanations are suggested for a passage of Scripture, I look for one that puts a biblical character in a better light. While I haven't a clue about poor Zebulun's exclusion, I can suggest a good reason why Benjamin gets so much attention. I believe the ends of chapters 8 and 9 are monuments to Jonathan and to his friendship with David.[27] Jonathan was worthy of honor, yet he was cut off in the midst of his days. Here in the boring parts, he and his posterity have their everlasting memorial. The genealogies give double honor to this man who loved the Lord's anointed and proved it by his deeds.

Jonathan's place in Scripture reminds me of Moses'. Though he served God well, for his sin at the waters of Meribah, Moses was excluded from the Promised Land.[28] God refused his last request to enter Canaan. He died in the desert, and "no one knows his grave to this day."[29] Similarly, after a lifetime of good works Jonathan was slain in battle beside his wicked father, and his body became a trophy for the Philistines. Yet in both cases the careful student of Scripture discerns a happy ending. Moses made it to the Promised Land after all; he was present at the Transfiguration of Christ. His seeming punishment turned out to be a blessing. Instead of walking through territory still occupied by sinful Canaanites, Moses saw the Promised Land and its fulfillment—the glorified Messiah. (So Fanny Crosby said she was content to be blind on earth, because the first thing she would see in heaven would be Jesus.) Jonathan died, but David, remembering his promise to his friend, honored his son Mephibosheth (or Merib-Baal). The chronicler faithfully records Mephibosheth's posterity through many generations, ending in the sons of Ulam, who were both archers and mighty men of valor.[30] Wouldn't that warm brave Jonathan's heart?

Thus the genealogies come to an end—with a monument to Jonathan. It says, in effect, that whatever may happen to us in this life, God will be faithful to honor our memory and to care for our families. How many brave Christians, do you suppose, who have perished before their time in this world, have such a memorial in the Lamb's Book of Life?

The Next Time Around

Originally, this chapter ended with the words you have just read. While I was working on The Law of the Leper (chapter 8), my daily Bible reading led me back to 1 Chronicles. The funny thing was, I got so much more out of it the next time around! That's how it is with the Scriptures; the more you know, the more you learn, even in the begats.

Of course the logical thing to do would be to integrate the new information with the original. This being the age of computers, there is no need to retype the whole chapter when adding a paragraph here and there. Therefore I trust you will not think laziness the motive behind this addition. No, as John Donne said of Christ, "Nor doth he by ascending, show alone, But first he, and he first enters the way."[31]

I must go before you in the study of the boring parts. Unless I expose my ignorance,[32] I cannot demonstrate how fertile the soil is in these dry places of Scripture. Prayerful study is the rain which makes this desert bloom. Having prayed and studied while writing this chapter, I harvested more the next time I passed through.

I have friends who used to go to Big Bend National Park in West Texas almost every spring to see the flowers there. (Only infirmity keeps them away now; old age alone couldn't do it.) They love the flowers so much, after many years they were asked to write a book about them, using their own photographs.[33] Their passion for and pleasure in the surprising beauty of nature now stimulates others to consider the lilies. Sure, I'd rather go to Big Bend than read the begats, but you can see the same wonder in both places. By the power of God:

> The desert shall rejoice and blossom as the rose;
> It shall blossom abundantly and rejoice,
> Even with joy and singing.
>
> (Isaiah 35:1–2)

When we water them with time and faith, the begats blossom forth abundantly. They live and grow, they live and grow in us! Here's a portion of my second growth in 1 Chronicles.

Fruits Worthy of Repentance

The first thing that struck me was the huge amount of space given to Judah's descendants. Chapter 2 (which is quite long), chapter 3, and half of chapter 4 are all devoted to the fourth son of Leah. Of the other patriarchs, only Levi and Benjamin have long genealogies, and neither of theirs compares to Judah's. (If we exclude the portions devoted to the Levites, Judah's genealogy is nearly as long as all the other tribes' put together.) Much of this disproportionate length is explained for us: "Judah prevailed over his brothers, and from him came a ruler" (1 Chronicles 5:2), whether David or Christ. Also, Judah was the most numerous tribe, and for centuries it formed an independent nation.

However, that's not the whole story. Judah's genealogy is indirectly a monument to the dangers of sin and the value of repentance. The sins of his three older brothers (and their lack of repentance) disqualified them from inheriting their father's chief blessing.[34] Judah's sins were not small, his election savors more of grace than of works, but at least he avoided breaking the letter of the Ten Commandments and, more importantly, he brought forth fruits worthy of repentance. He spared the life of Tamar, whom he could have destroyed, and never knowingly had intercourse with her.[35] His moving speech on Benjamin's behalf revealed his repentance for his crime against Joseph.[36] Judah's massive genealogy is a testimony to the mercy of God, who remembers the good and forgives the evil in His children with generous hearts.

When you read these begats, do you tremble for fear lest you should miss the mark, as Reuben and Simeon and Levi did? Are you encouraged by the life and genealogy of Judah? Do you perceive the wisdom of that ancient saying, "Judge none blessed before his death, for a man shall be known in his children" (Ecclesiasticus [Apocrypha] 11:28, KJV)?

The Woman and the City

One thing keeps bugging me in the genealogy of Judah. It is the name Ephrath or Ephratah (and its derivative, Ephrathite). Since I find it four times in these begats and seven other times throughout the Old Testament, surely it has significance.[37] The commentators tell us Ephratah was an ancient name for Bethlehem and the name of Caleb's wife (not Caleb the son of Jephunneh). The issue they never seem to address is the connection, if any, between the woman and the city. I cannot get rid of the idea that there is a connection, because two of Ephrath's descendants are called the father of Bethlehem.[38]

Genesis 35:19 tells us plainly that Ephrath and Bethlehem are the same place. It does not, as far as I know, prove which name is older, though Bethlehem seems to have been the current name when Genesis took its final form. (Their meanings are similar: Ephrath means fruitful, and Bethlehem means house of bread.) If we assume that Ephrath is the older name of the city, the easiest solution would be that the woman took her name from the place. But her husband was Judah's great-grandson:[39] She must have been born in Egypt or the wilderness, not in the Promised Land. We really can't say why this place and this woman have the same name. The only thing I feel sure of is that they are related by something more than coincidence.[40]

Some comparisons may be helpful to us at this point. Bethel and Hebron are the first two examples that come to mind of ancient Jewish cities with pre-Israelite names.[41] Bethel was formerly called Luz, and Hebron was known as Kirjath-Arba. There are some sixteen references to these two places by their older names, yet only one of them occurs after the book of Judges.[42] By contrast, of the dozen or so references to Ephratah and Ephrathites, over half of them are found after Judges. Another difference is that we are plainly told two times that Bethel had been Luz previously, and that the name of Hebron formerly was Kirjath Arba. But we are never told that the name of Bethlehem was previously Ephratah. A third difference is that there are no references to Luzites or Arbites, but Ruth's first husband and David's father are both called Ephrathites.[43]

Once again you may respectfully inquire, "So what?" ("A question to be asked," as Shakespeare's Falstaff would say.) I believe the Scriptures are telling us something, and we would do well to pay attention. Micah immortalized the name of Ephrath in his famous prophecy:

> But you, Bethlehem Ephrathah,
> Though you are little among the thousands of Judah,
> Yet out of you shall come forth to Me
> The One to be ruler in Israel,
> Whose goings forth have been from of old,
> From everlasting.[44]

The Old Testament would not give so much mention and glory to Ephrath, if it were only an obsolete name for Bethlehem. Whatever the connection may be between Ephrath the place and Ephrath the woman, much of the glory belongs to the woman.

Caleb's wife must have been a special person, for very few women are mentioned so often in the genealogies. Yet we do not know in what way she was remarkable. Probably she was an excellent wife and mother, for we hear of her in those capacities. All generations call Mary blessed,[45] because she was chosen to mother Jesus. Need we look further than motherhood for the reason of Ephrath's prominence in the Scriptures? Two of her closest descendants are distinguished by the title "father of Bethlehem." Her name is associated with Ruth and Jesse and the prophecy of Micah. Could more honor be given to a woman found only in the begats?

I believe Ephrath has suffered a fate similar to Mordecai's. You may remember that Mordecai, for saving the life of King Ahasuerus, had been mentioned in the chronicles of Persia.[46] Then he was forgotten. The night before Mordecai would have been hanged,

> the king could not sleep. So one was commanded to bring the book of the records of the chronicles; and they were read before the king. And it was found written that Mordecai had told of Bigthana and Teresh, two of the king's eunuchs, the doorkeepers who had sought to lay hands on King Ahasuerus. Then the king said, "What honor or dignity has been bestowed on Mordecai for this?" And the king's servants who attended him said, "Nothing has been done for him."[47]

To commemorate her goodness Ephrath is mentioned in the book of Chronicles. What honor or dignity have we bestowed on her? To our shame we must answer, "Nothing has been done for her." King Ahasuerus neglected Mordecai briefly; we have overlooked this mother of Bethlehem for two millennia. Shouldn't we, like Pharaoh's butler,[48] remember our faults this day? Shouldn't we honor Ephrath at least with recognition when we come across her name? In the Body of Christ, "If one member is honored, all the members rejoice with it" (1 Corinthians 12:26). Let us not fail to rejoice when God honors a mother in Israel.

Their Fathers Were Keepers

Last time I paid attention to 1 Chronicles 9:20, which says of Phinehas, "The Lord was with him." Yet I completely missed the previous sentence about the gatekeepers: "Their fathers had been keepers of the entrance to the camp of the Lord." This time it dawned on me: when they returned to Jerusalem from Babylon, Shallum and his brethren renewed the worship which God had ordained in the wilderness of Sinai, which their ancestors had performed a thousand years before them.[49]

Think about it. What were your ancestors doing a thousand years ago? Few people know, but surely it was different from what you're doing now. They couldn't have been reading a Bible study book, unless they lived in a Christian land, were learned enough to read, and were rich enough to buy handwritten manuscripts. (Remember that in those days many of the wealthy could not read. Lots of monks were reading and writing manuscripts, but they weren't supposed to have descendants!)

Consider how those gatekeepers felt. They returned from Babylon, built a temple from the ruins of Jerusalem, and worshiped God with the same rituals their ancestors used in the days of Phinehas. How shall we grasp what this meant to them? England has not been conquered from abroad since 1066. Imagine the English being subjugated by a Moslem power and taken captive to desert lands. After generations there a few of them return to the wreckage of London, build a church, and begin to worship Christ in the English tongue. Wouldn't they experience awe and gratitude beyond the comprehension of those who have always enjoyed (or endured) the privilege of Anglican worship? Wouldn't they treasure the soil and salvation their backslidden ancestors took for granted?

"A thousand years in Your sight are like yesterday when it is past" (Psalm 90:4). "Jesus Christ, the same yesterday, today, and forever" (Hebrews 13:8). Shallum and company were the physical and spiritual offspring of the gatekeepers in the camp of the Lord. Now, two millennia beyond the time of Shallum, we are their spiritual descendants. God's people have no temple built with hands. The genealogies of the Levites have been lost for centuries. Yet the Church of Christ still has leaders, and leaders need workers to assist them. If we usher or otherwise keep order in a church, we are the true successors of the gatekeepers of Israel. If we take care of buildings and grounds and provisions, or if we help our church leaders in some other way, we are the modern equivalent of the Levites. Our spiritual ancestors served in the wilderness with Moses, in the tabernacle with Phinehas and Samuel, in the temple with Solomon and Ezra. We have all come out of Egypt; we have all returned from Babylon. With awe and awareness let us gratefully say, "Our fathers were servants in the camp of the Lord."

6

THE TABERNACLE

(Exodus 25–40)

One of the delights of the Christian life is letting the Bible grow on you. Like a faithful spouse, after many decades it is ever new. The Word of God is living, never ceasing to surprise even its oldest and wisest readers. They have as much to look forward to as novices who have never read their boring parts. To study the Scriptures with the mind of faith is to obtain a foretaste of eternal life. He whose heart is set on heaven will often pasture there.

Jesus said, "If you believed Moses, you would believe Me; for he wrote about Me" (John 5:46). I used to give those words a narrow meaning. I thought they referred to Moses' prediction, "The Lord your God will raise up for you a Prophet like me, from your midst, from your brethren" (Deuteronomy 18:15). Over the years, I realized Jesus was saying more than that. The more I read, the more I saw that the genealogies, the history of the chosen people, even the tabernacle and its rituals—all pointed to Christ. Jesus was referring to *all* the writings of Moses; from the creation to the Promised Land, Moses wrote about Christ. More than any of us imagine, "He wrote about Me."

Most Bible readers can manage to get through the genealogies in Genesis and the laws of the covenant in Exodus 21–23. Most of us don't really hit the wall until we come to the tabernacle in Exodus 25. There the going gets tough. The good news is, you don't have to be tough to keep going. You just have to be flexible, patient, and in love with your Messiah. As you discern Moses writing about your Beloved, you will be both willing and able to pay attention.

Generally speaking, I would say the commentators have done a better job with the tabernacle than with Numbers 7 or the genealogies. Most of the older commentaries, and many of the new, can help you understand that the tent and its furnishings are symbols (or shadows) of Christ. As long as you avoid those scholars who discredit or dismember the Word of God, you will find something to enrich your reading. There are also books specifically devoted to the meaning and symbolism of the rites of Moses. I shall not attempt to duplicate those efforts. Rather, I shall pass through the end of Exodus, stopping here and there to point out things of interest, to glean the wisdom hidden in the worship of the Jews.

Exploring the Tabernacle

You Can't Miss It

The first thing to notice—and you can hardly miss it—is the repetition in these chapters. Why the Millennium, which generates so much Christian literature these days, is limited to one chapter in Revelation, while the boring parts, which generate next to none, pop up over and over again, I do not pretend to know. But so it is. In Exodus nearly everything gets a double mention. First, the Lord tells Moses what to make (chapters 25–28, 30). Then Moses tells us what was made, in nearly the same words we heard before (chapters 36–40). Through the mercy of God we have an intermission in chapters 32–34, where we learn about the golden calf, the shining face of Moses, and other things of interest.

Here is a portion of Matthew Henry's commentary on all this repetition:

> It may be thought strange that Moses, when he had recorded so fully the instructions given him upon the mount for the making of all these things, should here record as particularly the making of them, when it might have sufficed only to have said, in a few words, that each of these things was made exactly according to the directions before recited. We are sure that Moses, when he wrote by divine inspiration, used no vain repetitions; there are no idle words in scripture. Why then are so many chapters taken up with this narrative, which we are tempted to think needless and tedious? But we must consider, 1. That Moses wrote primarily for the people of Israel, to whom it would be of great use to read and hear often of these divine and sacred treasures with which they were entrusted. . . . That which they ought to read again and again . . . is written again and again. . . . 2. Moses would thus show the great care which he and his workmen took to make every thing exactly according to the pattern shown him in the mount. . . . Thus he teaches us to have

> respect to all God's commandments, even to every iota and tittle of them. 3. It is intimated hereby that God takes delight in the sincere obedience of his people, and keeps an exact account of it, which shall be produced to their honour in the resurrection of the just. . . . 4. The spiritual riches and beauties of the gospel tabernacle are hereby recommended to our frequent and serious consideration. Go walk about this Zion, view it and review it; the more you contemplate the glories of the Church, the more you will admire them and be in love with them.[1]

You will find many good things in this imperishable commentary.

A Little Golden Key

Before the boring parts of Exodus are even above ground, the Lord provides a way to make them all exciting. It's as if He said, "I'm building a ten-story cinderblock warehouse in your backyard. It may cramp your style a bit, but you won't mind once you use this." Then He gives us a little golden key, which opens every room in the drab-looking place. Inside we find rare and beautiful treasures beyond anything we ever imagined, each with its personal note to us saying "I just wanted you to have this." We'd be careful not to lose that key!

What is it? Exodus 25:8: "Let them make Me a sanctuary, that I may *dwell among them*" (emphasis added). Dwell among us? This is something new. God told Abraham He would be a God to him and his descendants.[2] After the Exodus He promised, "You shall be a special treasure to Me above all people . . . a kingdom of priests and a holy nation" (Exodus 19:5–6). Now at the first mention of the tabernacle, He says that He will dwell among us! To put this statement in its proper perspective, consider that the rest of the Bible is essentially the outworking or fulfillment of Exodus 25:8. Does that seem too much to claim for one little verse at the entrance to the boring parts?

"And the Word became flesh and dwelt among us, and we beheld His glory . . ." (John 1:14). A literal translation of this passage is, "the Word became flesh and *tabernacled* among us."[3] When the Old Testament was first translated into Greek (well before the time of Christ), the Greek noun derived from this verb was used to express the Hebrew words for tabernacle. Furthermore, the Hebrew word for tabernacle in Exodus 25:9 is derived from the word *dwell* in 25:8. In other words, the linguistic ties between Exodus 25:8 and Christ's dwelling among us could hardly be stronger.

John 1:14 is the first biblical use of that Greek word for dwell; its last use is equally instructive:

> Then I, John, saw the holy city, New Jerusalem, coming down out of heaven from God, prepared as a bride adorned for her husband. And I heard a loud voice from heaven saying, "Behold, the *tabernacle* of God is with men, and He will *dwell* with them, and they shall be His people, and God Himself will be with them and be their God. (Revelation 21:2–3, emphasis added)

The Interlinear Bible reads, "Behold, the tabernacle of God with men! And He will tabernacle with them. . . ." The Greek noun and verb are that closely related. The point of all this linguistic exercise is that the coming of Christ and the coming of His heavenly Bride are inseparable from Exodus 25:8. If you want to understand the end of Exodus, you must read your New Testament. And if you want to understand the New Testament . . .

Once you get the hang of it, with this little key you'll be able to open all the boring parts about the tabernacle and its rituals. Would a couple of examples help to strengthen your faith? We shall briefly consider the mercy seat and the robes of the High Priest.

The Mercy Seat

Clearly, the mercy seat was central in God's plan to dwell among the children of Israel.

> You shall put the mercy seat on top of the ark, and in the ark you shall put the Testimony that I will give you. And there I will meet with you, and I will speak with you from above the mercy seat, from between the two cherubim which are on the ark of the Testimony . . . (Exodus 25:21–22)

The symbolic presentation of divine love expressed in these holy objects is one of the most beautiful things in the Bible. I can hardly do it justice, but I will sketch it out a little for you.

As the gospel arose from and fulfilled the law of God, so the mercy seat completed the ark of the covenant. Though we think of the ark as an end in itself, it was really the foundation of the mercy seat.[4] Together they illustrate James' conclusion that "mercy triumphs over judgment" (2:13). The cherubim, symbols of God's power and presence, surround His dwelling place above the mercy seat.[5] Could not the three persons of the Trinity be hinted at here in the qualities we commonly associate with them—the righteous judgment of the Father, the covering mercy of the Son, and the ministering presence of the Holy Spirit?

From the beginning, the tables of the law were preserved in a perfect artistic representation of the redeeming work of Christ. We think of the Ten Commandments as given in fire and smoke and a fearful voice from heaven. This is a very incomplete picture. The whole story, known only to those who read their boring parts, is one of mercy triumphing through judgment, of God's intimate communion with men, and of the overshadowing power of the Holy Spirit. As the gospel first was preached before the doom of Eve and Adam,[6] the newborn law was swaddled in the shining love of God.

For Glory and for Beauty

The garments of the priests take up two full chapters (Exodus 28, 39). "You shall make holy garments for Aaron your brother, for glory and for beauty" (Exodus 28:2). Significantly, this is the first place our English translators use *beauty* to express the meaning of a Hebrew word. We were told in Genesis that women were beautiful, but here we encounter the concept of beauty itself. No one can sum up all the meaning in "for glory and for beauty," but here is one comment I particularly like:

> [Aaron's robes] were typical of the glory and beauty of Christ's human nature, which was as a garment put on, and put off, and on again, and in which he officiated as a priest, and still does: and which is now very glorious, and in which he is fairer than any of the children of men; [they also typify] the garments of his salvation, and robe of righteousness, in which all his people, his priests, appear exceedingly glorious and beautiful, even in a perfection of beauty.[7]

Didn't like what you saw in the mirror this morning? In the robe of Christ's righteousness you are exceedingly glorious and beautiful, even the perfection of beauty. Don't believe it? Read the last twelve verses of Ephesians 5, and meditate on them. Then read the Song of Solomon as the love song of Christ and His Bride, and feel the beauty of their love.[8]

I can't resist pointing out Exodus 39:3, which illustrates so well how the Lord slips in new information when He repeats a boring part. In 28:5 we were told, "They shall take the gold and blue and purple and scarlet thread, and fine linen, and they shall make the ephod. . . ." But in 39:3 something new is added: "And they beat the gold into thin sheets and cut it into threads, to work it in with the blue and purple and scarlet and fine linen thread, into artistic designs."

I find this quite interesting aside from its spiritual meaning. I like to know how things are made. I like being reminded of John Donne's telling his wife:

Our two souls therefore, which are one,
Though I must go, endure not yet
A breach, but an expansion,
Like gold to airy thinness beat.[9]

"That's very nice," you may say, "but what does thread-making have to do with Jesus Christ?" To answer that question we must understand the stuff in which the gold was woven.

I used to wonder about the choice of colors—blue and purple and scarlet—which were used in the high priest's garments and in the veil and tabernacle hangings. It wasn't until I wrote a sonnet about the veil that I realized it was the color of human wounds. Think about it. Have you seen a nasty wound? What we call black and blue is sometimes more like purple and blue. There is usually blood or red swelling around the injury. Could you sum up the coloration of a wound more accurately than blue and purple and scarlet? Purple and scarlet were colors worn by kings in ancient times, so there is certainly a note of royalty as well. Yet the dominant effect, I think, is to remind us of Him who was wounded for our transgressions.[10]

What does thread-making have to do with Jesus Christ? The gold, like our Lord, was beaten and cut. Then it was worked (twisted) into the thread. Do you think it was easy for a perfect and holy God to live among sinful men? "O faithless and perverse generation, how long shall I be with you? How long shall I bear with you?" (Matthew 17:17). Conversely, has it been an easy thing in your life for Christ to work His divine Spirit into you? Has the process been simple—just add water and stir—or has it been more time-consuming and difficult, like twisting golden wire into fragile linen thread?

Gold was used in the high priest's garment, but not in the veil. Perhaps I can suggest why. The veil represented the flesh of Christ,[11] which was torn for us, so His humanity and weakness were emphasized in its colors. But when "Christ came as High Priest of the good things to come, with the greater and more perfect tabernacle not made with hands, that is, not of this creation" (Hebrews 9:11), He came in His divine perfection. Like Melchizedek, He is both Priest and King. Therefore, gold (the royal substance, eternally bright, whatever form it takes) is proper for His priestly garment.

Bells and Pomegranates

Now we come to the pomegranates, the moment I've been waiting for, even if you haven't. (I had read about the pomegranates many a time, but until now I had never stopped to study them.) The high priest had alternating bells and pomegranates on the hem of his robe. The bells were of gold, and the pomegranates were—blue and purple and scarlet.[12] What strikes me right away is the difference in the materials used. Pure golden bells represent the divine call of the gospel and the intercession of Christ. (Dr. Gill points out that the bells were suspended from the high priest's blue robe, which symbolized the righteousness of Christ. In other words, His ability to intercede for us depends upon His righteousness.)[13] His divine work is both shown and sounded out by pure, imperishable gold!

The pomegranates were made of no such heavenly stuff. They were made of fragile cloth in colors reminiscent of human weakness. Why? The Bible mentions the pomegranate mostly in three places: on Aaron's robe, on the tops of Solomon's pillars, and in the Song of Solomon. I find little in the commentaries about the temple pomegranates,[14] but the comments on Solomon's Song are instructive. There, in the traditional interpretation of Christ's love for the Church,[15] the references to pomegranates are related to the Church and its growth. Could the pomegranate be, among other things, a symbol of the Church?[16] In these botanical descriptions does anything remind you of the blushing Bride of Christ?

> The pomegranate is of exceptional interest by reason of its structure, its history, and its utility. It forms a tree of small stature, or a bush. . . . The fruit consists of a hard leathery rind, enclosing a quantity of pulp derived from the coats of numerous seeds. This pulp, filled as it is with refreshing acid juice, constitutes the chief value of the tree. *The more highly cultivated forms contain more of it than the wild or half-wild varieties. . . .*
>
> Its peculiarities are so great as, in the opinion of many botanists, to justify its inclusion in a separate order. . . .[17] (emphasis added)

> The tree, or rather shrub, is but low . . . the blossoms of bright red or scarlet . . . the fruit, the glory of the land of Canaan, as big as a large apple. . . . The inside is full of small kernels, replenished with a generous liquor; in short, there is scarcely any part of the pomegranate which does not wonderfully delight and recreate the senses.[18]

Do you begin to see the bells and the pomegranates as something more than decorations? Next to each symbol of Christ's intercession is a symbol of those He died to save. Next to each reminder of the call of God is a reminder of those responding to the call. While our High Priest makes intercession for us in the heavenly places, He carries with Him tokens of His lover and His love: "A bell and a pomegranate, a bell and a pomegranate" (Exodus 39:26). Does a wedding ring remind you of your lover and your love? The hem of Aaron's robe is a pure love token too.

Not all of my research on the pomegranate was done at the library. I also went to the supermarket and purchased one. Eating and studying it was such a revelation, I bought more pomegranates for our family devotions and for an adult Bible study which I teach. It was interesting to see how both children and adults enjoyed this refreshing (and messy) departure from the usual routine. (This activity is not for Sunday school, unless the kids wear play clothes.) My little daughter kept finding hidden groups of seeds, exclaiming with each one, "Here's another church, Daddy!" And when at the Bible study I cut into a firm and perfect-looking pomegranate, only to discover all the insides were black and rotten, the adults seemed to comprehend the meaning without a word from me.

Closing Considerations

The Pattern

Before we leave our study of the tabernacle, there are several things I desire to point out. The first is the pattern God showed Moses on Mount Sinai.

> According to all that I show you, that is, the pattern of the tabernacle and the pattern of all its furnishings, just so you shall make it (Exodus 25:9).

King David had a similar experience with the temple he desired to build:

> Then David gave his son Solomon . . . the plans for all that he had by the Spirit . . . "All this," said David, "the Lord made me understand in writing, by His hand upon me, all the works of these plans" (1 Chronicles 28:11–19).

Without entering into the mysterious aspects of these communications, we can learn some vital lessons.

> Whatsoever is done in God's service must be done by his direction, and not otherwise. . . . When Moses, in the beginning of Genesis, was to describe the creation of the world . . . he gave a very short and general account of it, and nothing compared with what the wisdom of this world would have desired and expected from one that wrote by divine revelation; but, when he comes to describe the tabernacle, he does it with the greatest niceness and accuracy imaginable. He . . . has told us particularly the measure of every board and curtain of the tabernacle;

> for God's Church and instituted religion are more precious to him and more considerable than all the rest of the world.[19]

By making the model and drawing up the plans Himself, God showed how important the tabernacle was to Him.[20] As He mildly reproved Jonah,[21] may He not say to us, "Is it right for you to ignore the plans which I have made?"

God called two men by name to make the tabernacle and its furniture.[22] Bezaleel and Aholiab were specially gifted artists who carefully followed the divine pattern. When God has special work for a person to do, He gives a clear call and gifts to go with it. God's workers must search out and carefully follow His instructions. (Notice that for both tabernacle and temple, God gave the plans to one man, then called others to the work.) We may not have as clear a channel with God as Moses did, but he who seeks shall find. John Milton has given us, in the invocations of *Paradise Lost*,[23] an example of a great Christian artist seeking God's plan for his masterpiece. Like Bezaleel and Aholiab, Milton was a skilled worker before he began to "justify the ways of God to men."[24] Do you hope to do great things for God?[25] Be sure to master the fundamentals of your trade or calling. Then, should you receive a special summons, pay attention to the pattern which is shown you from above.

I could say more, but there is already a good book on this subject, *The Gift of Art* by G. E. Veith, Jr.[26] Though I wish Mr. Veith had emphasized the importance of the pattern more, I recommend his book to all who serve the Lord through their artistic gifts. He draws wonderful things out of the call of Bezaleel.

More Precious Than Silver

Between the altar of incense and the bronze laver in Exodus 30 we find Moses' account of the ransom money. This money was paid by every adult male to make atonement for himself. It was used to make the massive silver sockets of the veil and tabernacle.[27] Think of the symbolism here! The very foundation of God's house is laid in the price of atonement for the people of God. How beautiful the tabernacle not made with hands must be! For it is founded in something more precious than silver: "You were not redeemed with corruptible things, like silver or gold . . . but with the precious blood of Christ, as of a lamb without blemish and without spot" (1 Peter 1:18–19).

Though the ransom money was an occasional offering under Moses, it seems to have become an annual tribute in New Testament times.[28] For this, the commentators say, was the double drachma (or temple tax)

Peter paid for himself and his Master at the end of Matthew 17. How shall we understand Christ's meaning in those verses if we have never read about the ransom money or the way which it was used?

Have you considered the beauty and meaning of those wonderful words, "The rich shall not give more, and the poor shall not give less" (Exodus 30:15)? Let them roll off your tongue, let them roll through your mind. "The rich shall not give more, and the poor shall not give less." What resonance in saying we are equal in God's sight! What melody proclaiming we are purchased with a price! I have not heard such music (or such meaning) resounding from the Service which collects our revenue.

Cosmetology

Moses spends five verses in Exodus 30 on the instructions for and use of the bronze laver. Then he passes over its construction in one verse of Chapter 38. Ah, but that verse yields some extraordinary information! The bronze of the laver was different from the bronze used in the altar and in construction of the court.[29] "He made the laver of bronze and its base of bronze, from the bronze mirrors of the serving women who assembled at the door of the tabernacle of meeting" (38:8).

Surely there is meaning here! The word for assembled is a military term, suggesting that a large, highly disciplined group of women donated their polished bronze mirrors to make the laver. That vessel, which held water for the priests' required washings, symbolizes the holiness and purity of Christ, and the "washing of water by the word" (Ephesians 5:6), which He performs for His Bride. The giving up of the mirrors signifies renunciation of worldly vanity and all beauty which is not spiritual.

These women seem to have been way ahead of their time. In the Old Testament, we are often told of a woman's beauty, but there are no such statements in the New Covenant. Long before Isaiah spoke of turning swords into ploughshares, these ladies turned their instruments of vanity into a monument of spiritual beauty. Thus they anticipated the teaching of Peter and Paul:

> Do not let your beauty be that outward adorning of arranging the hair, of wearing gold, or of putting on fine apparel; but let it be the hidden person of the heart, with the incorruptible ornament of a gentle and quiet spirit, which is very precious in the sight of God. (1 Peter 3:3–4)

Or as a poet put it:

My dear wife's Cosmetologist
Is truly Master of His trade.
His touch no blemish can resist;
No beauty He bestows can fade.

He needs not gold or braided hair
To highlight all her winning features:
His flawless make-up makes her fair—
To me, the fairest of all creatures.

What is their secret? How does she
Bloom fresh as fields of new-mown clover?
He has her read First Peter Three,
And as she reads, He makes her over.[30]

7

The Sacrifices

(Leviticus 1–9)

Andrew Bonar noted: "There is no book, in the whole compass of that inspired Volume which the Holy Ghost has given us, that contains more of the very words of God than *Leviticus*. It is God that is the direct speaker in almost every page; his gracious words are recorded in the form wherein they were uttered. This consideration cannot fail to send us to the study of it with singular interest and attention."[1]

Exodus ends in a cloud of glory. The Lord is in His holy temple. Now things really ought to get interesting! Who knows what the Almighty will do next?

Just when we hunger for excitement, we come to Leviticus, the most unremitting of the boring parts. Just when we hope to be delivered from tedium, we come to the dullest book of the Bible. There is a valuable lesson to be learned in this predicament. Let's take a minute to make the most of it.

God is like a very indulgent father who happens to be employed as a Marine drill sergeant. (The funny thing is, the kids He so indulges are His former raw recruits. Such are the wonders of adoption.) He is able to be strict or lenient, hard or merciful, depending on what is best for His family. He knows the importance of mastering the basics and doing things by the book.[2] Woe to him who, like Saul, thinks that obedience is essential only at boot camp! Yet, as we see from the history of David, God can be very gracious to those who learn the basics and disappoint Him later.

Israel's Boot Camp

When Israel became a nation, God put all His kids through basic training. The program, you remember, was supposed to last a year. It was a hard course in the desert, but it was all necessary, even the thirty-nine years that were added for disobedience. When God is strict, or when He is tedious, it is for our good. He trains us to avoid disaster. A friend of mine, a former Marine sniper who is now a pastor, once told me about some of his basic training. He had to stand at attention on the beach, where the sand flies were at their worst, for many long minutes at a time. No matter how they bit him, he could not move a muscle. It wasn't until he got to Vietnam that he saw the purpose behind it—to save him the move that might cost him his life! Whatever objections he had to that training before he went into combat, he had none thereafter.

All the precise instructions about Levitical sacrifice lead us to one all-important conclusion: There is one way, and only one, to be saved from sin. We must follow God's instructions *to the letter*—or pay with our lives. When Nadab and Abihu, Aaron's oldest sons, perish before the Lord soon after performing their first sacrifice (Leviticus 10:1–3), the message could hardly be clearer. Do it My way or die; there is no other. Does this seem cruel or unnecessary to you? Have you considered the fate of the millions who speak much about God but are lost in their sins? Deceived by false teachers or personal pride, they trust in their own works (like Nadab and Abihu) and not in the sacrifice ordered by God. Do I mean only members of outlandish cults? No. There are nominal Christians who minimize sin, who think they are worthy of friendship with God. How little they know of holiness! How greatly they underestimate perfection! An awful fate awaits the soul persisting in delusion. The boring parts of Leviticus, if only we understood them, are stone walls built to keep God's flock from straying into hell.

God tutored His people in the law of the Levites that they might embrace the gospel of Christ.[3] A mind steeped in the sacrifices is a mind prepared for salvation. Have we, who no longer are schooled by the law, no need of disciplined minds? Have we nothing to learn from Leviticus 10? "Now all these things happened to them as examples, and they were written for our admonition, on whom the ends of the ages have come. Therefore let him who thinks he stands take heed lest he fall."[4]

If Christians were strong in the ground of the faith, if they knew the Rock from which they were hewn and the pit from which they were dug, I might be persuaded that knowing the rites of Moses is not essential to our well-being. But in this age of bloody cults and bloodless churches, of false teachers and female priests, in this new age of ancient heresy, it is a good thing to read Leviticus.

Hands-On Religion

As usual, I find something of interest in the very first section.[5] Right away we are told that he who would offer a sacrifice "shall put his hand on the head of the burnt offering, and it will be accepted on his behalf to make atonement for him. He shall kill the bull before the Lord . . . and he shall skin the burnt offering and cut it into pieces" (Leviticus 1:4–6).

One of our fashionable new words is the adjective *hands-on,* which Webster's[6] defines as "providing direct practical experience." Is your vocabulary up to date? Well then, Leviticus is hands-on religion. Let us consider the direct practical experience it required of Old Testament believers.

This laying hands on the sacrificial animal occurs more than a dozen times in Leviticus. Clearly, it is a central theme of the book, but before we can understand its meaning, we must free ourselves from modern prejudice. The children of Israel were not a barbaric or primitive people. They were not a bloodthirsty rabble of escaped slaves. They were the descendants of intelligent and sensitive men who had served the Lord for generations. They had long lived in, and held positions of power in, the most sophisticated culture of their day. Their leader was well educated in all the wisdom of that culture. It is true that they despised the dog, which was for them an unclean creature, but in general they were kind to animals.[7] (They also did not slaughter their children in the womb.)

The parable Nathan told King David in 2 Samuel 12 gives us an insight into the place of animals in Hebrew culture. Remember that Nathan's purpose was to arouse in David compassion for the oppressed and anger toward the oppressor. Anything bizarre or unusual in the story would distract David, who knew about sheep, and prevent him from identifying with the injured party. Therefore, we may assume that beloved household pets were not unknown in David's time. He lived in a culture where even a man with a houseful of children might treat his pet lamb like a daughter.[8]

No Supermarket, No Cellophane

There was one significant difference between the Jews' treatment of animals and our own. They never went to the supermarket for a leg of lamb wrapped in cellophane. When they wanted some meat, they killed a sheep or goat from their flocks. They were used to killing animals for food; most of us are not. However, we are not talking about killing animals for food. We are talking about destroying them before God to make atonement for our sins. The bull or sheep felt the wrath of God—divine wrath intended for the man whose hand was on it. Even the dullest sacrificer knew the animal he offered was a substitute for him. It is one thing to kill an animal to feed your family; it is quite another to slaughter one to pay for your misdeeds. Was it so much easier for a Jew in the desert to kill his atoning sacrifice than it would be for you or me? I doubt it. I think the chief difference is that we do not always face or feel the pain Christ suffered for us, because ours is not so directly a hands-on experience.[9] It is easier for us to avoid the ugly reality than it was for the Jews—but the ugly reality is just the same. The innocent dies for the guilty, the sinless for the sinner. We need to study the sacrifices because they bring home to us that we are the killers of Christ. Let him who is without sin among us first cast a stone at Annas and Caiaphas. We are the killers of Christ. A man who reads Leviticus with attention can hardly think otherwise.

Up to Your Eyeballs

Notice that in chapter 1 there are three different kinds of burnt offerings, one for the bull, one for the sheep, and one for the turtledoves.

> It appears that wealthier men generally selected *oxen* as their offering; and men less able took *sheep* or goats; while verse 14 shows that those yet poorer brought *doves.* God thus left sacrifice open alike to the *rich,* the *middle* classes, and the laboring *poor.*[10]

However, there were some differences in the way the three sacrifices were offered. The owner of a bull must kill it, skin it, and cut it into pieces. The man who brought a sheep must kill it and cut it into pieces, but he was not instructed to skin it. The poor man was only to "bring his offering of turtledoves or young pigeons." The priest performed the slaughter and preparation for him. Clearly there was a progression from much direct involvement for the rich to little involvement for the poor. I do not know the reason for this, but here are the explanations which come to mind.

The first possibility is that the rich man needs more hands-on religion to save him from "pride, fullness of food, and abundance of idleness."[11] It is no small job to slaughter and skin a bull. Like Hobbes' definition of life, the work is nasty and brutish, but it can hardly be called "short." The man who brought his bull for a burnt offering was not planning to spend the rest of the day skiing. Talk to a rancher or farmer who slaughters his own beef, and you'll get some idea of what's involved. It so happens that my friend the sniper turned pastor has sometimes raised and slaughtered his own livestock. He estimates that one man working alone would need half a day to slaughter and skin a bull, *if he only quartered the carcass.* It would take longer to divide the meat into pieces small enough to burn completely on the altar. When were you last so fully involved in such a memorable statement of your guilt before God? When were you last so humbled, so exhausted in the presence of the Lord?

The man who is truly poor in spirit, no matter how little he brings to God, will find it well received and graciously accepted. As for the poor man in Leviticus, we can say that he was either deprived of the honor, or spared the disgrace, of having to slaughter his offering. Perhaps the best way to view the whole business is to look at it spiritually. The man who is proud or rich in spirit will find himself making a bloody mess of things, hacking and hewing all day for his sin, before he enjoys either rest from his labors or peace with God. The larger the portion, spiritually speaking, he has in this life, the harder he must struggle to free himself from it. We would do well, it seems, when we come before our King, to appear as Esther did, with nothing ours and everything our Keeper's,[12] mistrusting self-reliance and the riches of the world. Unless, of course, you like being up to your eyeballs in bull fat on a desert afternoon.

Fire and Salt

The grain offerings in the second chapter of Leviticus can teach us many things. In the Bible wheat is a symbol for man, especially the people of God.[13] God is pleased when we devote ourselves to Him and to the support of His chosen ministers. (Most of the grain offering was eaten by the priests.) What is offered to Him must be the finest we have, and it must be mixed with oil, a symbol of His spirit. The portion burned on the altar was also combined with frankincense, making "a sweet aroma to the Lord" (2:2).

The grain offering must be without leaven and honey, which are both fermentable. Leaven is a well-known symbol of corruption.[14] Honey may represent worldly delight, and it is reported to have been a common element in pagan sacrifice.[15] What every sacrifice must have, on the other hand, was salt (2:13). Jesus referred to this passage when he said:

> Everyone will be seasoned with fire, and every sacrifice will be seasoned with salt. Salt is good, but if the salt loses its flavor, how will you season it? Have salt in yourselves, and have peace with one another (Mark 9:49–50).[16]

The importance of this thought is shown by the prominent location of the parallel passage in Matthew 5:13. After the introductory beatitudes, this is the first verse of the Sermon on the Mount: "You are the salt of the earth; but if the salt loses its flavor, how shall it be seasoned? It is then good for nothing but to be thrown out and trampled underfoot by men." This Preacher was not afraid to draw His illustrations from the boring parts of the Bible.

The Sweet Aroma

Chapter 2 of Leviticus caused me more difficulty than any boring part we have encountered so far. I found good things in it, to be sure, but they were already elucidated in the commentaries. I hungered for something more. "No surprise for the writer, no surprise for the reader," said Robert Frost.*

> Step by step *the wonder of unexpected supply* keeps growing. . . . [The poem] must be a revelation, or a series of revelations, as much for the poet as for the reader . . . [then] it can never lose its sense of a meaning that once unfolded by surprise as it went.[17]

The wonder of unexpected supply—that's our third strategy for reading the boring parts.[18] But how shall my readers strike water from a rock if I can't do it myself? I wanted a fresh insight, a different point of view, but what could it be?

Then, I noticed something. In verses 2 and 9, when the priest burned the grain offering on the altar, it became "a sweet aroma to the Lord." However, in verse 12 the Lord says offerings of first fruits "shall not be burned on the altar for a sweet aroma." Though a grain offering could be made from first fruits, apparently it must be in the form of whole grain, not flour. When the priest burned part of it on the altar (2:16), there is no mention of a sweet aroma to the Lord.

---

* Reprinted by permission of Henry Holt and Company, Inc., "The Figure A Poem Makes," quoted in *Complete Poems of Robert Frost,* copyright © 1967.

Why should one offering give a sweet aroma[19] to the Lord and not another? I started looking around a little. All three burnt offerings in chapter 1 produced the sweet aroma. Then I noticed a discrepancy among the peace offerings (in chapter 3) similar to the one that puzzled me among the grain offerings. The bull or cow (3:5) and the goat (3:16) made a sweet aroma, but the lamb (3:11) did not. Why would a lamb not make a sweet smell to the Lord? I had no idea, and I found no complete answer in the commentaries. I got out my Hebrew concordance and discovered there were some thirty-nine passages in the Pentateuch which mention the sweet aroma. So much for strategy #3; now it was time to travel slow and dig deep.

The Thirty-Nine Passages. I made a list of all the thirty-nine passages, with a brief description of each one, and a corresponding list of offerings burnt on the altar but not causing a sweet aroma. Yes, it took time to make the lists. Yes, I had other things to be doing. So why did I do it? I knew no better way to discover what makes one offering sweet smelling to the Lord and not another. (Of course I knew that sweet aroma could be a remark meant to apply to all the sacrifices, and just thrown in here or there to save space. Yet I also knew, as I trust you do by now, that saving space is not a top priority in the boring parts.) Was there a pattern in the two lists, a clear way of distinguishing the sweet aroma offerings from the others? I trust the suspense is more than you can bear. (Too bad this book is not being published in installments, like some of Dickens' novels, with each installment ending in mystery or surprise. This would be a fine place to leave you hanging!)

Here's what I discovered. All the burnt offerings which are described in detail,[20] with one exception (Leviticus 9:12–14), produce the sweet aroma to the Lord. All the sin and trespass offerings, with one exception (Leviticus 4:27–31), do not produce it. The grain and peace offerings nearly always cause a sweet smell to the Lord. Why would all burnt offerings but one have this effect, and only one sin or trespass offering produce it? I think the tendency is much too clear to be explained away as accidental, and the exceptions seem sufficient only to prove the rule.

As every sacrifice must be salted with salt, every new notion about the sacrifices must be taken with a grain of salt. Including this one. But here's what I came up with. After much study of the sweet aroma, I believe the New Testament explains and confirms the tendency we noted in the different offerings. The Greek words for sweet aroma in the New Testament appear in the context of self-sacrifice and total giving.

> Walk in love, as Christ also has loved us and given Himself for us, an offering and a sacrifice to God for a sweet-smelling aroma. (Ephesians 5:2)

> Indeed I have all and abound. I am full, having received from Epaphroditus the things which were sent from you, a sweet-smelling aroma, an acceptable sacrifice, well pleasing to God. (Philippians 4:18)

I believe these passages show us that voluntary devotion and self-sacrifice are the qualities which smell good to God.[21] We find an echo of this in Mary's pouring out her costly oil upon Jesus. Then "the house was filled with the fragrance of the oil" (John 12:3). I could say more about these New Testament connections, but we are studying the boring parts. How will all this help us with the rites of Moses?

Which of the sacrifices best symbolizes total devotion to God? When Abraham was tested, what kind of sacrifice was he asked to make? The answer to both questions is the burnt offering. All the sacrifices foreshadow Christ, but the burnt offering best expresses His total devotion and love. In the sin and trespass offerings, the emphasis is more on His dying for our wickedness. Neither wickedness nor the death of an only son could ever delight a holy and loving father. That is why the sin and trespass offerings do not produce the sweet aroma, and why the only one that does is the atypical sacrifice of a female goat.

The Four Exceptions. We have explained the vast majority of the sweet aroma sacrifices by saying that they represent total, selfless devotion to God, whether in the offerer or in Christ Himself. We consider the sacrifices without aroma to be reminders of Christ's dying for our sin. We see a clear pattern, a significant difference between the two groups. So far, so good. What about the exceptions? I find four we need to account for, and I shall take them in order.

- The first exception is the grain offering of first fruits in Leviticus 2:14–16 (the one that started all this trouble). Notice in how many ways this sacrifice symbolizes Christ and His sufferings.

  > These are *"ears of corn,"* a figure of Christ (John 12:24). . . . They are *"dried by the fire,"* to represent Jesus feeling the wrath of his Father. . . . *"Beaten out of full ears,"* represents the bruises and strokes whereby he was prepared for the altar. . . . In all this he is *"First-fruits,"* intimating that many more shall follow.[22]

  I suggest that because this offering is redolent of Jesus' sufferings, it could never produce a sweet aroma to the Lord. It hits too close to home to be included with the other grain offerings.

- I believe the same criteria apply to our second exception, the peace offering of the lamb (Leviticus 3:6–11). I see no difference between this sacrifice and the ones before and after it, except the kind of animal offered. I do not recall Jesus being compared to a bull or a goat, but He is clearly called the Lamb of God on a number of occasions.[23] (If you do not accept my "too-close-to-home" explanation, I think you will have to resort to saying the sweet aroma is interjected into the sacrifices at random. Otherwise you must find some significant difference among the peace offerings in chapter 3 which has eluded me, and base your distinction on that.)

- The third exception is the lone sin offering which *does* give off a sweet aroma to the Lord (Leviticus 4:27–31). This is the atypical sacrifice of a female goat referred to earlier. It was to be offered when "anyone of the common people sins unintentionally." This seems less grievous than intentional sin or the sin of a ruler or priest, who ought to know more about the Law than others. I think the difference here is due once again to the kind of animal offered, and also to the rank of the sinner and the sin.

  (I do not feel that I can or that I must devise systematic answers to cover everything in the Bible. I strive to do my best, and when I feel unsure of my answer, as I do here, I say so. This is a principal difference among Bible expositors. Many feel that everything must fit into their systems. They take pains to account for every detail, rarely if ever admitting a weak point in their arguments. Others do not insist on completion or perfection; they can say, as Matthew Henry does, "I cannot account for this.")

- Our last exception is comprised of three different sacrifices in close succession. These are the very first burnt, grain, and peace offerings actually performed by the newly consecrated priests in Leviticus 9:12–21. We do not expect a sweet aroma from the sin offering, but why is there none from those that usually produce it? I take my answer from the end of the chapter: "Then the glory of the Lord appeared to all the people, and fire came out from before the Lord and consumed the burnt offering and the fat on the altar. When all the people saw it, they shouted and fell on their faces" (Leviticus 9:23–24).

  Surely this is exceptional. God Himself consumed the sacrifices at the start of the Levitical ministry. I believe this is why there is no mention of the sweet aroma in chapter 9.

Summary

I have gone on at some length. Have we anything to show for our labors? As I see it, God is like a successful businessman whose son became a missionary to a sinful and backward people. After years of labor and suffering the son was martyred by that ungrateful rabble, for whose sake he had given up his privileged position. Yet his work among them produced fruit that lasted, bringing thousands to the truth. The father often remembers his son with a mixture of pride and grief. When he thinks of the sin and the evil that bereaved him, he has no joy except in knowing what his son's converts were saved from. Otherwise, it is a painful experience. Yet the father loves to dwell on the son's selfless devotion and his all-absorbing love. He remembers how he trained him in the family business, instilling truth and nobleness at every opportunity. He realizes it was not in vain. He thinks of the disciples his son made, how they resemble their master, and how they carry on his work. Those meditations and memories are like a sweet smell, an odor of rest to the old man. They fill him with peace and with love. They soothe him and comfort him. Thus I interpret the sweet aroma to the Lord.

Three Items of Interest

Having spent so much time on the sweet aroma, I shall pass over most of the sacrifices without further comment. I shall notice only the peace offerings, the animals burned outside the camp, and the guilt incurred through ignorance.

Peace Offerings

The ritual of the peace offerings emphasized man's fellowship with God and his joy in the presence of his Maker. After bringing his peace offering to the Lord, a man could eat some of the flesh and share it with his family and friends.[24] Thus it was distinguished from the other animal sacrifices. The burnt offering was wholly burned up to God. The sin offering was partly offered to God and partly eaten by the priests. Only the peace offering was shared by all: the Lord, the priests, and the people each had their set portion.

The time of the peace offering was a time of joy, the joy of real obedience to God. Before honor is humility; before the joy of holiness there must be sacrifice for sin. (Thank God that our holiness is in Christ and not in the filthy rags of our own righteousness!) In Leviticus 9 the peace offerings were offered after the burnt offering and the sin offering. After sanctification and sorrow for sin comes the time for fellowship with God. Thus we celebrate the Lord's Supper after an interval of self-examination and repentance:[25] "Thou hast turned for me my mourning into dancing; Thou hast put off my sackcloth and girded me with gladness . . ." (Psalm 30:11, KJV).

How good and how pleasant it is to bring peace offerings after sacrifice for sin! How important it is to move on from repentance to holy joy! In the place that God chooses for His worship,

> There you shall bring all that I command you: your burnt offerings, your sacrifices, your tithes, the heave offerings[26] of your hand, and all your choice offerings which you vow to the Lord. And you shall rejoice before the Lord your God, you and your sons and your daughters, your menservants and your maidservants, and the Levite who is within your gates. . . . (Deuteronomy 12:11–12)

Is your worship full of holy joy? Do your family and friends share joyfully in your peace offerings to God? (How often I hear the sad story of a Christian home that was not good or glad!) May your peace offerings be like Solomon's,[27] too many and too large to fit upon your altar!

Blood in the Sanctuary

Are you familiar with this touching passage in the last chapter of Hebrews?

> We have an altar from which those who serve the tabernacle have no right to eat. The bodies of those beasts, whose blood is brought into the sanctuary by the high priest for sin, are burned outside the camp. Therefore Jesus also, that He might sanctify the people with His own blood, suffered outside the gate. Therefore let us go forth to Him, outside the camp, bearing His reproach. For here we have no continuing city, but we seek the one to come. (Hebrews 13:10–14)

I find that last sentence especially affecting. In it the New King James translators echo and excel the language of Tyndale, which was wisely retained in the Geneva and Authorized versions. We should certainly applaud when modern scholars touch us with "soul-animating strains—alas, too few!"[28]

If we would grapple with this mystery expressed in Hebrews, we must research the parallel passage, Leviticus 6:30:[29] "No sin offering from which any of the blood is brought into the tabernacle of meeting, to make atonement in the holy place, shall be eaten. It shall be burned in the fire."

The sin offerings which fit this description are the bulls sacrificed for the sins of the priests and the sins of the people, and the bull and the goat killed on the day of atonement.[30] The question I can't get rid of is, Why were these particular sacrifices, and no others, singled out to be burned and not eaten? I'm sure there's an answer, but I've not been able to come up with a comprehensive one, nor have I found one in the commentaries. I wish I had a clear explanation that would make everything fit perfectly, but I don't.[31]

> Ah, but a man's reach should exceed his grasp,
> Or what's a heaven for?[32]

If you know or if you should discover a good answer, I would be happy to hear from you. In the meantime I reluctantly take the advice of the gravedigger in Hamlet:

> Cudgel thy brains no more about it,
> for your dull ass will not mend his pace with beating.[33]

It's better to concentrate on the things we understand. I like the way Matthew Henry explains what the author of Hebrews is saying:

> The apostle infers the advantage we have under the gospel above what they had under the law; for though the blood of Christ was *brought into the tabernacle, to reconcile within the holy place,* yet we have a right by faith to *eat of the altar* (Hebrews 13:10–12), and so to take the comfort of the great propitiation.[34]

We have greater privileges than the sons of Aaron had. We also have the honor of sharing Christ's reproach, of being cast out of the worldly Jerusalem for sharing in His righteousness. Only those who are willing to be led or cast out of the city of sin escape the destruction sure to come upon it. Remember Lot's wife.[35]

Once again our main point is the intimate relation between the Testaments, especially between Leviticus and Hebrews. How shall we understand the one without the other? If we refer to the boring parts only as we need them for background to the New Testament, our knowledge will be spotty and incomplete. We shall resemble the immigrant cab driver in Manhattan, who learned the city from his riders, instead of buying a map and preparing himself in advance. How much would you tip a cabby who asked directions at every corner south of Houston Street?

Sins of Ignorance

I cannot leave the sacrifices without some discussion of Leviticus 5:17, a verse full of meaning for us today: "If a person sins, and commits any of these things which are forbidden to be done by the commandments of the Lord, though he does not know it, yet he is guilty and shall bear his iniquity."

There's an up side and a down side to maturing in Christ. The up side is discovering more of the glory of God and His love for His children. The down side is learning more about sin, especially our own. What we never gave a thought to in our early walk with Christ, we later see as sinful and defiling. The closer we draw to God, the more we see how unworthy we are of His fellowship.

> The cases referred to here are evidently those wherein *holy things, or things connected with worship,* were neglected or defectively performed. It is that class of cases wherein—it may be through ignorance—the Lord was defrauded of what was due in his worship.[36]

We are not Old Testament Jews. We don't have to abstain from shellfish or swine, or fear a dead lizard may keep us from God.[37] How shall we apply this Scripture to ourselves?

The way we most commonly defraud God in our worship is by trusting in our own righteousness. To think that we are good enough for God, that we can go to heaven because we try to be good, is a terrible insult to Christ. Imagine offering to die in the place of a convicted felon, only to have him swear at you for saying he's guilty! That's the true relationship between Christ and many a nominal Christian. The ram without blemish which atones for such sin is a repentant and grateful heart. Christians don't need to go around scourging themselves and wallowing in their wickedness. But they do need to acknowledge their guilt before God and their gratitude to Him who took it all away.

We may also sin against the Lord by neglecting prayer, by neglecting or diluting tithes and offerings, or by not giving them with a cheerful heart.[38] Yet the chief thing we should gain from Leviticus 5:17 is an awareness of our need to know all of God's law. Ignorance is no excuse. The Christian who wishes not to offend his Maker learns and keeps His commandments. Whether or not they are exciting is not his chief concern.

Consolation

Let me close with a word of consolation. I have studied the sacrifices but never mastered them. The longer I boil each one in my brain, the more they all seem to come out scrambled. What's waved and what's heaved? What's sprinkled, what's poured? Why a bull or a goat?[39] Is it trespass or sin? With a preschooler's comprehension of these mysteries, why shouldn't I sound like a Dr. Seuss book? I hope you derive some comfort from my confusion. Better yet, I hope you don't need any comfort, because Leviticus is clear as day to you. But, if so, keep it to yourself, willya? Don't sing songs to a heavy heart, and don't parade your uniformed lucidity around my tattered thoughts. Misery loves company, but not the friends of Job.

You just had to be there to know what some things are all about. To me the Levitical rites will always be one of them. But I think God has a purpose even in this. As I lift my befogged brain from the shadows of Leviticus, what a blessing it is to see the one clear Son shining down from the heavens. I do understand that Christ died for my sins, that He is my peace and He is my righteousness. "O glorious, golden, glad sun, the only true lamp—all others but liars!"[40]

8

The Law of the Leper

(Leviticus 13–14)

The early chapters of Leviticus may not be exciting, but at least they are short. Chapters 13 and 14, on the other hand, contain nearly sixty verses apiece. Together they are half as long as the first nine chapters! It's not their length, however, but their meaning, that interests me. Surely there's a reason for this accumulation of detail. Surely there is wisdom in the law of the leper.

It doesn't matter much to me what particular disease this leprosy was. Whether or not it still exists today,[1] the question is how to apply these ancient regulations to modern life. Most of us aren't worried about catching leprosy, and we certainly can't go to the sons of Aaron for treatment. So what can we do with these chapters, except skip or suffer through them? You know by now I can find something of interest in any boring part. Whether or not it stimulates you, I'm sure to find something that fascinates me. "How will he do it here?" you inquire. Come and see.

Something Worse Than Acne

After reading only a few verses of chapter 13 I start to feel desperate. This stuff about scabs and sores is totally lost on me. I've got to travel very light and very fast here, if I stick around at all. Unlike Ulysses Grant, I have no intention of fighting it out on this line if it takes all summer. I'm ready to run at the first scream of the mortars. So what can

I do? First, I try not to panic. I'm not going to suffocate; it just feels like it. Next, I try to neutralize the feeling that I *have* to read this. Pressure of that kind incapacitates me. Once I've calmed down a little, then I can be creative. I'm not getting anything on VHF; could UHF be better? AM's not working; what about FM? In other words, that totally hopeless feeling, properly understood, instructs me to look for a different angle or another level of meaning. Why not try it? I've got little to lose, and it's certainly more dignified than heading for the hills.

Okay. Slow and steady now, and back to the beginning. What's going on here? When a man has something wrong with his skin, he shall be brought to the priests. Why the priests? I don't recall anything about the priests healing people. Well, maybe they didn't have doctors. But Pharaoh had physicians, and Job called his friends worthless physicians.[2] They must have had some kind of medicine, even in the wilderness. Let's keep that on the back burner and look a little further. Verse 3 says, if "the sore appears to be deeper than the skin of his body, it is a leprous sore." A sickness that's more than skin deep. Hmm. Then the priest isolates the patient and waits to see if the sore is spreading (vv. 5–8). If it spreads, the priest must pronounce him defiled, or unclean. It is leprosy.

Before we go further, let's see what else we know about leprosy from other parts of the Bible. Who was the first person to get it? Miriam, the sister of Moses. When she did, her partner in crime cried out, "Do not lay *sin* upon us!" Then he said, "Do not let her be as one *dead!*"[3] Why did he use those words?

You can learn about a disease from its treatment. However, there is no treatment for leprosy. Throughout the Bible, it is healed directly by God or not at all. (Chapters 13 and 14 say nothing about treating or healing. They tell how to diagnose leprosy and what to do when a leper is healed.) There is only one person in the Bible who did something which helped to cure his leprosy. That was Naaman the Syrian.[4] He didn't do much, but what he did was significant. He washed seven times in the Jordan River. Naaman couldn't wash and be healed in any other river, despite his raving about it—only in Jordan. Let's see. Where else in the Bible is washing in the Jordan significant? (You don't have to be Thomas Aquinas to figure out the symbolism here.)[5]

God has a funny way of telling us things in Scripture. He gives us a pile of laws, stories, and letters and says, "Read this." No index, no forty-volume commentary, no "paragraph 44, subsection C." Seems like He wants His Book to be different from traffic codes or textbooks. We get some things plain as day—"Love one another"—and others, like the meaning of leprosy, in a roundabout fashion. To catch His meaning in hints and symbols and stories, you have to spend time in His Book. You have to exercise the logical and creative sides of your brain. Sure it takes time and it takes work. But when the Bible comes together for you, it's like Goliath's sword: "There is none like it; give it to me" (1 Samuel 21:9).

Let's look at what we've learned. Leprosy is more than skin deep, likely to spread, and dangerous enough to make a fuss about. A priest, not a doctor, must diagnose it, and he may need several appointments to do so. The first time someone caught it, the high priest begged for deliverance from sin and death. The only thing that seems to help is responding to the Word of God by washing in the Jordan River. Now it's time for a riddle. What is there in modern life that seems to fit this description? What could make us hopelessly unclean in the eyes of God, and unable to fellowship with His people? (No doubt the teenagers will cry, "Acne!", but it's something worse than that.) You will not be bored by the law of the leper if when you see *leprosy* you substitute *sin*.

Difficult to Diagnose

Let's try it. Let's stop looking at the physical and start looking at the spiritual. Let's look at these chapters as manuals for the discovery and cleansing of sin.

There seems to be an inordinate amount of space devoted to the proper diagnosis of this disease. It doesn't take forty-six verses to tell if you have measles or mumps.[6] Is sin really so hard to discern? Hear the testimony of Richard Baxter, a great seventeenth-century pastor, a man well qualified to speak on this subject: "It is not so easy a matter to discern a man to be certainly graceless, as many imagine it to be."[7] And Matthew Henry says, "It is a work of great importance, but of great difficulty, to judge of our spiritual state."[8]

The intricate instructions in chapter 13 were designed to aid the priest in making a difficult and momentous decision. The man whom he pronounced unclean must "cover his mustache and cry, 'Unclean! Unclean!' . . . He is unclean, and he shall dwell alone; his habitation shall be outside the camp."[9]

Even the king, if he were a leper, must dwell alone, as the story of Uzziah shows.[10] What a horrible fate it would be for a clean person to be pronounced leprous by the priest! One could hardly be too careful or too patient in discerning this uncleanness.

Let's apply this to modern life. How careful and patient are we in judging whether a man is clean (or acceptable) in the sight of God? Do we patiently observe him over time? Do we carefully analyze his symptoms in accordance with the Word before drawing our conclusions? Have we taken care to sanctify ourselves before looking at our brother? Seen in this light, the law of the leper is full of instruction.

The basic analogy here is between the leper and the lost sinner. The lost are banished from the camp of Israel: the Spirit cannot tolerate the fellowship of sin.[11] Until he is healed by the power of God, the sinner is an exile from New Jerusalem. Therefore, Christians must be able to judge the spiritual condition of others, to know the clean from the unclean.

> To know man is vital to a (Christian) worker. . . . Our effectiveness in service is closely related to our discernment of man's spiritual condition. If God's Spirit enables us through our spirit to know the condition of the person before us, we can then impart the appropriate word.[12]

If we would take Leviticus 13 seriously, we would be well on our way toward having this essential knowledge. We would not make snap judgments about the salvation of others. We would not condemn the innocent or bless the guilty. We would testify to the lost of their need for Christ, and we would encourage our brothers and sisters who are weak in the faith. Woe to us if we encourage the sinner and discredit the saint!

A secondary application of this principle will help us to deal with sin in believers. We all have sins and weaknesses, but we do not have them all alike. As C. S. Lewis has said, a man who fears cats may display more courage in picking one up than some naturally brave men do when they go into battle. What a blessing we are to others when we understand this, when we know how to give a word in due season. Is what we see a superficial blemish, or a mark of corruption in the soul? Is it the last vestige of pride in a man of God, or is it the sign of a rebellious spirit? I assure you I ponder these things when I read the law of the leper.

Lord, help us to be serious about sin. Give us the patience and wisdom to know the clean from the unclean. Forgive our past presumption, and help us to be faithful ministers of your truth. Amen.

Quotes from the Masters

I find some things in the commentaries too precious to withhold. First, some fine language from Dr. Gill: "*The plague of leprosy* . . . was an emblem of sin . . . with which every man is defiled, and which renders him infectious, nauseous, and abominable; and of which he is only to be cured and cleansed by Christ."[13]

Infectious, nauseous, and abominable—say it out loud to yourself (unless you're in the library!). The sound and the meaning work together for good. Who would have thought the boring parts could move methodical Dr. Gill to Shakespearian utterance? For what can rival his description but this immortal line: "The rankest compound of villainous smell that ever offended nostril"?[14] (I know Falstaff and the good doctor make strange companions, but here they have the field to themselves.) If only we avoided sin as Falstaff did work, or the Jews lepers! Then it would be well with us.

Here is a portion of Andrew Bonar's stimulating commentary on Leviticus 13:12–17:

> At first sight it seems strange, to ordain that the man should be reckoned *clean,* if the leprosy were out upon him, and covered him wholly. . . . It seems meant to teach that the Lord has a deep abhorrence of a *corrupt nature*—deeper far than merely of corrupt actions. We are ever ready to take home the guilt of *evil deeds,* but to palliate the evil of a *depraved heart.* But the Lord reverses the case. His severest judgement is reserved for *inward* depravity. . . . And yet more. Is it not when a soul is fully sensible of entire corruption, as Isaiah 1:5, that salvation is nearest? A complete Saviour for a complete sinner?[15]

These are some of Matthew Henry's thoughts on the same place.

> If men freely confess their sins, and hide them not, there is no danger comparable to theirs that cover their sins. . . . There is more hope of the profane than of hypocrites. The publicans and harlots went into the kingdom of heaven before scribes and Pharisees. In one respect, the sudden breakings-out of passion, though bad enough, are not so dangerous as malice concealed.[16]

And concerning verses 18–23, Mr. Bonar tells us:

> Marks, or remnants of former sins, may remain, though the *leprosy* be not there. Remains of an old peevish temper, of a proud, haughty demeanor, of a hasty judgment, of a taste for some earthly things, may exist in a pardoned man. They are remnants—scars—of an old wound. But if these indicate a tendency to spread, or show that they are "deeper than the skin," then the leprosy is there—the man, in spite of other appearances, is really an unforgiven, unsaved man.[17]

Valuable as his comments are, some recent books on Leviticus do not even list Bonar's commentary in their bibliographies. The tyranny of fashion, it seems, has subjugated more than models and designers.

Leprosy in Garments

Speaking of clothes, the end of chapter 13 is devoted to leprosy in garments (vv. 47–59). Most of the older commentators agree with John Calvin: "This kind of disease, God, in His infinite clemency, has willed to be unknown to us. . . . What the leprosy of garments may be, is unknown."[18]

Some more modern expositors think it was "in all probability nothing but so-called mildew."[19] While preferring the older view, I think it more important to find a relevant application of these Scriptures than to solve the biological puzzle they present. As you will see, I apply them differently from the commentators I have read.

Generally, if they find any symbolism here, the commentators say the garment stands for whatever is closest to us. Our friends, our employment, our possessions, our personal habits, all of these if impure may become dangerous to us. We must treat them with caution, and cut ourselves off from them if they cannot be reformed. We are referred to the passage where Jude speaks of "hating even the garment defiled by the flesh" (Jude 23). I think this sort of interpretation is valid; it just doesn't do much for me. I get more zip out of this passage by coming at it from a different angle.

Taking a hint from Isaiah and Hebrews, where the earth and the heavens are compared to a garment,[20] I use these verses to meditate on the big picture. God is the Priest; we and the land we inhabit are the garment. When a nation or a culture becomes infected, God in His wisdom carefully inspects it. He waits and watches; does it have a spreading leprosy, one so virulent the culture must be destroyed (Leviticus 50–52)? If He sees signs of hope, He washes it with the washing of water by the Word.[21] His servants make His will known, and He waits again to see if the people will repent (vv. 53–54). If the washing produces no change, destruction is inevitable. If there is a change, if a remnant responds to His Word, God tears out the infected part and preserves the rest (vv. 55–56). If the plague of sin breaks out again, the land is doomed: judgment shall accomplish what mercy could not. Yet the chapter ends on a hopeful note. If a nation is washed in the Word, and the plague disappears, "then it shall be washed a second time, and shall be clean" (58). The land which was so dangerously infected shall once again be acceptable in the eyes of God.

If you can relate to this kind of interpretation, you must admit the "leprosy of garments" is only too familiar to us. The sins of our culture are as red as scarlet. Isaiah admitted as much when he said:

Woe is me, for I am undone!
Because I am a man of unclean lips,
And I dwell in the midst of a people of unclean lips. . . .[22]

Yet God in His mercy was patient with Jerusalem. He cleansed it in the time of Hezekiah. He tore out the infected part in the reign of Josiah.[23] Only when the infection reappeared after Josiah's death was the city destroyed. That was more than 150 years after the vision of Isaiah.

I do not pretend to know the future of our culture. I know that our sins are great, and that God is merciful. The most I would venture is that God has not yet told us to stop praying for our land and its people.[24] In other words, there is still hope. The Priest is still waiting to see if this garment, or part of it, can be saved. It is our job to stop the plague from spreading. As He fingers the fabric, is not the Priest asking, "Who is on My side? Who?" (2 Kings 9:32).

Rituals of Cleansing

Leviticus 14 is a beautiful chapter, well worthy of attention from our finest artists. Have we no painter's vision of the cleansed and sprinkled leper glimpsing his last of the liberated dove? (Let it not be said!) Many a song might amplify the theme, but this old hymn comes to mind:

O happy! O happy day!
When Jesus washed He washed my sins away![25]

(You haven't lived until you've heard a soulful choir sing it!)[26] If you get no joy from this chapter, the boring parts must be your personal Sahara.

Some things are too lovely to analyze. I don't melt down my wedding ring to guarantee its goldenness. I don't think about spondees and anapests when I read Milton's sonnets. Whether you're into baseball or ballet, you know the time when awe is better than analysis. The cleansing of the leper requires such response. Marvel at it. Paint it in your mind, or picture it on instant replay, but fill your soul with its symbolism. Don't worry about what it means. Just absorb it. It will do you good.

A Question to Be Asked

There are two rituals in chapter 14 each of which has a single parallel in Scripture. First, the two "living and clean birds" of verses 4–7 have no equivalent except the two goats on the Day of Atonement.[27] (One of those goats was killed and the other set free.) However, I will practice what I have just preached to you, and leave that first portion undisturbed.

Second, the blood and oil on the right ear, thumb, and toe of the leper (Leviticus 14:14–18) have no parallel except in the consecration of Aaron and his sons.[28] In that ceremony, the blood of the ram of consecration was applied to the same three places on the bodies of the priests. What I had never noticed before, however, is that the cleansed leper has *oil and blood* placed on his ear, thumb, and toe, while the priests receive nothing but blood. Why does a priest get blood, when a cleansed leper gets oil and blood? A question to be asked.

When I spot something like this, after having missed it entirely in prior readings, my Geiger counter starts ticking. I know some spiritual truth is being illustrated for us, but I don't know what it is. Let's see if we can find out.

When I started to write this book, I considered the godly commentators to be Olympians of the spiritual realm.[29] They dwelt apart; and while I noticed their peculiarities, they seemed, like the wiles of Juno or the rage of Mars, a part of their divine nature. Somehow that changed as I wrote the chapter on Numbers 7. I realized the commentators were to me what Peter was to Cornelius—a specially favored (and sometimes fallible) member of the same fallen species. I began to see that I could not always go to them for the answers to my questions. Whatever the value of the questions might be, if I was to have answers, I must find them myself. Then I started to recognize *which* questions I would have to answer, *before* I researched them. I began to sense that certain subjects were long-unfurrowed ground.[30] And so it proved here. One commentary approached the question in my mind, but neither asked nor answered it.[31] Gradually, as I meditated on the Scriptures and browsed among my books, the following thoughts took shape.

The union of oil and blood. The union of oil and blood is significant. It completes both the anointing of the priest and the cleansing of the leper.

> Then Moses took some of the anointing oil and some of the blood which was on the altar, and sprinkled it on Aaron, on his garments, on his sons, and on the garments of his sons with him; and he sanctified Aaron, his garments, his sons, and the garments of his sons with him. (Leviticus 8:30)

In the law of the leper, by placing oil "on the blood of the trespass offering" the priest makes atonement for the leper.[32] Thus in both ceremonies the union of oil and blood signifies completion. However, there are some differences between the two rituals. The priest is sprinkled with anointing oil and blood, which fall mostly on his garments.[33] The leper brings more ordinary oil for his cleansing, and on his ear, thumb, and toe that oil is mingled with the blood. I believe that an examination of these differences will help us to answer our original question.

The first thing that strikes me is that the oil and blood are combined on the *body* of the leper, but they are sprinkled mostly on the *garments* of the priest.[34] The reason for this, I think, is that the priest and the leper are types, or symbols, of different things. The priest represents Christ as our High Priest, and he also represents those who minister in Christ's name.[35] Here we shall examine only the latter aspect, that gospel ministry which Christ has given to us. The priestly garments symbolize the righteousness of Christ and His other attributes. No one who trusts in his own merits may minister in Jesus' name. Whatever the ministry, celebrating or preaching, evangelism or hospitality, the Christian is totally dependent on the grace and merits of his Savior. He must be personally washed in the blood of Christ; therefore the blood is applied to his ear (hearing), thumb (doing), and toe (going).[36] His ministry is not his own, but the Lord's. Let us learn from this sprinkling of the oil and the blood; unless we are wrapped in the finished work of Christ, we shall do nothing well.

There is a memorable scene in Bertolt Brecht's play *The Life of Galileo.* It starts with the Pope seated in his underwear, discussing important issues with the Inquisitor. As they speak, a servant brings a succession of garments to his master. The first ones are simple linen; the last are gorgeous silk. By the time they finish talking, the Pope is resplendent in his finest robes. We have witnessed the transformation of a mere man into the Vicar of Christ. Whatever Brecht's purpose in this scene may have been, he illustrates for us a spiritual truth. Any person who truly ministers in the name of Christ undergoes this transformation. The power and purity of our ministry is not in ourselves but in Him who called us. The light we beam in dark places is not ours but our Master's. The blood and oil fall largely on our robes to remind us that we are His ambassadors. If we read Leviticus 8 with wisdom, we will not forget it.

The leper is a type or symbol of the sinner saved by grace. In the ritual of his cleansing the emphasis is on his person, not his garments. He must have the blood of Christ applied directly to his soul. He must be anointed with the Spirit of Christ.[37] Then he is saved. Over time, the sinner will become an effective servant of Christ, a Christian minister, for the cleansed leper of the New Covenant becomes a priest as well. But in the moment of his cleansing, it is enough for him to exhibit God's plan of salvation. Receiving the blood and the Spirit, he enters into fellowship with the children of God. He is no longer a stranger to all that is good, but a member of the commonwealth of Israel. The outcast is joined to the Body of Christ. The exile embraces his siblings in the family of God.[38] What other ceremony interprets so beautifully our spiritual resurrection from the dead?

When a baby is born, no one worries about clothes. The emphasis is on new life, not new garments. Even the most fashionable mother thinks her newborn looks grand in a hospital towel. (At least then we understand the body is more than raiment!) When we are born again, the angels of heaven rejoice like delighted parents. They are as pleased by our infant cries for grace as by any anthem we shall sing when mature. Later they will watch us grow in the Spirit, making sure that our garments are sprinkled like Aaron's. But not at our birth. You don't dress up a baby in a celebrant's robes.[39]

Why does the leper receive oil and blood on his ear, thumb, and toe, when blood is enough for the priest? They symbolize different aspects of God's love; therefore, their ceremonies are differently ordered. The leper is the sinner saved; the priest is the bearer of Christ. The leper rejoices in his salvation; the priest carries that joy to others. The leper stands still and receives the salvation of the Lord; the priest labors in Christ's vineyard. Oil and blood they both require, and both display God's glory. Their differences arise from the facets of redeeming grace which each of them foreshadows.

The poor leper. Verses 21–32 are devoted to the ceremony of cleansing for a poor leper. He must still bring a lamb for a trespass offering; it must be lamb's blood on his ear, thumb, and toe. The oil of his cleansing may be mingled only with the blood of a lamb. But he might substitute doves for the two lambs of sin offering and burnt offering. Noticing this, Andrew Bonar was inspired to remark:

> Probably, the Lord was pleased with this arrangement for another reason, viz., it gave occasion to the more frequent display of Jesus as the *dove*—the holy, harmless, undefiled One, made sin for us. And it is beautiful to observe how the exigencies of his creatures, instead of puzzling Divine wisdom, call forth a display of his resources, and furnish opportunities for manifesting his love.[40]

Though I had to look up *exigencies,* which Noah Webster defined as urgent needs or pressing necessities, I love that last sentence. How true it is. Our urgent needs do furnish opportunities for God to show His love. Our poverty does call forth His gentleness and generosity. The "wisdom that is from above" (James 3:17) is never puzzled by our problems. Remember that the next time you think you're in a fix.

Leprosy in Houses

The last third of chapter 14 concerns leprosy in houses. Here again there are different ideas about what this plague was and what it symbolized. I trust you won't mind if I ignore the controversies and give you a practical application. This passage is a manual for helping troubled families, particularly the family of God. There are several principles illustrated here to which we should pay heed.

The first is, when great difficulties arise, no man should be the sole judge of what is nearest and dearest to him. He must get help from an objective person, one trained in the things of the spirit. The tentative language of verse 35, "It seems to me that there is some plague in the house," contrasts sharply with the rash judgments to which men are prone. Remember Judah's? "Bring her out and let her be burned!" And Saul's? "You shall surely die, Jonathan."[41] Before an unruly child is banished from home, before a church member is cut off from fellowship, we must seek the patient counsel of godly people who are not caught up in the passions of the moment. Admittedly, there is too little discipline in our homes and churches today. However, if those who dare to discipline in the midst of this laid-back generation would proceed according to the law of the leper, they would find others falling in behind them.

He who examines a leprous house must not be fooled by appearances. He must be able to see its structure and foundation.

> Then the priest shall command that they empty the house, before the priest goes into it to look at the plague, that all that is in the house may not be made unclean; and afterward the priest shall go in to look at the house.[42]

Any experienced landlord knows that tenants put rugs and pictures over damaged places when they hope to recover their deposit. Isn't the Lord of the law of the leper the most veteran landlord of all? He has more real estate than Ahasuerus, more tenants than Joseph's Pharaoh, and more patience than Job. He knows all our tricks. He knows that we'll promise Him anything as long as we need lodging, and that there's nothing we won't do once we think the place is ours. You who are called to examine houses, take a tip from the Master. Don't begin until you're sure that nothing can be hidden.

Second, if, after patient examination, we see that the plague is spreading in the house, we must take action. The rebellious child who will not respond to proper discipline, the church member who defies the church—these must be removed from the house (Leviticus 14:40), lest the house should come to ruin. Remember the balance in Paul's admonition: "Do not keep company with him, that he may be ashamed. Yet do not count him as an enemy, but admonish him as a brother" (2 Thessalonians 3:14–15).

Third, once the infected stones are removed, the rest of the house must be scraped clean. I find verses 41 and 42 especially interesting. After the gap is repaired, the whole house must be replastered. In other words, we must treat the stones which remain very carefully. They must be scraped (as with a stiff wire brush) and all the scrapings carted off to long-polluted places. When every taint of evil is removed, then it's time to replaster. We may lovingly restore the house to its pristine condition.

A member of my church runs his own auto body shop. From him I've learned how much labor goes into a good paint job. If a car has poor paint or rust spots, it must be stripped to the metal. The chrome must be removed and the body repaired. Only then is the car ready for painting. Three coats of primer (with sanding between each coat) and three coats of finish paint must then be applied. (Special treatments may require more.) This type of paint job may cost ten times as much as the mask-spray-and-sell job which looks good to an untrained eye. But you get what you pay for. The real thing will last. Now consider our two most venerable institutions—those trusty old Studebakers—the family and the Church. The Lord who built them, despite jeers and mocking offers from demonic new car dealers, has always kept them running. How many times, when they seemed ready for Satan's Scrap and Wrecking, has He restored them to perfection? When you pull your church or your family into the Lord's body shop, which kind of paint job do you think He'll recommend?

The last resort. We must, alas, consider the fate of houses to which the plague returns. They shall be broken down, and all their stones and timbers carried off to unclean places. Two times, as a last resort, the Lord did this to His own family and Church. Yet each time He carefully applied the principles of the law of leprosy in houses. How careful He was to empty the house before He entered it in judgment! The uncontaminated things were lovingly watched over. In the reign of Nebuchadnezzar many Jews were removed to Babylon before the burning of Jerusalem. Among them were Daniel and his friends, Ezekiel, and Kish, the ancestor of Mordecai. We know also that the lives of Jeremiah, Baruch, and Ebed-Melech the Ethiopian were spared.[43] O Israel, trust in the Lord!

Centuries later Jesus warned His disciples:

> When you see Jerusalem surrounded by armies, then know that its desolation is near. Then let those in Judea flee to the mountains, let those who are in the midst of her depart, and let not those who are in the country enter her. For these are the days of vengeance, that all things which are written may be fulfilled. (Luke 21:20–21)

We know from more than one ancient writer that Christ's advice was followed. Here is Eusebius' account, written early in the fourth century:

> The whole body, however, of the church at Jerusalem, having been commanded by a divine revelation, given to men of approved piety there before the war (with Rome), removed from the city, and dwelt at a certain town beyond the Jordan, called Pella. Here, those that believed in Christ having removed from Jerusalem, as if holy men had entirely abandoned the royal city itself, and the whole land of Judea, the divine justice, for their crimes against Christ and his apostles, finally overtook them (the unbelieving Jews), totally destroying the whole generation of these evildoers from the earth.[44]

About the same time that unwary thousands were streaming into Jerusalem to celebrate the Passover, the followers of Christ fled the doomed city. Josephus tells us that more than a million Jews perished in the siege,[45] yet, as one commentator remarks, "there is not evidence that a single *Christian* perished in Jerusalem."[46] How consistent this is with Leviticus 14:36.

From the time of Lot to the time of Titus, the Roman commander, we see the Lord, when He must destroy a house, separating the clean from the unclean before the final judgment. Yet we also know that many good Christians have suffered for their faith. From the Roman circus to the Soviet gulag (or the jails of Atlanta), Christians have been grievously persecuted. How can we reconcile these things? Does the Lord care for some of His people and not for others? I read the facts differently. They tell me that Christians never agonize alone. The God who is able to deliver His children, when He leaves them to suffer (as He did His dear Son), attends them "with groanings which cannot be uttered" (Romans 8:26). When we understand this as clearly as Peter and John, we shall be found rejoicing when we suffer for His name.[47]

No Stone upon Another

After I finished this chapter, a friend steered me to Duncan Derrett's article, "No Stone upon Another: Leprosy and the Temple."[48] This impenetrable piece of scholarship[49] contains a very interesting idea. Derrett suggests that when Christ cleansed the temple, He fulfilled the law of leprosy in houses. He cleared out the moneychangers to inspect the house for sin. I find this interpretation helpful. To me, it explains why Jesus' visit to the temple fills the interval between the cursing of the fig tree and its withering away in Mark 11. He used the temple and the tree as two graphic illustrations of one theme—the judgment sure to fall upon corrupt and fruitless people.

The priest who examines a house for leprosy shall not destroy it until his third visit.[50] Jesus examined the temple twice.[51] Forty years later came the final visit—and utter destruction at the hand of the Romans. Foreseeing this, Jesus told his disciples, "Do you see these great buildings? Not one stone shall be left upon another, that shall not be thrown down" (Mark 13:2). Was He thinking of Leviticus 14:45: "And he shall break down the house, its stones, its timber, and all the plaster of the house . . . ?" Another question to be asked.

On a Positive Note

I am happy to say that the law of the leper closes on a positive note. The house in which the plague has not spread shall be pronounced clean (14:48). Since we can never have too much of something so beautiful, that cleansing is celebrated with the same ineffable ceremony (of the two birds) with which the chapter opened. Assuredly, I say to you, I have not found its equal, not even in the exciting parts of Scripture.

9

Ezekiel's Temple

(Ezekiel 40–48)

The boring parts, like judgment, begin at the house of God. They also end there. The first extended boring part is Moses' description of the tabernacle. Ezekiel's vision of the temple is the last. They end where they begin, but the glory of the latter house is greater than the former.[1] The vision of Ezekiel excels the temple made with hands. And so it should. God never does anything twice without doing it more gloriously the second time. Ask a resident of New Jerusalem. Or ask a man who loves a woman.

Since Ezekiel's temple excels the tabernacle, is the end of his book more tedious than the end of Exodus? I believe this is an area of Christian liberty. Let everyone be fully persuaded in his own mind. As for me, I used to think the prophet's vision the hardest of the boring parts,[2] but I've had so much fun writing this book that I can honestly say, "What—me worry?" There's gold in them-thar hills, I've learned, and God will help me find it. May He grant you, Reader, the same blessed assurance.

The Key to the Vision

The key to Ezekiel's vision is in the first verse: "In the twenty-fifth year *of our captivity* . . . in the fourteenth year *after the city was captured* . . . " (40:1, emphasis added). The prophet was writing to a people whose hopes in this world were utterly destroyed. Jerusalem was only a memory to them, and another generation must pass before their liberation under Cyrus. God gave this vision to His people at perhaps the lowest moment in their history, almost precisely at the midpoint of their seventy-year captivity.[3] (It's as if in 1950, when Stalin reigned supreme, the peoples of Russia and eastern Europe received a vision of 1989.) I believe the Lord's first purpose in making it known was to encourage the exiles, to assure the chosen people that they were not forgotten. Whatever application the prophet's vision may have in modern times, it was specifically given to the captive Jews of Babylon.[4] It was relevant to them. We should not seek abstruse or later meanings until we understand the first and plainest one.[5]

Ezekiel's vision is an elaborate description of a temple and a city. It includes a bewildering variety of measurements and dimensions, of laws for the priest and laws for the prince, of instructions for worship and dividing the land. What could all this mean to an Israelite in Babylon? The Lord says clearly that if the Jews will forsake their past idolatries, "I will dwell in their midst forever" (43:9). This is the ultimate promise of the Bible, one we have already followed from Mount Sinai to New Jerusalem. It is also the meaning of Ezekiel's temple. God is telling the Jews what He told them before. When the tabernacle was shown to Moses, when Solomon was building the temple,[6] the Lord made the same (conditional) promise. Whatever the literal fulfillment of the vision may be, its meaning to the captives is clear. "You have all you need. This temple and this city are greater than those which I destroyed. Keep My law, and trust Me to provide the temple and the worship, the city and the land you long for. Behold this prophetic monument to My faithfulness, and rejoice." Or as the hero in a western put it, "Take heart, little lady."

You may think four words from the good guy better than nine chapters from the prophet. But you won't when you know how to apply the vision to your own life. Has your family been destroyed by sin? Is your church or your personal life in ruins? If not, you should still take note, for "man is born to trouble, as the sparks fly upward" (Job 5:7). However shattered your surroundings appear to you, they are not more shattered than the hopes of Ezekiel's audience. What gave hope and strength to them may strengthen you today. Here's how it works.

Remember Numbers 7, that monument to God's sacrificial love? Ezekiel's temple is a larger monument to His faithfulness. It shows the Old Testament God of wrath (as some conceive Him) to be a most incurable optimist. He has just torn down the house and marched His delinquent kids off to reform school, and now He's sending them blueprints of the new mansion He's building. Can you imagine the impact on the kids? "Wow! Look at this! He's building a new house for us, one bigger and better than we had before!" If you were stuck in Nebuchadnezzar's College of Etiquette, wouldn't those blueprints cure your depression and help you to cope with the rigors of Babylon? Sure they would, but there's a hitch. The plans only help kids who believe Dad means what He says. If you think about past failures, if you concentrate on the times when you imagine He let you down, then His plans will seem like a cruel joke.[7] But for kids who know their Father loves them, the stack of blueprints couldn't be too thick. They just love to look at them. They don't care if it's the electrician's diagram for the bathroom; they like it just fine. "Here's what my Daddy is building for me! Isn't it grand? Wanna see the broom closet? It's got places to hide in. And look at this banister! Won't that be fun to slide on?" Actions speak louder than words, and plans are more tangible than promises. It's hard for kids to keep things neat with blueprints spread all over, but God rejoices in a mess that stems from simple faith.

In one of their movies, the Marx brothers have a scheme to get rich quick. They're so sure it will succeed that they start drawing up plans for the mansion they'll build with the profits. Then they get in a big fight over who gets the room next to the maid's room. (They all want it; I guess they envision Mae West as the maid.) Well, what's the difference between us and the Marx brothers? How can we know we're not just fantasizing? If we say, "We're looking at God's plans, not our own," and that's the whole truth, we shall be blessed indeed. But are we using God's Word in a way which pleases Him? Any fool who's made a wreck of his life can apply some scrap of Scripture to his wounds and tell himself he's okay. Or he can use the Scriptures as scaffolding, nailing them together any which way to prop up the walls of his fantasy. To guard against this kind of construction, we need to ponder the time and setting of the prophet's vision.

When Ezekiel saw God's temple, Nebuchadnezzar was at the height of his power. He was, everyone agreed, supreme ruler of the world. He had no challengers to speak of, and any lands unconquered lay very far away or had nothing he wanted. Compared to Nebuchadnezzar, Stalin in 1950 was not even on the scoreboard. Though he ruled the Soviet empire with an iron hand, a rival power with hydrogen bombs was present to withstand him. His dominion was limited. Nebuchadnezzar had crushed his rival empires; he could be humbled only by the God of heaven.[8] There was no earthly power in whom the Jews could hope. They were a broken people.

Israel had now been captive for a generation. Though Jerusalem had been destroyed only fourteen years before, Daniel and many of Judah's finest had been hostages in Babylon for two decades prior to that.[9] In other words, God kept His blueprints to Himself when His delinquents landed in reform school. He made them wait. He knew it was easier to demolish a house than to destroy a family's delusion. When that harder work was accomplished, then He sent blueprints.

Ezekiel's vision is for those whose earthly hopes have long been in ruins. They know what it is to wait for the Lord; they know because they have no alternative. If God does not deliver them, they shall never be delivered. They know the truth of that saying, "You cannot expect too much from God, or too little from man."[10]

Before we examine God's blueprints, let's examine our hearts. Are we the kind of people for whom the blueprints were written? Have we repented of our own sins and the sins of our fathers? Is the Lord our only hope, or do we wait for another? Are we simple enough to believe Him and humble enough to obey? Take a minute and think about it. If you do, you will not despise Ezekiel's vision or dismiss it as too boring.

Literal or Symbolic?

There are different ideas about what Ezekiel's temple represents. In fact there are tons of ideas about it. These may be roughly divided into two categories: the literal and the symbolic. Those who interpret the vision literally say that it represents either Solomon's temple, or a plan for the second temple, or a temple to be built by converted Jews in time to come. Others see it as a symbol encouraging captive Jews to believe that true worship would be restored.[11] The traditional view, which prevailed in the Christian Church until the nineteenth century, is that Ezekiel's temple signifies the gospel church expressed in Old Testament terminology.

Too Much to Learn

The reason there's so much fuss about Ezekiel's vision is that one's views of it will affect one's views of Revelation and the end times.[12] May I remind you that our goal is to enjoy the boring parts? Since I do not enjoy tearing down positions held by others, or defending my own, I would simply say that I prefer the symbolic interpretations, were it not for one passage which I cannot ignore. There's too much to learn about *homo sapiens* (that most peculiar species) from the ways he tries to cope with Ezekiel 42:15–20.

You should resist the urge to skip this section because it is too technical. Rather you should consider it a brief and diverting anthropological expedition. Where else will you find a gentle and sympathetic guide, a layman much like you, to lead you through the briar patch of textual criticism? "Well," you say, "I have no interest in this particular briar patch. It does not concern me." Ah, but surely you are interested in having a good time. Good things and good times are often found in unlikely places. Which leads me to the following anecdote.

The Whole (and Sordid) Truth

I grew up in Washington, D.C., only an hour's drive from Baltimore. To tell the whole (and sordid) truth, to one raised in an affluent section of D.C., that historic port was little more than a train stop on the way to New York. I and my friends rarely went *to* Baltimore; we only went *through* it. As far as I was concerned, except for its marvelous train museum, Baltimore hardly existed.[13]

My best friend in adolescence later became a city planner. For several years he lived in and worked for the city of Baltimore. One day in my late twenties, I accepted his invitation to visit him there. He took me on a tour of the city, including places little known to tourists. What a revelation! Seen through the eyes of one who knew and loved it, Baltimore was an exciting city, full of life and wonderfully different from D.C. We ended the day in Little Italy with a meal I wish I could forget. The lasagna I ordered was so good, so perfect to my taste, that all subsequent lasagnes have been found wanting.[14] The peril of visiting Baltimore, I discovered, is that in some things it is so much richer than Washington.

When I told my friend what I was feeling, he summed it all up with a story. He told me of a Pittsburgh native, who had become a professor at George Washington University in downtown D. C. Sometimes the professor would tire of white-collar, unindustrial Washington. He remembered a simpler life. He hankered for home. "When I want a *real* city," he told my friend, "I go to Baltimore."

The City of Textual Criticism

Though nothing there equals lasagna in Little Italy, yet come with me to the city of textual criticism. You'll find things there you never found at home.

Verses 16–20

Ezekiel 42:15 is easy enough: "Now when he had finished measuring the inner temple, he brought me out through the gateway that faces toward the east, and measured it all around." But all purgatory breaks loose in verses 16–20. The question is this: Does Ezekiel's guide measure the temple in cubits or in rods?[15] In other words, is the temple 875 feet on each side or a mile on each side? Is it the size of a stadium or the size of a city? If you read only one Bible, you are likely to think there is no problem. If you consult several translations, however, you are sure to be amazed.

Let's look at how some English versions deal with this passage. Most translators use either rods or cubits in verses 16–19. Some have no unit of measurement in verse 20, because the Hebrew has none, and some supply their unit of choice to make things uniform. (In the following list, those with an asterisk have no unit of measurement in verse 20.)

RODS (or REEDS)	CUBITS
Geneva (1560)	Revised Standard Version
King James (1611)	Berkeley[16]
Noah Webster (1833)	The Bible—An American Trans.
Revised Version (1885)*	New English
American Standard (1901)*	New International (NIV)
A. Harkavy's translation (Jewish)	Good News[16]
Young's Literal Translation*	New American (Catholic)
Emphasized Bible*	Living Bible[16]
New American Standard (NASB)*	Jerusalem and New Jerusalem*
The Interlinear Bible*	
NIV Interlinear* (Kohlenberger)	

Clearly, we have a major division of the translators here. The older versions and the more literal modern versions use rods, while the modern versions which translate more freely use cubits.[17] If you ask, "How did these differences arise?" or "On what are these translations based?"—I can only reply, "Thereby hangs a tale." I hope you find it interesting.

It's All Greek to Me

The Hebrew clearly expresses everything in rods,[18] except that in verse 20 it reads simply "five hundred." There is, as far as I know, no Hebrew manuscript in existence which reads "five hundred cubits." So where do the translators get their cubits? *From the Greek.* "From the Greek?—but the Old Testament was written in Hebrew." You are correct, but the Hebrew was translated into Greek some two thousand years ago. And it is from the Greek that most advocates of the cubit mine their material.

The early Greek version of the Old Testament is known as the Septuagint, from the seventy translators supposedly employed in the work.[19] In Ezekiel 42:15–20, the Septuagint never uses *rods* and twice (vv. 17 and 20) uses *cubits.* What caused the Septuagint translators to switch to cubits? Was it the peculiar Hebrew of verse 16 (see note 18)? Was it that a square mile of temple area seemed too big to them? Did they work from a Hebrew manuscript different from those we possess? The answer to all these questions is, "We don't know." We only know that they went for the cubit, and after twenty centuries they have found their followers.

Why do so many translators of this passage favor the Septuagint over the Hebrew? I think it's because today so many people expect the temple to be rebuilt. They take Ezekiel's vision literally, and they look for its fulfillment. Obviously it is hard to imagine the Jews building a new temple with over a square mile of holy ground. So believers in the new temple look for one which is five hundred cubits on a side. Here we see an oddity of textual criticism. Those who believe Ezekiel's vision shall be literally fulfilled forsake the Hebrew wording. Conversely, those who take his vision figuratively translate the Hebrew literally. (I told you we were going to an unusual place!)

Should an early translation overrule every manuscript in the original language? Let's imagine a similar situation in the New Testament in which the apostle John tells us about the New Jerusalem: "The city is laid out as a square, and its length is as great as its breadth. And he measured the city with the reed: twelve thousand furlongs. Its length, breadth, and height are equal" (Revelation 21:16).

Twelve thousand furlongs! That's something like fourteen hundred miles on a side! This city is as big as half the United States and fourteen hundred miles high! But nobody worries about it. Why not? Well, first, we figure the Architect knows what He's doing; but mostly it's because, unlike Ezekiel's temple, we don't interpret John's vision literally. No one's theology is threatened by the size of *New* Jerusalem.

However, let's imagine that sixteen hundred years ago a scribe is translating the New Testament into Syriac, Coptic, or Armenian. For some unknown reason he decides that John's city is too large. He changes the "twelve thousand stadia" of the Greek to "twelve thousand cubits." Should our translators then ignore hundreds of Greek manuscripts to follow this scribe? Should they make the city three miles on a side instead of fourteen hundred? To judge by what's happened in Ezekiel 42, our answer would be, "Only if their theology requires it!".

Am I overstating the case against the cubits? Where that measure is derived from the Septuagint, as in the New International Version and other recent translations, I think not.[20] Let our theologies be what they will; we should not tamper with the sacred words of Scripture. It is much better to say, "Here is my system of theology, and here are the Scriptures which support it. There, I admit, is a verse hard to reconcile with my system." Such honesty is commendable. It is also very rare. Every school of Christian scholars tends to distort or, as in this case, even to change the words of Scripture, in order to strengthen its doctrine.[21] The more fierce the debate, the greater the temptation to do so. I believe there is a better way. Let us admit that some words or passages don't fit in with our ideas. Instead of changing or denying the words handed down to us, let us retain and honor them, and let our man-made systems shift for themselves. Let God be true, and every man a liar. Is that too much to ask?

Bedfellows and Friends

Textual criticism can make the strangest bedfellows and part the dearest friends. Let's start with the bedfellows.

You may have noticed some omissions in my list of English Bibles. I left out the Douay, New Catholic, and New King James versions because they use rods and cubits too. They agree in reading "five hundred rods" in verses 16–19, but then they all read "five hundred cubits" in verse 20. As strange as it may seem, there are reasons for this rendering. In verses 16–19, where the Hebrew says "rods," the three amigos faithfully translate it "five hundred rods." In verse 20, where no unit of measurement is mentioned, the translators supply the unit they prefer—cubits! How they reconcile these measurements I neither know nor ask. But I delight in their unexpected concordance, and I appreciate their honesty. For they have retained the inconvenient rods, which so many others have changed to cubits.

In The NIV Interlinear Hebrew-English Old Testament we see how textual criticism, like a whisperer, separates the best of friends.[22] The NIV Interlinear contains the Hebrew text, and under each Hebrew word a literal translation of that word, with the NIV printed in the margin. In other words, it offers a literal English equivalent of each Hebrew word as well as a translation into idiomatic English. This has unusual consequences in Ezekiel 42:16–20. There the word-for-word translation follows the Hebrew, reading "five hundred rods" in 16–19, and simply "five hundred" in verse 20. Meanwhile the NIV (in the margin) follows the Septuagint and reads "five hundred cubits" straight through. To my mind this has a disconcerting effect on the reader, like the anxiety a child feels when his parents argue in public. Or it's like trying to buy acreage from a real estate firm whose agents give conflicting accounts about the size of the property. Sooner or later you're bound to ask, "Is there another Realtor in town?"[23]

Messrs. H. and Z.

So much for borrowing cubits from the Septuagint. What about getting them directly from the Hebrew? I have run across two commentators who attempt to do this, Hengstenberg and Zimmerli.[24] Of course, not being a Hebrew scholar, I cannot properly evaluate their arguments. However, I can understand them, more or less, and I can compare them with the work of other scholars who argue for the rods. Having done so, I am left with an impression. I am reminded of the poem "O sweet spontaneous" by E. E. Cummings:

> O sweet spontaneous
> earth how often have
> . . . religions taken
> thee upon their scraggy knees
> squeezing and
>
> buffeting thee that thou mightest conceive
> gods. . . .*

Far be it from me to suggest that any scholar's knees are scraggy! (I myself am not in great demand as a model for Bermudas.) Yet I confess

---

* Reprinted from *Tulips & Chimneys* by E. E. Cummings, edited by George James Firmage, by permission of Liveright Publishing Corporation.

to thinking Messrs. H. and Z. are not above squeezing and buffeting the Scriptures that they might conceive cubits. Allow me to explain.

Hengstenberg fastens on the "five cubits rods" of verse 16.[25] After some intricate reasoning about vowel points in Hebrew, he concludes that the proper translation of verse 16 is, "He measured the east side with the measuring-reed, *five hundred cubits in reeds,* with the measuring-reed around."[26]

"Five *hundred cubits* in reeds?" This is having your cake and eating it too. (In the wonderland of textual criticism, we often dispense with reality.) Hengstenberg gets two words, *hundred* and *cubits,* from one Hebrew word. No one else seems to attempt this.[27] Other commentators choose between *five hundred rods* or *five cubits rods.* Since there is a marginal reading in the Hebrew, I see how one can derive either word from the text. But how to get both at the same time is beyond me. Hengstenberg's "five *hundred cubits* in reeds" are, I believe, what Huckleberry Finn would call a stretcher. I give Hengstenberg high marks for ingenuity and creative criticism, but not for faithful rendering of the text. Yet I much prefer his reasoning to the "method" I am about to relate. For, as Huck said of Mark Twain, "There was some things which he stretched, but mainly he told the truth."[28]

Mr. Zimmerli relies on the most common stratagem of modern textual critics: when in doubt (or inconvenience)—revise the text! Make it say what it ought to say.[29]

> Verses 16–19 lead to a total measurement for the temple precinct of three thousand by three thousand cubits. This cannot be made to coincide with the five hundred by five hundred cubit which results from the information given hitherto.[30] Thus the suggestion that the (rods) in the measurement figures in verses 16–19 is of secondary origin is highly probable. It has been inserted because . . . [31]

There follows a mass of conjecture passed off as fact. Whenever a commentator starts to speculate on which words of Scripture are not original (but glosses, insertions, or conflations)—beware![32] You are about to be had. Does the Word of God judge us, or do we judge it? You can't have it both ways. (In the wonderland of textual criticism, not everyone understands this). Zimmerli ends his theorizing by saying that "undoubtedly"(!) the cubit was the original unit of measurement. It just happened to be stuck into verse 16 in the wrong place, due to someone's misunderstanding what the original author meant. Lucky for us we have Mr. Z to make the rough places smooth! (Otherwise we might have to wait for God to do it.)[33]

A Most Unusual Argument

Imagine my surprise when, reading along in Hengstenberg's commentary, I stumbled on this: "Had the prophet wished all these things to be regarded as mere figures, he must have explained this in the clearest manner. The apagogical argument for this view. . . . "[34]

Apagogical! Make my day! I couldn't believe my eyes. When at last I sobered up, I started looking. Nope, not in *Webster's Ninth New Collegiate Dictionary.* Not in *The American Heritage Dictionary.* Not in my one hundred thousand word spell checker (and no guesses, either). Then I struck pay dirt in the original Webster's:

> APAGOGICAL, *a.* An apagogical demonstration is an indirect way of proof, by showing the absurdity or impossibility of the contrary.[35]

(*Rats!* I thought to myself, *nothing about gorillas.*) As it turns out, however, there is both an amusing and a serious application of this unusual word. I believe students may fairly amuse themselves by dropping *apagogical* into one of their papers. They should use it correctly, of course, and in work of a serious kind. What response, if any, such surprising erudition might draw from instructors, should be interesting to discover.[36]

The serious side of *apagogical* (I admit to struggling with the concept!) has to do with our Lord Jesus Christ. For the word is derived from *apago,* a Greek verb meaning to draw aside or to lead away. Jesus used it twice in the Sermon on the Mount.

> Enter by the narrow gate; for wide is the gate and broad is the way that *leads* to destruction, and there are many who go in by it. Because narrow is the gate and difficult is the way which *leads* to life, and there are few who find it. (Matthew 7:13–14)

The same word is used, by the wisdom of God, to describe Christ's entrance into the narrow gate appointed for Him. All four evangelists utilize *apago* to relate the fate of Jesus in the hands of the wicked.

> Then when they had mocked Him, they took the robe off Him, put His own clothes on Him, and *led* Him *away* to be crucified. (Matthew 27:31)

> So he delivered Him to them to be crucified. So they took Jesus and *led* Him *away.* (John 19:16)

O Lord, may no argument from the world, the flesh, or the devil, as to the absurdity or impossibility of imitating Christ, lead us away from following our Savior. Amen.

Among the Oases

The Lord in His mercy intersperses things of interest among these nine chapters. I find three long passages which I cannot call dull. Notice how they are spaced: Ezekiel 43:1–12, 44:1–9, and 47:1–12. It seems they were prepared to refresh the thirsty pilgrim. (We never have more than three chapters [40–42] in a row which deserve the title "boring.") The first two of these oases describe the visible glory of the Lord in His temple; the last reveals the wonderful river of healing. It would be against my principles to comment on such stimulating sections, but I cannot pass them by without proclaiming with the psalmist:

> Oh, give thanks to the Lord, for He is good!
> For his mercy endures forever.
> Let the redeemed of the Lord say so . . .
> They wandered in the wilderness in a desolate way;
> They found no city to dwell in.
> Hungry and thirsty,
> Their soul fainted in them.
> Then they cried out to the Lord in their trouble,
> And He delivered them out of their distresses.
> And He led them forth by the right way,
> That they might go to a city for habitation.
> Oh, that men would give thanks to the Lord for His goodness,
> And for His wonderful works to the children of men!
> (Psalm 107:1–8)

A Parallel for Numbers 7

Between the first two oases we find a description of the altar and its consecration. "Seven days they shall make atonement for the altar and purify it, and so consecrate it" (Ezekiel 43:13–27). Thinking the best of us, though we little deserve it, the Lord assumes that we understood Numbers 7. He does not separately describe the offering for each day, as He did there. Clearly, this is a parallel passage for Numbers 7, one which confirms the special significance of the altar of sacrifice. Having spoken of this at length in chapter three, I will be brief about it here.

There is only one other consecration in Ezekiel's vision. Three verses suffice for the cleansing of the sanctuary, to make atonement for the temple (Ezekiel 45:18–20), but nine verses are devoted to the dedication of the altar. Notice that there is no consecration of the priests, no anointing of the Prince, and no dedication for the altar of incense. The special attention given to the altar speaks for itself. May we have ears to hear it.

A Mysterious Building

Before taking leave of Ezekiel's vision, I would like to point out two of its more intriguing features. In 41:12 the prophet mentions "the building that fronted the separating courtyard at its western end." What is remarkable about this building is how little we know about it. We are told its dimensions, but nothing about its function or its entrances, if it has any. While the commentators have various notions about it, I like Dr. Gill's statement: "What building is here meant is not easy to say, there being nothing in the first or second temple which answered to it: it seems to be a new building; and what the mystical sense of it is cannot be easily guessed at."[37]

This is fine for Dr. Gill, who measures the temple in rods and does not expect it to be built. Those who measure in cubits and look for a new temple tend to have more specific ideas about the building. Let us suppose for the moment that the temple rebuilders have their day at last. I would like to observe the first session of the committee which determines the use of this structure. From what I know of human nature, it won't be a ten-minute meeting.

The Sons of Zadok

Four times in the vision the Lord refers to the priests as "the sons of Zadok."[38] (Zadok, whose name means just, or righteous, became high priest of Israel in the time of Solomon, completing the fall of the house of Eli.)[39] The priests are never called the sons of Zadok in Scripture, except in Ezekiel's vision. There must be a reason why. These four passages emphasize two things: the sons of Zadok are those who draw near to God, and the sons of Zadok "did not go astray when the children of Israel went astray, as the Levites went astray." Like everything else in the vision, the sons of Zadok causes difficulty to, and disagreement among, the various commentators. Is this primarily a reference to the restored priesthood of the second temple? Or does it symbolize the redeemed ones who illuminate this darkened world with the righteousness of Christ? Either way, the sons of Zadok evokes images of sheep replacing goats, of promises fulfilled after centuries have passed, and, most appropriately, of restoration and a second chance to serve the living God. Whatever the meaning of Ezekiel's temple, those who minister in it must be the sons of righteousness.

PART 3

THE LISTS OF THE BIBLE

10

CENSUS AND ITINERARY

(Numbers 1–3; 26; 33)

There are lists in the Bible. There are lots of lists in the Bible. Some lists are repeated, and some are repeated more than once.[1] Do you wish there were fewer lists in the Bible? I don't. "It is the Lord. Let Him do what seems good to Him" (1 Samuel 3:18). The more I read and learn, the more I see the wisdom of God in the Book of His Word. He has reasons for making mountains and deserts in the world, and He has reasons for putting lists in the Bible. The more I study the boring parts, the more good reasons I find for their existence. That God may have other reasons which I cannot comprehend does not trouble me at all. Who am I that I should grasp the wisdom of my Maker?

The lists of the Bible tend to be about people, not about things. The only major exceptions are the sacred things and the sacred land. Lots of attention is paid to sacrificial animals and furnishings for the temple, and whole chapters are devoted to the borders of Israel. But these are things special to God, symbols of things in heavenly places. They are not the things of this world. People and heavenly things are what matter most to God. You can tell from the lists He has left in His Word.

A few of the lists are not boring, so I shall not discuss them. Among these I include the lists of incestuous and immoral relationships in Leviticus 18 and 20. Technically these chapters might be considered boring parts, but human nature being what it is, they do not make dull reading. Leviticus 26 and Deuteronomy 28 are lists of blessings and curses which come upon cultures which obey God or forsake Him. These may be inspiring or frightening, but they are hardly tedious. Last, there is a list of the rebellions of Israel in Deuteronomy 9. Even people who hate history or repetition, if only they would consider the list of their own rebellions,[2] should find this passage moving.

Like many Americans I seem to have a bit of the pioneer spirit, a desire to go where few have gone before. For example, how many authors can you name who have written books devoted to the boring parts? Probably not many. Which brings me to a question: Does it take one to know one? Before I ever thought of making this book, I had met and liked several people who later wrote extensively on one of the boring parts. Seeing no reason to duplicate their efforts, I shall simply give them a plug and go my way.

Mitch and Zhava Glaser of Jews for Jesus have written *The Fall Feasts of Israel.*[3] This is a thorough treatment of Leviticus 23:23–44. The Glasers describe the celebration and meaning of Rosh Hashanah, Yom Kippur, and Sukkot (Tabernacles) in Old Testament, New Testament, and modern times. They glean among the sheaves of Jewish learning, and all the finest grain they offer unto Christ. What more could you ask?

Jim Jordan, minister, author, and Bible scholar, has written a series of papers on the dietary laws of Israel.[4] These include a lengthy commentary on Leviticus 11 and Deuteronomy 14, where the lists of clean and unclean animals appear.

Of course there are other works about the lists of the Bible. These are just two, whose authors I happen to know, which contain a wealth of knowledge beyond what I can offer. What's wonderful about the books (and their makers) is that they are scholarly but not insipid, detailed but not dull. Would God that all the Lord's people wrote so well about the boring parts!

The Censuses

Now to our lists. Since my friends have already written on the foods and the feasts of Leviticus, I shall begin with the census in Numbers 1. (This is the famous boring part from which the book of Numbers takes its name.) The census seems to be closely connected, or even identical with, the numbering of the people who paid the ransom money in Exodus 38. Though they were taken months apart,[5] the total number of men is the same in both counts.[6] Commentators have various ways of explaining this, but we cannot be sure of the true solution. What matters most to us, I think, is to find the relevance of these Scriptures to our own lives.

The First Census

I have already discussed the ransom money in chapter 6 of this book.[7] Here, from a different perspective, is a wise man's comment on the collection and use of those half-shekels of silver.

> The silver, derived from the atonement-money of the numbered Israelites, was chiefly appropriated to the sockets of the tabernacle. . . . Each socket would contain the ransom-money of 6,000 men (3,000 shekels): and each board, therefore, stood upon the ransom money of 12,000 men; for each board stood in two sockets. . . .
>
> Each man could affirm, that the very dwelling-place of God rested on the ransom-money which he had paid for his soul. He could look upon the sockets, and say—my silver half-shekel has gone to make up the hundred talents, of which they are formed. May we not, in like manner, say that the new creation of God, His everlasting dwelling-place in glory, rests upon the redemption of the Church? If one ransomed sinner were to fail of reaching the heavenly city, a living stone would be wanting in the super-structure; and there would also be a defect in the very foundation of the city itself.[8]

All of God's people are written and numbered in His Book of Life.[9] On the days when you feel out of it, unwanted or unneeded in this hyperactive world, think on these things. Take time to stroll around the tabernacle, to view its precious foundation. Reflect on the half-shekel of silver, on the blood beyond price which was paid for your at-one-ment with the true and living God. Assure yourself that, no matter how this world may shake, your portion in your Father's house remains. You can afford to be out of it.

The Historical Reality

God promised Abraham: "I will make you a great nation" (Genesis 12:2). In Numbers 1, we see His Word fulfilled. Not only do we have the history of that nation, we also have its census records. This is most unusual. No other ancient sacred book compares with the Bible in its wealth of historical detail. The very lists we call boring distinguish the Word of God from the counterfeits of man. They say, in effect, "This actually happened. These names, dates, and places, these tedious facts, testify to the historical reality of the sacred story." I am not Max Müller; I have not read all the sacred books of the East. What I have read, however, and what I've read about them, convinces me that none of them are like the living Word.[10] Sure, we've discovered complex records on the clay tablets of ancient cities, but they do not comprise a sacred history. And we have religious books full of philosophical teaching, but which of them contains a precise historical narrative, one for which archaeology is even relevant? If you consider the importance of history to religion, you won't despise the lists of the Bible.

Not all the teachings of the Bible are unique. For example, some passages in *The Bhagavad Gita* resemble thoughts expressed in the New Testament: "Only by love can men see me, and know me, and come unto me. . . . Those who set their hearts on me and ever in love worship me, and who have unshakable faith, these I hold as the best Yogis."[11]

Also, there are ancient myths in pagan literature about dying gods who attained some form of resurrection. But no other sacred writing intersects human history the way the Bible does.[12] For it is the historical facts of Christ's life, death, and resurrection that separate God's Word from all others. There are, of course, unique doctrines in the Bible,[13] but if those doctrines had no relationship to human history, our faith would be in vain.

Do you begin to see how the boring parts figure in all this? Throughout the Old Testament we see the finest saints, Abraham, David, and Job, falling into sin. Almost no one escapes unscathed.[14] Therefore, when we come to Christ and find all the New Testament writers agreeing that He was sinless, what can we say against it? If the New Testament were preceded by official, self-serving biographies of Herod and other luminaries, we would reject its testimony to Christ out of hand. Instead, we are compelled by the honesty of the Scriptures to bow the knee before Him. In the same way, the boring parts prepare us to accept the historical accuracy of the evangelists. Anyone who has waded through the lists of the Bible and who has even the dimmest awareness of their uniqueness among sacred writings will find it difficult to reject New Testament history. To start with census records and nine chapters of legal boundaries,[15] only to end in fairy tales, would certainly be peculiar. Until you have read the boring parts time and again, as I have, it is hard to conceive how much their sheer weight can add to your faith in the biblical record.

Perhaps the best use we can make of the first census is to regard it as a monument to the sin of unbelief. Of its 603,550 men of war, 603,548 died in the wilderness.[16]

> For who, having heard, rebelled? Indeed, was it not all who came out of Egypt, led by Moses? Now with whom was He angry forty years? Was it not with those who sinned, whose corpses fell in the wilderness? And to whom did He swear that they would not enter His rest, but to those who did not obey? So we see that they could not enter in because

> of unbelief. . . . For indeed the gospel was preached to us as well as to them; but the word which they heard did not profit them, not being mixed with faith in those who heard it. (Hebrews 3:16–4:2)

What can a mortal author add, that will not detract from this message? Meditate on the apostle's words—and read the whole census.

The Second Census

As the first census is a monument to unbelief, the second census (Numbers 26) is a monument to God's faithfulness. When He judged the people for their lack of faith, He also made a promise: "But your little ones, whom you said would be victims, I will bring in, and they shall know the land which you have despised" (Numbers 14:31). God kept His word, and the number of little ones who were able to go to war thirty-eight years later was just 1,820 less than the original number. Those who, by man's wisdom, were sure to perish in the wilderness were the very ones to inherit the land.[17] Has not God chosen the weak things of the world to put to shame the things which are mighty?[18]

One of the fascinating things about the second census is that as soon as it starts, it digresses (vv. 9–11). Imagine our census bureau interrupting its statistics to report on the wickedness and punishment of some of our ancestors! (That'll be the day, won't it?) And then, in verse 11, the pearl of great price: "Nevertheless the children of Korah did not die." Hallelujah! In the midst of a census of the Reubenites, we are told that the sons of Korah, the wicked Levite, did not die for his sin. The children of Dathan and Abiram were destroyed, but not the children of Korah. Do you see how the boring parts go out of their way to proclaim the Lord's mercy? If it were not for this digression, you might have thought that Korah's children died with him.[19] It's a good thing they didn't, for centuries later two very godly men came forth from Korah's clan. Who were they? You can find out in 1 Chronicles 6:33 (connecting to Korah in 6:37).[20] What suspense! Don't tell *me* you're not curious!

Though all the men of war died in the wilderness, it's possible some of their widows survived to settle in the Promised Land. As far as I know, there is no information about what happened to the *women* who left Egypt. Should we assume they perished with their husbands? Why? Experience teaches us that women are survivors, physically and spiritually. From my unofficial survey of the Church, there are going to be a lot of older women (with incorruptible bodies) in the kingdom of heaven. Couldn't they have entered as well into that symbol of heaven, the Land of Promise? (If you want to have friends in high places, visit the faithful old ladies in your congregation.)

The Son of Uzziel

The census of the Levites in Numbers 3 brings us to Elizaphan the son of Uzziel (v. 30). Since I managed to read the Bible a dozen times without noticing him, I will assume most readers are unfamiliar with this great-grandson of Levi.[21] When at last my eyes were opened, I thought he was like Serah the daughter of Asher, worth mentioning to believers who feel unimportant. However, the more I studied him, the more I saw that Elizaphan was really a significant Israelite, a man highly honored by the Lord. Allow me to introduce you to him.

I shall relate my discovery in some detail, because it shows how wonderfully the boring and exciting parts of the Bible work together for good. Elizaphan (or Elzaphan) is mentioned five times in the Scriptures.[22] I happened to notice him in the last of them, 2 Chronicles 29:13, during my daily Bible reading. (In other words, I overlooked him in all my research for this book.) Second Chronicles 29 describes Hezekiah's cleansing of the temple and his restoration of true worship. Verses 12–14 catalogue the chief Levites who were active in the cleansing and divide them into seven categories, as the descendants of seven men. Six of these men I knew, as would many students of the Old Testament. Gershon, Kohath, and Merari were the three sons of Levi.[23] Heman, Asaph, and Jeduthun were the lead singers under King David.[24] I drew a complete blank on the seventh name—Elizaphan. "Hmm," I thought, "this guy is in pretty distinguished company. How come I don't know who he is?" So I went looking.

My topical Bible led me to the places where our hero is mentioned. As I studied them I realized that he is specially honored in four of the five passages. In Leviticus 10:4, in a moment of crisis, Moses asked Elizaphan and his older brother Mishael to carry the bodies of Nadab and Abihu outside the camp. When those rebellious sons of Aaron were consumed, soon after their consecration as priests, every one present must have been in shock. No doubt Moses called on men whom he trusted: loyal men who would obey without a moment's hesitation. Elizaphan was such a man.

Returning now to our list, we read:

> And the leader of the fathers' house of the families of the Kohathites was Elizaphan the son of Uzziel. Their duty *included* the ark, the table,

> the lampstand, the altars, the utensils of the sanctuary with which they ministered, the screen [veil], and all the work relating to them. (Numbers 3:30–31)

When the Jews journeyed through the wilderness, the Kohathites carried the most holy things,[25] and Elizaphan was in charge of them. This honor is the more remarkable because Elizaphan was the second son of the *youngest* son of Kohath. His older brother and all his first cousins had more fleshly reason to hope for his position than he did. He must have been a spiritual man, one specially favored by the Lord, as David was, to be chosen before all his relatives.

Do you remember how David's oldest brother resented his election?[26] Elizaphan may have suffered a similar fate. Dr. Gill, the master of Talmudic lore, guided me to this interesting speculation of Rashi, the great medieval commentator of the Jews, concerning the rebellion of Korah.

> What induced Korah to quarrel with Moses? He was envious of the princely dignity held by Elizaphan the son of Uziel, whom Moses had appointed prince over the sons of Kohath, although this was by the express command of God (Numbers 3:30). Korah argued thus: "My father and his brothers were four in number—as it is said (Exodus 6:18), 'and the sons of Kohath were [Amram and Izhar and Hebron and Uziel]'. As to Amram, the eldest, his two sons have themselves assumed high dignity, one as king and the other as High Priest; who is entitled to receive the second (the rank next to it)? Is it not I who am the son of Izhar, who was the second to Amram amongst the brothers? And yet he has appointed as prince the son of his (Amram's) brother, who was the youngest of them all! I hereby protest against him and will undo his decision."[27]

To me this idea seems cogent, even compelling. (A threefold cord of strands diverse as Rashi, Gill, and Rosenbaum should not be quickly broken.) Once again, paying attention to the dull minutiae of the Bible has added something crucial to a long-familiar story. Korah may well have been grinding his own ax when he claimed to be speaking for "all the congregation" (Numbers 16:3). Behind his facade of concern for others, we discern his true motive—envy. He accused Moses of the sin of which he himself was guilty, exalting himself by his own power. Let us earnestly pray to the Lord that when He honors others, He may save us from the sin (and the judgment) of Korah.

First Chronicles 15 adds further luster to the name of Elizaphan. There it is found in another list of Levites,[28] and once again the circumstances and the company are remarkable. After failing at his first attempt to bring the ark of God to Jerusalem, King David wisely decided to consult the law of Moses. He assembled the priests and Levites, for they alone were appointed to carry the holy ark. In this list the Levites are divided into six categories, as the descendants of six men. Three of them, Gershon, Kohath, and Merari, are sons of Levi. Two of them, Hebron and Uzziel, are Levi's grandsons. The only one of Levi's many great-grandsons named here is Elizaphan. Why is he alone exalted in this way? Surely there is a reason. "Therefore humble yourselves under the mighty hand of God, that He may exalt you in due time" (1 Peter 5:6).

Let's summarize our findings and see what we can learn from them. After Elizaphan is introduced to us in the genealogy of Moses, we encounter him four more times. In each of them he seems special. We see him as a useful servant, as a distinguished leader, and twice as a man remembered centuries after his death. Not bad, not bad at all. Yet for every Bible reader who knows about Elizaphan, there are thousands who remember his jealous cousin Korah. If you seek the honor which comes from God, you may not be as famous (or infamous) as some of your relatives. The world may forget you ever existed. Yet God will not forget you, and He may cause His negligent people to cherish your name in times and in places beyond your comprehension.

Five Young Ladies

In Numbers 26:33, in the middle of the second census, we find the daughters of Zelophehad. Zelophe*who?* Zelophehad. He's mentioned eleven times in Scripture, as often as Haggai the prophet. His five daughters, Mahlah, Noah, Hoglah, Milcah, and Tirzah, are named only four times each,[29] but that's more often than Lydia or Zacchaeus. These five young ladies came before Moses to plead, not for themselves, but for the name of their father. Though technically their touching interview with the lawgiver in Numbers 27 is too interesting for us to examine, repetition makes this family too conspicuous to ignore.[30] The Lord approved of these daughters, as well as their cause, and He shows us His pleasure by rehearsing their names.

Matthew Henry writes perceptively about the children of Zelophehad. He says they showed:

> (1.) A strong faith in the power and promise of God concerning the giving of the land of Canaan to Israel. Though it was yet unconquered, untouched, and in the full possession of the natives, yet they petition

> for their share in it as if it were all their own already. . . . (2.) An earnest desire of a place and name in the land of promise, which was a type of heaven. . . . Their example should quicken us with all possible diligence to make sure our title to the heavenly inheritance, in the disposal of which, by the covenant of grace, no difference is made between male and female (Galatians 3:28). (3.) A true respect and honour for their father, whose name was dear and precious to them now that he was gone. . . .[31]

And Dr. Lange comments:

> They thus secured the law with respect to the inheritance of daughters, and with it a significant elevation of woman in her social dignity; although it did not amount to an equality with man. Their common and confident appearance before Moses, before the high-priest, the elders and the whole congregation, was itself an act of true moral elevation, which must have had a lasting effect, and therefore they well deserved to have their names rescued from oblivion, by a double record here and in chapter 36:10. . . .[32]

And when the daughters state that their father "died in his own sin" (Numbers 27:3), the doctor adds, "Indeed these daughters of Zelophehad possessed a fair faculty for doctrinal discriminations."[33] Is it any wonder such bold, tactful, and intelligent heiresses all managed to find husbands close to home?[34]

The Itinerary

My desire to get to Numbers 33 is so strong that I shall pass over the division of the spoil in chapter 31 (vv. 25–47). Suffice it to say that close study of the passage will give you insight from the Lord about motivating people, profit-sharing, tithing, and other subjects of interest in our time.

What could be so intriguing about Numbers 33? Haven't we already seen every conceivable kind of boring part? Nope. There's a lot of variety in the lists of the Bible. Numbers 33 is an itinerary, one written at God's express command, a list of the Jews' campsites in the wilderness. It tells us the places where Israel journeyed, between Goshen in Egypt and Gilgal in Canaan.

The Journeys of Our Lives

Before I tell you what Numbers 33 can do for your study of the Bible, let me tell you why I look forward to it so. Some years ago, I was assistant director of a year-round wilderness school for troubled (and troublesome) boys. The idea behind the program was that life in the woods, in shelters they built themselves, was better for the boys than being locked up in reform school, taking tranquilizers in a mental hospital, or raising cain in special education class. One of my duties was to assist and supervise the counselors in planning itineraries for backpack and canoe trips. Many's the night I spent looking at relief and road maps, figuring where they might camp, or get water, or portage canoes.

Did they have adventures on these trips? My favorite story is about the counselor and boys who were steering their canoe through low-hanging branches along a swift and curving stream. Turns out there was a snake in the branches, and the snake fell into the canoe. With the canoe, the boys, and the snake all moving at once in different directions, the counselor earned his meager day's pay in a hurry. (They later discovered the snake had no venom; but who teaches taxonomy in a white-water rapid?)

What's this got to do with Numbers 33? (Too bad you had to ask: I've got lots more stories. . . .) Though Moses wrote this itinerary down either day by day or in retrospect, it was known to God before the foundation of the world. This trip was not planned by young counselors, or suggested by an assistant director. It was conceived, guided, (prolonged), and brought to its conclusion by the true and living God.

> Whenever the cloud was taken up from above the tabernacle, after that the children of Israel would journey; and in the place where the cloud settled, there the children of Israel would pitch their tents. At the command of the Lord the children of Israel would journey, and at the command of the Lord they would camp. . . . (Numbers 9:17–18)

We can only view the journeys of our lives as Moses did, retrospectively or moment by moment. Yet no matter how long we tarry in the wilderness, there is One who knows each stopping place before we first set out.

Do you journey at the command of the Lord? Do you camp where He suggests? Do you have confidence in your Guide, no matter how foreign (or scary) the place He provides? If you study this list, and take it to heart, you will not consider it strange if fiery trials come. Remember how often God has cared for you in the deserts of your own disobedience, and trust in the Lord. Verily, you shall be fed.

Gleaning Knowledge

Though most of the places mentioned in Numbers 33 are doubtful or unknown, we can glean important knowledge from the chapter.

Verse 4 relates at least two things revealed nowhere else. It says that when the Jews departed Egypt, "The Egyptians were burying all their firstborn, whom the Lord had killed among them." They were too busy burying their dead to bother with the Jews. Unfortunately for the Egyptians, once all the dead were buried, Pharaoh remembered the children of Israel. . . . In the same verse we are told, "On their gods the Lord had executed judgments." These judgments were prophesied in Exodus 12:12, but only here, I believe, are we told of the prophecy's fulfillment.

Verse 10 informs us that after leaving Elim, the Jews "camped by the Red Sea." Exodus does not mention this. Dophkah and Alush (in verse 13) would also be unknown to us if this itinerary were omitted. Whoever hopes to determine the Jews' route to Mount Sinai will surely pay attention to Numbers 33.[35]

Any good reference Bible will enable you to compare the campsites on the list with the history related in Exodus, Numbers, and Deuteronomy. In general, the sites mentioned early and late in Moses' list are known to us from other Scriptures, while those in the middle are not. We have little knowledge about the places mentioned from verses 19 through 29. Will they always remain obscure to us, or will we someday know more about them? (I think we have things to learn about Tahath and Terah, about Rissah and Mount Shepher. When we do, I trust we'll be more grateful that the Lord embalmed their names.) Meanwhile, Numbers 33 provides a good checklist for following the sequence of events in the first and last years of the Exodus.

Nearly all the boring parts contain something essential to our comprehension of a familiar story, and verse 38 is a prime example. It tells us the exact date of Aaron's death. We know that everything which follows must have occurred in the last year of the Exodus. Without this information, how should we understand the sacred narrative? I shall apply it to a sequence of events which can only be called pathetic.[36]

Comparing Numbers 33 with Numbers 20, it seems almost certain that Miriam died only a few months before Aaron. It was after the death of Miriam that Moses and Aaron sinned at the waters of Meribah.[37] In other words, only after forty years in the wilderness, only after innumerable provocations which he successfully resisted, did Moses commit the sin which cost him so dearly. His was truly a case of so near, and yet so far. Why after forty years of obedience, should he suddenly ignore the Lord? I believe he transgressed while grieving for his sister. We cannot excuse the sin, but surely we can sympathize with the sinner. Let us beware of grief, lest it cause us to depart from God. And let us be charitable toward those who sin while grieving, for even Moses our rabbi (as the Jews call him) succumbed to that temptation.

Consider how humbly Moses bore the punishment of his sin, his exclusion from the Land of Promise. He did not belabor God with a list of good deeds he had performed. He did not whine for a second chance when his one request was denied.[38] He did not moan and groan about his cruel fate, God's unfairness, or anything else. He did what he was told—and died. (Go thou and do likewise.) And whom did the Lord choose to stand with Elijah on the Mount of Transfiguration?

11

The Division of the Land

(Joshua 12–21)

Between the conquests of Joshua and Nebuchadnezzar the Jews inhabited the land of Canaan for nearly a thousand years.[1] If you think the formal records retained in Scripture from this period are excessive, you must have little familiarity with the publications of modern governments. On a slow day the Government Printing Office of the United States churns out more reports and statistics than we find in all the historical books of the Bible.[2] The clay-tablet archives of the ancient Near East indicate that there was also no shortage of record-keeping in Old Testament times. The lists of the Bible are not random, but carefully selected and preserved by God for the edification of His Church. If you don't believe me, try scanning the thousands of tablets dug up at Ebla or Nineveh. Or take the easy way out and read this chapter.

Nearly all the lists from this period fall into two categories. Either they describe the lands conquered by Joshua (and others), or they record the officers of the theocracy ruled by David and Solomon. We have almost no lists from the time of the judges or from the divided kingdom. The Bible passes over periods longer than the history of the United States without leaving us a single boring record. This is a considerable proof of the goodness of God.[3]

Joshua 12

Joshua 12 prepares us for the description of the Promised Land by recording the kings who once ruled it. I assure you there is more spiritual treasure in this list of kings than I can now present. I was amazed to find that the more I studied the chapter, the more of value I found in it. By now, of course, I should know better than to underestimate the boring parts. Either I'm a slow learner, or the treasures of this desert are truly inexhaustible.[4]

Conquered Kings

The first six verses of chapter 12 rehearse the kings conquered under Moses on the east side of Jordan. If you remember Moses' descriptions of the kingdoms of Og and Sihon,[5] you may be tempted to ask why we must hear it all again. Judges, chapter 11, provides one reason for the repetition. There Jephthah, that "mighty man of valor," gives the hostile king of Ammon a lengthy answer from the books of Moses and Joshua. I can think of nothing like it in Scripture. Jephthah shows himself to be a wise, peaceable, and learned man, very different from the filicidal[6] monster most of us envision. I believe his scholarly reply and Hebrews 11:32 are two good reasons for us to think better of Jephthah than we do.[7] In any event, Jephthah based his answer on Joshua 12 and the parallel passages in the books of Moses. The Lord had provided him plenty of ammunition to prove His people's right to their land.

There is also a spiritual application of this list of conquered kings. The Bible tells us that we are "heirs of God and joint heirs with Christ."[8] We have a right to our inheritance, as Israel had a right to the land of Sihon. Both rights are based in military conquest and the gift of God. When Jesus said, "Be of good cheer, I have overcome the world" (John 16:33), He used a word which means I have conquered. And John tells us, "For this purpose the Son of God was manifested, that he might destroy the works of the devil" (1 John 3:8). Unless we keep in mind the conquests of Christ, as Jephthah did those of Moses, how shall we maintain our right to them? For our adversary the devil sneaks about like an experienced confidence man, seeking whom he may defraud of his inheritance. When you read about Og and Sihon, remember the kingdoms of sin and death, and the One who for your sake shattered their legions.

Speaking of Og and Sihon, have you ever wondered why they're so famous? Og is named more than twenty times in the Bible, and Sihon some thirty times. Many a great emperor goes unnoticed in Scripture, but these petty potentates are known round the world. Why? Theirs were the first kingdoms taken by God's people. Whether you apply their example to a sin you put to death through the Spirit or to the Church's victory over her Roman persecutors, first triumphs in Christ deserve celebration. Most of us have days when we flee from the men of Ai or from the armies of Muhammad.[9] In those disgraceful times, what shall better bandage our wounds than the banners of Og and Sihon?

Og seems to have been a remarkable monarch. Verse 4 tells us that he had two residences and that he "was of the remnant of the giants." (Moses even tells us the size of his bedstead.[10]) Yet his stature, his riches, and his armies were no help to him against the wrath of God. When you're facing giants in spiritual battle, recall the vain prowess and strength of King Og.

A Mystery in Chapter 12

Most of the thirty-one kings listed in chapter 12 were rulers of places we have heard about in Scripture. For example, David hid in the cave near Adullam, and Micah prophesied, "The glory of Israel shall come to Adullam."[11] And the last king mentioned ruled Tirzah, a city immortalized in the Song of Solomon:

> O my love, you are as beautiful as Tirzah,
> Lovely as Jerusalem,
> Awesome as an army with banners!
> Turn your eyes away from me,
> For they have overcome me.[12]

You can use a concordance to find other references to any of the known cities. However, it's the preamble to this list (Joshua 12:7–8) which interests me the most. Notice how it begins: "And these are the kings of the country which Joshua and the children of Israel conquered on this side of the Jordan." The word *conquered* is significant, for it brings us to one of the mysteries of the Bible.

Joshua 12:8 lists six nations which were conquered by Israel. All six were mentioned by Moses in Deuteronomy 7:1 as nations cast out of the Promised Land by God. But there Moses speaks of "*seven* nations greater and mightier than you." What nation is missing from the list, and what happened to its people? The Girgashites are the seventh nation, but what became of them no one knows for sure. They are not mentioned at all in the book of Judges, though all the others are. Thus it appears that the Girgashites ceased to be a problem for Israel after the time of Joshua. Matthew Henry comments:

> Seven nations they are called (Deut. 7:1), and so many are there reckoned up, but here six only are mentioned, the Girgashites being either lost or left out. . . . Either they were incorporated with some other of

> these nations, or, as the tradition of the Jews is, upon the approach of Israel under Joshua they all withdrew and went into Africa, leaving their country to be possessed by Israel, with whom they saw it was to no purpose to contend, and therefore they are not named among the nations that Joshua subdued.[13]

There are some Scriptures which tend to support the Jewish tradition about the Girgashites. Though *destroy* is the verb usually applied to the Canaanites, *drive out* also appears a numbers of times. We find both verbs in Deuteronomy 9:3: "[The Lord] will destroy them and bring them down before you; so you shall *drive them out* and *destroy them* quickly, as the Lord has said to you" (emphasis added).

Why drive them out? Why not just destroy them? Is this a foreshadowing of the Lord's mercy to the Girgashites? Nobody knows. All we know for sure is they are conspicuous by their absence in Joshua and Judges, and we are never specifically told that Joshua destroyed the Girgashites.[14]

If this Jewish tradition is correct, the Girgashites seem to be the heathen equivalent of On the son of Peleth. (You don't remember On the son of Peleth?) The co-conspirator of Dathan and Abiram, his name occurs only in Numbers 16:1. When the rebels were punished, On's name does not recur.[15] Presumably, he either dropped out of the rebellion, or was consumed with the others whose names are repeated. (You can guess which alternative I prefer.)

What happened to the Girgashites? I also will ask you a question: What happened to On the son of Peleth? If you say, "We do not know," then neither will I tell you what happened to the Girgashites.

General Principles

Now we come to the division of the land, nine chapters of predominantly boring parts.[16] I shall lay out some general principles relevant to the study of the whole section. Then I shall select one item of interest from each chapter. (If I were to attempt an exhaustive commentary on every boring part, though the world might contain all the books that would be written, surely my brain and my hard disk would not.)

The Last Shall Be First

The last verse of these nine chapters provides the first general principle for their interpretation: "Not a word failed of any good thing which the Lord had spoken to the house of Israel. All came to pass (Joshua 21:45)."

These chapters are a monument to God's faithfulness, a detailed, historical monument. Unlike some earthly fathers, God doesn't make empty promises to His children. He keeps His word. And when His promises are fulfilled, His servants keep records for posterity. (He knows how quickly we cease to be grateful.) Has God made promises to you? As you read these chapters, think about the time when those promises shall be as completely fulfilled and documented as God's promise to Abraham.

Let's get specific. Opening this section at random, I read (from Simeon's inheritance) ". . . Hazar Shual, Balah, Ezem, Eltolad, Bethul, Hormah, Ziklag, Beth Marcaboth, Hazar Susah . . ." (Joshua 19:3–5). Even though I've heard of Ziklag, where David lived in exile, and Hormah, where the Jews fled from the Amalekites,[17] this is not exciting reading. But it is when I put it in perspective. Not all of God's promises are blessings. He promised Simeon. . . .

❧ ❧ ❧

The boring parts are a funny way to learn the Scriptures! I was just going to refer to Jacob's cursing the sin of Simeon, in his last words to his sons, when I remembered that Moses also had a parting word for each tribe. Turning confidently over to Deuteronomy 33, I looked for Moses' prophecy to Simeon. Imagine my surprise as I discovered there is no prophecy to Simeon! (I know: a humble man would have been less surprised.) Anyway, as Matthew Henry puts it:

> The tribe of Simeon is omitted in the blessing, because Jacob had left it under a brand, and it had never done any thing, as Levi had done, to retrieve its honor. It was lessened in the wilderness more than any other of the tribes. . . . Or, because the lot of Simeon was an appendage to that of Judah, that tribe is included in the blessing of Judah.[18]

Either way Simeon's omission is a form of disgrace. But that only reinforces the point I was going to make.

❧ ❧ ❧

The Lord promised Simeon and Levi, "I will divide them in Jacob and scatter them in Israel" (Genesis 49:7). The Levites were scattered among the twelve tribes, and Simeon became an appendage to Judah.[19] God kept His promise. Yet look at the blessings which came to Simeon.[20] He received seventeen cities in the south of Judah "and all the villages that were all around these cities." He has his portion in Ezekiel's temple (no appendage there!), and twelve of the 144 thousand sealed with Christ are his.[21] Not bad for a murderous son whose sin was hateful even to his father.

And what about you, dear Reader? Have you sinned against God? Has He decreed a punishment for you? How you ought to rejoice in the names of Balah, Ezem, and Eltolad, for they are your hope. Beth Lebaoth and Sharuhen are God's tokens of peace and prosperity to His rebellious children. I don't know about you, but with my past, I'd consider seventeen cities an incredible blessing. Ain, Rimmon, Ether, and Ashan are beautiful names to me.

> Oh, that men would give thanks to the Lord
> for His goodness,
> And for His wonderful works
> to the children of men!
>
> (Psalm 107:8)

A Reward for Each

Here's another general principle relevant to these nine chapters. *God has prepared a reward for each of His children.* As Jesus put it,

> In My Father's house are many mansions; if it were not so, I would have told you. I go to prepare a place for you. And if I go and prepare a place for you, I will come again and receive you to Myself; that where I am, there you may be also. (John 14:2–3)

Joshua 13–21 is a detailed illustration of this statement. Each of Jacob's sons had a reward laid up for him in the Promised Land, a reward inherited by the tribe of his descendants. The Promised Land was always there, waiting to be claimed by its rightful heirs. As soon as those heirs had a little faith in God's promises, they were fully able to possess their inheritance.

To see how this applies to us, we need to review something we noted in "The Return of the Begats." In 1 Chronicles 2–8, we saw that three tribes take up the vast majority of the chronicler's genealogies. Judah, Benjamin, and Levi each receive a chapter (or more) devoted exclusively to them. By contrast, Naphtali has only one verse, while Dan and Zebulun are not mentioned at all. The other tribes' genealogies take up anywhere from five to twenty verses. (It's interesting to note that Simeon leads the pack with twenty verses.[22]) Do you see the contrast between Joshua and 1 Chronicles? In Joshua, every tribe has its portion.

Some are larger than others, but all have a goodly inheritance. Centuries later, in the second begats, things are much less equal. Not every son of Jacob receives the lion's share. We have, at best, only partial knowledge of the developments behind this seeming discrepancy, but here's how I apply it to our life in the Spirit.

God has faithfully prepared an abundant reward for each of His children. Even though some have grieved Him greatly, as Reuben, Simeon, and Levi did, He has been generous to all. Only a Canaanite or an envious son of Israel could possibly object to the distribution under Joshua. Yet in the later begats, Judah gets the most attention, while the others have much, little, or none. All His sons are loved and provided for by their heavenly Father, but they are rewarded in the long run according to their works. We are all loved, but we are not all equal in faith and works.

> Now he who plants and he who waters are one, and each one will receive his own reward according to his own labor. . . . Each one's work will become manifest; for the Day will declare it, because it will be revealed by fire; and the fire will test each one's work, of what sort it is. If anyone's work which he has built on it endures, he will receive a reward. If anyone's work is burned, he will suffer loss; but he himself will be saved, yet so as through fire. (1 Corinthians 3:8, 13–15)

Recognizing the imperfection of our analogy, we might say that through faith we inherit a portion of the Promised Land, but through works we maintain it. As James inquired, "What does it profit, my brethren, if someone says he has faith but does not have works"(2:14)? Perhaps I can make myself clearer by getting more personal.

You are, I trust, a true believer in Christ. As He allotted a portion of land to each of Israel's children, God has reserved for you a heavenly dwelling place. A portion of paradise is yours, but you shall not have it without effort. You must fight in the Spirit against sin and unbelief. You must put on the whole armor of God. Truly God shall be with you, and you shall be more than a conqueror.

Now come a little nearer, and remember, "Faithful are the wounds of a friend" (Proverbs 27:6). Are you content with a small portion of your inheritance in Christ? Are you allowing the Canaanites to live on your land? You have been granted a great property, but have you conquered it and kept it? Is it bringing forth fruit for the Lord? Or have you made a truce with sin? When the roll is called up yonder, when the last and most important of the boring parts appear, will you look more like Judah or like Naphtali?

These nine chapters were not written to make you complacent, but to invigorate your faith. When your heavenly mansion seems like pie-in-the-sky, turn to the boring parts of Joshua. For there you'll find in black and white the deed to your inheritance, notarized and stamped with a raised seal. It's an important document, to be sure, but one more suitable for framing than for keeping in a safe.

Items of Interest

I promised you something of interest from each chapter in the division of the land. We'll start with Joshua 13.

Balaam, the Diviner

In verse 22 we are told, "The children of Israel also killed with the sword Balaam the son of Beor, the soothsayer, among those who were killed by them." This is the only place in Scripture where we are plainly told that Balaam was a soothsayer, or diviner.

Moses told us that "the elders of Moab and the elders of Midian departed with *the diviner's fee* in their hand, and they came to Balaam and spoke to him the words of Balak" (Numbers 22:7, emphasis added). New Testament writers make it clear that Balaam had an inordinate interest in the diviner's fee,[23] but with that information alone we cannot accuse him of more than greed. Moses and John tell us Balaam counseled the king of Moab to tempt the Jews with immorality, thus provoking the plague of Peor.[24] So we already know that Balaam is no saint. However, Joshua 13:22 completes our portrait of the man. The Hebrew word for diviner employed there occurs a number of times in Scripture, nearly always in a strongly negative way. (This is where a Hebrew concordance comes in handy.) In Deuteronomy 18, the Lord employs it twice to tell Israel that there must be no diviners among His people.[25] And it is used twice more in the account of Saul's fall from grace:

> For rebellion is as the sin of *witchcraft,* and stubbornness is as iniquity and idolatry.[26]
>
> So Saul disguised himself and put on other clothes, and he went, and two men with him; and they came to the woman by night. And he said, "Please *conduct a séance* for me, and bring up for me the one I shall name to you."[27]

Balaam must have needed another nail in his coffin, for the Lord supplied one when He called him Balaam, the diviner. And I think I see why He did it. Balaam seems rather attractive when we first meet him. Doesn't he bless Israel, even though Balak offers him great riches to curse the chosen people? The prophet seems to have a clear channel with the Lord, and he resists the temptation of worldly wealth. Surely he must be a good man. But the Scriptures prove that he was wicked. I believe that all the passages concerning Balaam are carefully ordered for our edification. He is a warning to us. He illustrates perfectly Paul's doctrine of "covetousness, which is idolatry" (Colossians 3:5). And by appearing admirable at first, with the magnitude of his wickedness revealing itself little by little, he exemplifies this warning from Jesus:

> Not everyone who says to Me, "Lord, Lord," shall enter the kingdom of heaven, but he who does the will of My Father in heaven. Many will say to Me in that day, "Lord, Lord, *have we not prophesied in Your name,* cast out demons in Your name, and done many wonders in Your name?" And then I will declare to them, "I never knew you; depart from Me, you who practice lawlessness!"[28] (emphasis added)

A Mountain in Mind

I trust you need no help from me to take an interest in Joshua 14. Caleb's testimony there is one of the most memorable in the Bible. I love how it builds and builds in verses 6 through 11, like a wave mounting to its crest or a thundercloud swelling with rain. Then the climax: *"Now therefore, give me this mountain. . . ."* Reader, do you have a mountain in mind? Do you have a promise from the Lord, the fulfillment of which you patiently await? Do you expect to say to Him someday, "Now therefore, give me this mountain?" I hope you do. And if not, when are you going to start praying for one—*mañana?*

There once was a lady who said to a great English painter,[29] "Why, Mr. Turner, I never see sunsets like the ones you paint!" To which he replied, "But, Madam, don't you wish you did?"

Those Infamous Bad Guys

Reading about David and his mighty men fighting with the Philistines, I used to imagine that those infamous bad guys were a legitimate, though troublesome, nation. They just seemed to have difficulty getting along with their neighbors.[30] Joshua 15 shows how wrong I was about them: there three of their five principal cities are given to Judah.[31] Also, Joshua 13:2 tells us that "all the territory of the Philistines" had yet to be possessed by Israel. This information puts the battles of David's time in a different light. The Philistines were occupying land which the Maker of heaven and earth had given unto Israel. The Jews were not supposed to buy Ashdod or Gaza, if they desired to live there; they were to take them by force.[32] We know from the begats that the Philistines were descended from Ham's son Mizraim.[33] Therefore, they were not involved in the curse of Noah upon Canaan and his descendants (Genesis 9:25). Yet their land was clearly given by God to the children of Judah.

Jewish and Christian commentators agree that the Philistines were inhabiting land which originally belonged to Canaan and therefore was included in God's gift to Abraham.

> This is the land that yet remains: all the territory of the Philistines and all that of the Geshurites, from Sihor, which is east of Egypt, as far as the border of Ekron northward (which is counted as Canaanite); the five lords of the Philistines—the Gazites, the Ashdodites, the Ashkelonites, the Gittites, and the Ekronites. . . . (Joshua 13:2–3)

The point is that Ekron was the northernmost of the five Philistine cities; therefore all of them were counted as Canaanite. Thus, the land belonged to Israel by the will of God and ought to be taken, though the Philistines themselves did not have to be treated as Canaanites.

One spiritual application of this boring part is that only God can turn evil to good. When wicked men usurp and seek to improve what other sinners have begun, they cannot escape the judgment of God. God is not willing to deal with us as some modern bankruptcy judges do. We may not dissolve our corporation, repudiate our debts, and hop back into sinful behavior under some new name, as if we were a new creation. Only God can make a new creation. Only Jehovah can turn the land of the Canaanites into the Promised Land. There are plenty of modern-day Philistines who do not understand this. They think that by their own power they can transform evil into good. They do not recognize the sovereignty of God; they do not believe the land belongs to Him. Though God raises up Samson and David to convince them of their folly, they walk on in darkness. Yet their doom is sure. One little word shall fell them.[34]

Wonder what I'm talking about? From a host of possible examples, I select the theory of evolution. This fantastic acreage has been Canaanite from the beginning. Rationalists in sheep's clothing have imagined that once they occupy it, it somehow becomes acceptable to God. "This land is no longer Canaanite," they say. "Can't you Bible-bangers understand that we have conquered it? It is no longer theirs, but ours." Yet, in the eyes of the Lord, the land of the so-called Christian evolutionists "is counted as Canaanite." It can never be clean until every falsehood is destroyed. God has given the truth of creation to His people, and He waits for them to reclaim it. Dr. Gill tells us, "Ekron was . . . never possessed by the Israelites."[35] Brothers and sisters, isn't it time?

The King's Companion

In chapter 16 we learn that the border of the children of Joseph "went out from Bethel to Luz, passed along to *the border of the Archites at Ataroth,* and went down westward . . . "(vv. 1–3). As a charter member of the Hushai the Archite Fan Club, I will grasp any straw which provides an excuse to magnify my hero. Remember Hushai? He was David's friend and the answer to David's prayer when he fled from Absalom.[36] Long before I realized that either of us was a poet,[37] I admired Hushai for his position in the official list of David's officers. While most of the men are mentioned in some mundane capacity, such as scribe or keeper of camels, Hushai is listed as the king's companion. Whatever the salary, I have always thought he had the best job of all.[38]

We do not know why Hushai is always referred to as the Archite, rather than as Hushai, the son of so-and-so. We also do not know who the Archites were. All we know is that Hushai was one of them. Either Archi was a remarkable place, or more likely, the Archites were a remarkable people. The Lord has remembered them in the boring parts, and the only Archite we know of figures prominently in a rousing part as well. When you pass by "the border of the Archites at Ataroth," think on these things.

Chariots of Iron

In chapter 17, we encounter once more the persistent daughters of Zelophehad. They did not rest on their laurels after their interview with Moses in the land of Moab.[39] They came before Eleazar and Joshua to remind them, "The Lord commanded Moses to give us an inheritance among our brothers" (Joshua 17:4). When it came to honoring their father, these five females were not at all passive. Is that why God keeps bringing them to our attention?

Our new item of interest for this chapter comes from its last verse. Charles Spurgeon preached a sermon on this text, "For thou shalt drive out the Canaanites, though they have iron chariots, and though they be strong" (Joshua 17:18, KJV). Since I read Spurgeon's sermon seven years ago, and much of it is still with me, I thought it would be good to share the gist of it with you.

You will see, then, dear friends, that Canaan is hardly a full type of heaven. It may be used so in a modified sense; but it is a far better emblem of that state and condition of soul in which a man is found when he has become a believer. . . . He has come to take possession of the covenant heritage, but finds the Canaanite of sin and evil still in the land. . . . Before he can fully enjoy his privileges he must drive out his sins. . . .

Our first reflection shall be—WE MUST DRIVE THEM OUT. It is a command from God—"Thou shalt drive out the Canaanites." Every sin has to be slaughtered. Not a single sin is to be tolerated. Off with their heads! . . .

There are certain sins that, when we begin to war with them, we very soon overcome. . . . But certain other sins are much tougher to deal with. They mean fight, and some of them seem to have as many lives as a cat. There is no killing them. . . . They may be said to have chariots of iron. . . .

Perhaps one of the things that is worst of all to a Christian is, that *certain sins are supposed to be irresistible.* It is a popular error, and a very pernicious one. "These chariots of iron," the Israelites said, "it is of no use to try to contend with them." So they gave up the plains to the Canaanites.[40] It is a sad calamity when a Christian person says, "I can keep straight in everything except *that.*" . . .

I have said that we must drive them out. The second head is that THEY CAN BE DRIVEN OUT. I do not say that we can drive them out, but I say that they can be driven out. It will be a great miracle, but let us believe in it; for other great wonders have been wrought. Note first that *you and I have been raised from the dead.* . . . It can be done. The raising from the dead is the evidence that it can be done. . . .

We close with our third head, and that is, THEY SHALL BE DRIVEN OUT. They must be driven out; they can be driven out; they shall be driven out. . . . *This is what Christ died for. . . . This is what the Holy Spirit is given for. . . .*

If you be living children of the living God, lay hold upon that promise, "By little and by little, I will surely drive them out."[41]

No doubt the reason I was so impressed by this sermon is that I had a sin with chariots of iron. It troubled me for decades. With fear and trembling, lest a worse thing come upon me, I testify to you that it oppresses me no more.[42] May God be glorified!

Do you have a besetting sin? Have you tried to conquer it? Have you read all the books and been to all the conferences? Are you sick of hearing about everyone else being delivered but you? Ah, Reader, it's a miserable condition, I know. But it's a lot better than giving up hope. Let me try to tell you why.

Consider the daughter of Abraham, whom Satan had bound for eighteen years (Luke 13:10–17). Do you think she knew something about hopeless conditions? She attended a synagogue so corrupt, the ruler of it rebuked Jesus for healing on the Sabbath! Yet despite that creep and despite her disability, she had likely been worshipping there faithfully for years.[43] Then one day, out of the blue, she was healed. Maybe it wasn't such a dumb thing to do after all, going to that synagogue sabbath after sabbath.

I'm a big believer in going to church services and retreats, getting prayed over, and so forth, *even when you know it won't do any good.* Huh? Why go if it won't do any good? Well, first of all we can never be quite sure: we might get healed as the daughter of Abraham did. But even if we don't (and it didn't happen to me that way), there's a good reason to go. It's a form of beggary: "Here I am, God, at my 432nd prayer meeting since coming to Christ. You know, despite all the good things that have happened, this particular sin is worse now than when I began. I've been preached at and prayed over; I've fasted and prayed; I've read the old timers and the best-sellers, and still I'm no better. But I just thought I'd come down here tonight to show You that I know I'm a beggar. I am totally dependent on You. The Canaanites have chariots of iron, and I haven't got a pogo stick. I could have stayed home, but I thought I'd come just because I'm a beggar, and 'beggars must be no choosers.'"[44]

Sound like a peculiar way to get healed? No doubt it is, but it worked for me. Through trying to be faithful, and by doing the Lord's will *in things that seemed totally unrelated to my sin,* I found myself healed. He really had noticed me begging all those years! He really did have a plan to implement, after all my plans had failed! Yes, we really shall drive out the Canaanites, though they have iron chariots, and though they be strong.

As I Have Done to Shiloh

There is more than meets the eye in the next verse: "Then the whole congregation of the children of Israel assembled together at Shiloh, and set up the tabernacle of meeting there. And the land was subdued before them" (Joshua 18:1).

As soon as they were secure, the Jews set up the tabernacle in Shiloh, a beautiful spot in the land of Ephraim (Joshua's tribe). The ark, which had been moved so often in the wilderness, would move no more for centuries.[45] What a hopeful time in the life of God's people! Their own land, freedom to worship, and abundance of all things were theirs at last. Surely Shiloh would be a synonym for *blessing.* Surely Shiloh would mean celebration!

Shiloh! What strange emotion that word evokes, at least in an American reader. In the war between the states, Shiloh was the first big battle to disappoint both sides. Much has been written and sung about it.

> Skimming lightly, wheeling still,
> The swallows fly low
> Over the field in clouded days,
> The forest-field of Shiloh—
> . . . .
> Foemen at morn, but friends at eve—
> Fame or country least their care:
> (What like a bullet can undeceive!)
> But now they lie low,
> While over them the swallows skim,
> And all is hushed at Shiloh.[46]

The eerie side of the American mystique about Shiloh is that it dovetails so well with the biblical one. For ultimately the Shiloh of the Promised Land also became a symbol of disappointment and disaster. The name, some commentators say, means rest. But the rest of Shiloh is either that of a Mississippi graveyard or a sorry ruin among the hills of Ephraim. For the sins of Eli's sons, the ark of God was taken, never to return to Shiloh.[47] The first permanent home for the ark and tabernacle ended up as prime material for prophetic warnings.

> But go now to My place which was in Shiloh, where I set My name at the first, and see what I did to it because of the wickedness of My people Israel. And now, because you have done all these works, says the Lord, and I spoke to you, rising up early and speaking, but you did not hear, and I called you, but you did not answer, therefore I will do to this house which is called by My name, in which you trust, and to this place which I gave to you and your fathers, as I have done to Shiloh. (Jeremiah 7:12–14)[48]

How many untried armies have marched off gloriously to the slaughter? How many splendid churches are now mosques, or ruins, or concert halls? What a storehouse of dashed hopes and disappointments is the history of man! Nor do the faithful escape the miasma of this fallen world. Remember Jonathan, and Job, and John the Baptist. Remember Solomon's mysterious warning: "The end of a thing is better than its beginning" (Ecclesiastes 7:8). Remember the Lamentations of Jeremiah. When you have realized the vanity of worldly hope, when you are thoroughly purged of fleshly optimism, when you know that God is in heaven and you upon earth, then you may utter and understand the fearful name of Shiloh.

The First Textual Critic

I thought I would divert you with a botany lesson in chapter 19. Spotting the "terebinth tree in Zaanannim" in verse 33, I thought it would be good to discuss the Author's interest in natural phenomena. Was I wrong! Worthy as that subject is, the phenomenon I uncovered in verse 33 was most unnatural—the briar patch of textual criticism from which we just escaped.[49] Don't worry, though; I wouldn't take my dog, much less my trusting reader, in there twice in the same ramble through the biblical countryside.

It turns out that where the New King James confidently reads "terebinth tree," other translators and commentators read "Allon,"[50] "oak," "oak forest," "large tree," and the LORD only knows what else. (I stopped looking as soon as I realized what was happening.) Part of the difference arises from the fact that some scholars question the first vowel point of the Hebrew word. One vowel makes the word *terebinth;* another makes it *oak.* (*Large tree,* I gather, is a compromise.) Though I no longer flee the boring parts of God, I think heading for the hills a sensible reaction to many of the disputes of men. Follow me—and the first textual critic take the hindmost.

Skipping to verse 35, it seems remarkable that most commentators pass over the word *fortified,* or *fenced,* without comment. Why is it that, among all the holdings of all the tribes, only here we are told that the cities are fortified?[51] I don't know, but I think this may help us to explain some seeming discrepancies in these chapters. Surely a list of fortified cities would be different from a list of other populated places. Until we determine what criteria were used for these records, we ought to refrain from assuming that they are incomplete or imperfect.[52] Perhaps they are, but how would we know?

A Native of Gath Hepher

Looking for verses relevant to the previous paragraph, I noticed the name Gittah-hepher, or Gath Hepher, in Joshua 19:13.[53] This is too important to omit. Why? Centuries later, that obscure village brought forth a native son whom all the world knows now. And it is only from this list that we know where Gath Hepher was—in the land of Zebulun.[54] But where was the land of Zebulun?

> The land of Zebulun and the land of Naphtali . . .
> By the way of the sea, beyond the Jordan,
> In Galilee of the Gentiles.
> The people who walked in darkness
> Have seen a great light;
> Those who dwelt in the land of the shadow of death,
> Upon them a light has shined.
>
> (Isaiah 9:1–2)

Remember that wonderful prophecy?

Now we're ready to look at one of the exciting parts of Scripture. When the Pharisees got upset with Nicodemus, they said to him, "Are you also from Galilee? Search and look, for no prophet has arisen out of Galilee" (John 7:52).[55] I'd love to know if Nicodemus remembered this little passage from 2 Kings: " . . . the word of the Lord God of Israel, which He had spoken through His servant Jonah the son of Amittai, *the prophet who was from Gath Hepher*" (14:25, emphasis added).

Do you think those Pharisees were the last learned men to invoke the Scriptures with great vehemence—and be totally wrong? I doubt it. Evidently they did not muse upon the boring parts. For not only was there a prophet from Galilee, but a prophet who prefigured the Messiah's rising from the dead and His preaching to the Gentiles.[56] Even the nastiest cloud has a silver lining. In setting the classic example of how *not* to pontificate upon the Scriptures, these hateful men provided Bible readers everywhere a very useful warning.

You can discredit any group of people by looking at its worst representatives, and Christians need to be wary of doing so.[57] The group I have in mind, those who skip their boring parts, are my potential readers, whom I would do well not to slander or offend. May I respectfully point out, then, that as we need to avoid the hardness and pride of the Pharisees, we need to avoid their spotty knowledge of the Bible?

If our Lord judged the Pharisees by their own words, they would certainly have been in trouble. For, as is commonly the case,[58] they were guilty of the sin they attributed to others. What did they say just before "Search and look . . . "? "This crowd that does not know the law is accursed" (John 7:49). Lord, let us add to our faith virtue, and to our virtue knowledge;[59] but let us not add to our hypocrisy such haughty condemnation. Amen.

Our City of Refuge

The twentieth chapter of Joshua, like the fourteenth, is short and intriguing. Therefore, we shall be brief. A manslayer who fled to a city of refuge must remain there "until the death of the one who is high priest in those days."[60] Why until then? Nowhere else in the Bible is such a sentence imposed. Whatever the reason for that unpredictable term in Joshua's day, it has a beautiful symbolism now.[61]

> We cannot think these cities of refuge would have been so often and so much spoken of in the law of Moses . . . if they were not designed to typify the relief which the gospel provides for poor penitent sinners, and their protection from the curse of the law and the wrath of God, in our Lord Jesus, to whom believers flee for refuge. . . .[62]

To which I add: we must *experience* the death of our perfect High Priest to be free from the curse of the Law.

Of All the Real Estate

Chapter 21 lists the cities given to the Levites, forty-eight in all, the exact number prescribed by Moses.[63] The same list is repeated with minor variations in 1 Chronicles 6. (We looked a little at the chronicler's list in "The Return of the Begats.") The interesting thing to me is simply the repetition. Of all the real estate recorded in Joshua 12–21, only the Levites' and the Simeonites' are fully catalogued again. How carefully God defends the rights of those whom He has "divided and scattered in Israel" (Genesis 49:7)! Sometime after the return from Babylon, the Lord had His chronicler write down the cities of Simeon and Levi. Why should they receive special treatment?

The cities of the Simeonites are rehearsed in 1 Chronicles 4:28–33. This list may have reestablished their title to regions they had inhabited "until the reign of David." Remember that the Simeonites were a small tribe whose land lay within the boundaries of Judah, the largest tribe. Possibly after David's reign the Simeonites ceased to have any meaningful autonomy. But they had something better than strength preserving their right to their land. They had something longer than the long arm of human law. They had on their side the infinite memory of the King of Kings.

God told the Levites a number of times that they would have no inheritance in the Promised Land.

> You shall have no inheritance in their land, nor shall you have any portion among them; I *am* your portion and your inheritance among the children of Israel. Behold, I have given the children of Levi all the tithes in Israel as an inheritance in return for the work which they perform, the work of the tabernacle of meeting. (Numbers 18:20–21)

If we fail to tithe to the Levites, we are making God a liar. He has promised His servants, those employed in His work, the tithes of His people as an inheritance *from Him.* When they don't get what they're entitled to, how reliable do the promises of God appear? If you do not tremble to think of this, you must have little knowledge of the Bible. For God is a jealous God, and He is very jealous of His honor. "Those who honor Me I will honor, and those who despise Me shall be lightly esteemed" (1 Samuel 2:30). God has entrusted us with the responsibility of caring for His ministers. When we fail to fulfill that sacred trust, it is not only the ministers whom we have despised.

Before I stopped counting, I found a dozen verses in Numbers, Deuteronomy, and Joshua which tell us the Levites had "no inheritance" in the land. Even for the boring parts, this is a lot of repetition. And nearly as often as the Lord tells His servants they have no inheritance, He tells them His wealth is theirs. "They shall eat the offerings of the Lord made by fire, and His portion" (Deuteronomy 18:1). These things are said so frequently, there must be meaning in them. Here's how I apply them to the lists of the Levites' possessions.

After the destruction of Jerusalem, only one tribe has its cities listed extensively—the tribe with no inheritance. The Lord went out of His way to make sure that His servants retained what was theirs. He looks after those who abandon the pursuit of riches to minister in His name. The smaller your portion in this world, the more concerned the Lord is about your right to it. The more you devote yourself to Him, the more He looks after the things that are yours. Jesus put it this way:

> Therefore do not worry, saying, "What shall we eat?" or "What shall we drink?" or "What shall we wear?" For after all these things the Gentiles seek. For your heavenly Father knows that you need all these things. But seek first the kingdom of God and His righteousness, and all these things shall be added to you. (Matthew 6:31–33)

In the peculiar language of the boring parts, the lists of the Levite cities say the same.

12

THE OFFICERS OF THE KINGDOM

(1 Chronicles 23–27)

First Chronicles has two major boring parts. We have already examined the genealogies of the first nine chapters. Now it's time to look at chapters 23–27 and the officers of David's kingdom. Before we do so, however, let's thank the Lord for the adventures He has placed between the boring parts. Chapters 10–22 contain a lively history of David's reign (omitting his sin with Bathsheba and all its dire consequences). The weary pilgrim who has struggled through the begats may refresh himself there in abundance of excitement. By the time he gets to the officers, he shall be rested and ready for the challenge. "The Lord is good to all, and His tender mercies *are* over all His works" (Psalm 145:9).

Some Shorter Boring Parts

There are, it must be conceded, some shorter boring parts in the historical chapters. A list of David's mighty men ends chapter 11, and the records of his army fill chapter 12. Yet unless you're hard to please, you won't object to these chapters. For in terms of excitement, the list of mighty men is justified by the famous stories which precede it (1 Chronicles 11:11–25). And the army roster contains gems of poetry:[1]

Some Gadites joined David
At the stronghold in the wilderness,
Mighty men of valor, men trained for battle,
Who could handle shield and spear,
Whose faces were like the faces of lions,
And as swift as gazelles on the mountains. . . .

Then the Spirit
Came upon Amasai,
Chief of the captains:
"We are yours, O David;
We are on your side, O son of Jesse!
Peace, peace to you,
And peace to your helpers!
For your God helps you."
(1 Chronicles 12:8, 18)

Have you heard such language from the Joint Chiefs of Staff, or from the heads of NATO?

1 Chronicles 11

There is a list of mighty men in 2 Samuel 23, but it ends, significantly, with Uriah the Hittite. This later list includes sixteen new names after Uriah's (1 Chronicles 11:41–47), men about whom we know nothing for certain. The Lord gave these worthies a place among the mighty, which says more for their valor than medals or ribbons. Notice that there are three sets of brothers among them, and that the names of their fathers are duly set down. These three fathers were in the physical realm what Zebedee was in the spiritual—the sire of two great warriors of God. "A man shall be known in his children,"[2] especially in the boring parts of the Bible.

Just after the brothers, we encounter Ithmah the Moabite in 1 Chronicles 11:46. His name may be derived from the word for orphan, which leaves us with two mysteries about him. Was he a Moabite, or a Jew who lived among the Moabites, as Naomi's husband did? Was he an orphan, and if so, has that something to do with his being called the Moabite? (The two men after Ithmah are listed by first name only, which leads me to believe there's a story in his name.) If you think it strange to wonder about such things, remember that we are to live by every word of God.

Remember Sheshan's daughter Ahlai from the begats? Whether or not Zabad the son of Ahlai is her descendant, there is something remarkable about him. He comes between Uriah, the last man on the first list, and Adina the Reubenite in 1 Chronicles 11:41–42. Though our Bibles say of Adina "and thirty with him," Dr. Gill maintains, plausibly enough,[3] that the phrase should be rendered, "but the thirty were superior to him," meaning that the men added to the second list were of lesser note than the first thirty.[4] Zabad, however, coming between the first and second groups, may have taken the place of one of the original mighty men. (Elika the Harodite appears in the first list of thirty, but not in the second.)[5] If Dr. Gill's theory is correct, Zabad may have been to the mighty men what Matthias was to the twelve apostles,[6] one chosen to replace an original member. Since Asahel died young,[7] and yet is found at the head of the thirty in both lists, I reluctantly suppose that Elika lost his position for another reason, and that Zabad took his place.

1 Chronicles 12

There are many things of interest in chapter 12. We see in verse 15 an exploit of the daring and courageous sons of Gad. We learn of the children of Issachar that they "had understanding of the times, to know what Israel ought to do" (1 Chronicles 12:32). Blessed is the leader who has such wise men under him! However, our focus shall be on verses 27 and 28, on "Jehoiada, the leader of the Aaronites," and on "Zadok, a young man, a valiant warrior."

The Aaronites were all priests, for Aaron's male descendants inherited the priesthood.[8] Thus Jehoiada led thirty-seven hundred men who were qualified to be priests, and they were all "equipped for the war."[9] Zadok is singled out from the others as a valiant warrior. What kind of priests were these? There is nothing to suggest that they were only chaplains to the soldiers. These clergy came to fight.

We should not be surprised by this, for we have soldier-preachers in our history. In Woodstock, Virginia, where I used to live, they still speak of the farewell sermon the Reverend John Peter Muhlenberg delivered in January 1776. His text was Ecclesiastes 3:1: "To every thing there is a season, and a time to every purpose under heaven." At the end of the sermon he disrobed, revealing an officer's uniform beneath. That very day he began the long journey to New England to reinforce George Washington's troops, and a number of his hearers marched beside him. For his distinguished service to the Continental Army he was promoted to brigadier general in 1777 and to major general at the war's end.[10] (One need not share all of his views to admire the man and his courage.)

Both Jehoiada and Zadok were the fathers of valiant men.[11] We have already spoken of Ahimaaz, the son of Zadok in chapter 5. Benaiah, the son of Jehoiada, whom we find among the second three of the mighty men in 1 Chronicles 11:22–25, became the head of David's bodyguard and the leader of Solomon's army. In fact, the same day that Solomon promoted Benaiah, he made Zadok, now an older man, the high priest of Israel. (Both of these worthies had supported him during the usurpation of Adonijah.)[12]

Why is this important? Because we are " . . . a holy priesthood . . . a royal priesthood" (1 Peter 2:5, 9), and we need to know what that means. Evidently, it does not mean a bevy of effete counselors whom men speak well of, but an army ready for spiritual battle.

> Finally, my brethren, be strong in the Lord and in the power of His might. Put on the whole armor of God, that you may be able to stand against the wiles of the devil. For we do not wrestle against flesh and blood, but against principalities, against powers, against the rulers of the darkness of this age, against spiritual hosts of wickedness in the *heavenly* places. Therefore take up the whole armor of God, that you may be able to withstand in the evil day, and having done all, to stand. (Ephesians 6:10–13)

Jehoiada, Zadok, and their sons are not the Rambos of yesteryear, fantastic heroes created for our amusement. No, they are models for us to emulate today, if indeed we are the warriors of God.

The Proportion of Levites

Now we come to the five chapters of officers in 1 Chronicles 23–27. The first thing to observe is the proportion of Levites to men in positions which we would call secular. Even if we include the warriors in chapters 11 and 12, the Levites take up more space than the twelve tribes of Israel, for the men who ran the kingdom are confined to chapter 27. The emphasis is on the house of God. Thus, the treasurers of the temple receive more notice than the treasurers of the kingdom.[13] There must be a reason why the boring parts devote so much attention to the tribe of Levi. But what is it, and what can we learn from it?

God's priorities are different from ours. Compare these chapters to a list of government officials in your county or state (or shire or province) and you'll see what I mean. How many priests and choir directors do you discover there? "Ah," you say, "but we have separation of church and state. Of course the lists are different." Well then, look in a volume of *Who's Who,* or consult the index of some brief, authoritative history of your country, and you'll find the same result. We are long on leaders and legislators, on merchants and scientists, and short on gatekeepers and musicians. The Lord's focus is on the things which are spiritual and eternal,[14] even in the mundane parts of the Bible. We would do well to remember this.

It would be easy to conclude, "I get it. The Church is where it's at. I'll become a missionary or a pastor." Or if you're older, "I missed the boat when I chose a secular occupation. The Lord will hardly care about my labors in the office, farm, or factory." Yet both these conclusions would be terribly wrong if they failed to take into account one all-important fact: *The Levites were called to their work.*

God took the tribe of Levi as his own, exchanging them for the first-born of Israel.[15] Then He assigned particular kinds of work to the different families of Levites.[16] Each Levite had a particular job to do, a job assigned him by the Lord. The Levites were called.

We have fallen so far from this concept of calling, or vocation,[17] that remedial instruction is required.

> The gospel teaches us that *every* man is capable of receiving a vocation, a special call, which distinguishes him from his kind and endows him with an inalienable dignity to the degree to which he obeys the call. This is the fundamental principle of any social order that can be called Christian. . . . An ideology which denies personal vocation, or a social regime which deprives man of the freedom to obey his vocation, is incompatible with Christianity.[18]

Before we can make a proper use of the lists of the Levites, we need to understand the call of God in our own lives.

Our Personal Calling

The best work I have seen on our personal calling was written by William Perkins about A.D. 1600. Here are a few of Perkins' remarks on the subject at hand.

> *A vocation or calling is a certain kind of life ordained and imposed on man by God for the common good. . . .*
>
> Every person of every degree, state, sex, or condition, without exception must have some personal and particular calling to walk in. This appeareth plainly by the whole word of God. Adam so soon as he was created, even in his integrity had a personal calling assigned him by God, which was to dress and keep the garden. . . .

> Every man must judge that particular calling in which God hath placed him to be the best of all callings for him: I say not simply best, but best for him. . . .
>
> The action of a shepherd in keeping sheep . . . is as good a work before God as is the action of a judge in giving sentence, or of a magistrate in ruling, or a minister in preaching. . . .
>
> Men of years make choice of fit callings for themselves when they try, judge, and examine themselves to what things they are apt and fit and to what things they are not. And every man must examine himself of two things: first, touching his affections; secondly, touching his gifts. . . . He may say that is his calling because he likes it best and is every way the fittest to it. . . .
>
> That [parents] may the better judge aright for what callings their children are fit, they must observe two things in them: first, their inclination; secondly, their natural gifts. . . . And here all parents must be warned that the neglect of this duty is a great and common sin, for the care of the most is that their children may live, nothing regarding whether they live well and do service to God in a fit calling or no. And the truth is that parents cannot do greater wrong to their children and the society of men than to apply them unto unfit callings. . . .
>
> He that is fit for sundry callings must make choice of the best. . . .
>
> We may not leave our callings when we please, but the prescribing thereof belongs to God.[19]

Did you notice that Adam was given a secular occupation? Come to think of it, the Second Adam had one too, *until He was called by God* to other work. The same for the twelve apostles. Get the picture? It's not in the work; it's all in the call of God. It will be a great day for the Church when all her children are following their true vocations.

Now we can appreciate the officers of the kingdom. Some were singing praises, and some were herding sheep, but all were serving God. "Every man must judge that particular calling in which God hath placed him to be the best of all callings for him." (If you have been ignorant of your calling, be ignorant no more. If you have heard but not responded to your calling, now is the time to repent. A broken and a contrite heart the Lord will not despise.)

Do you remember my asking, about Caleb's conquest of Hebron, "Reader, do you have a mountain in mind?" If you have a calling from God, rest assured that you have a mountain as well (and giants to go with it). When God gives you your calling, He may not show you the mountain at first, lest you run from the path of duty. Just follow His lead; He'll know when you're ready to see the whole picture.

Whatever our calling, we should glorify God in it. We should bring to the workplace the same outlook that God brings to the lists of the Bible—an emphasis on what is spiritual and eternal. I cannot say too strongly that the best way to do this is to do good work.[20] If your job is merely an opportunity to preach the gospel to your fellow workers, you cannot fulfill your calling. Evangelists in employees' clothing have much in common with people who work only for money. They both misunderstand that we are called to serve our employers. Let your excellent service glorify your God. Let your deeds proclaim Him, and He will bless your words. Good workers make the best evangelists; the apostles caught fish before they caught men.

The Great Commodity

Let's look at some particulars. There are several things in chapter 23 which we find nowhere else. In the last year of his life, David gathered all the leaders of Israel. Then he divided the Levites according to their families and appointed a work for each. (The details of these appointments continue on for three more chapters.) David ordered the kingdom and provided workers for the temple *before the temple was begun.* He recognized that God had given His people rest, that the ark was no more to be carried about,[21] and therefore he gave new assignments to the Levites. We can learn something from this.

God spends a lot of time training and organizing His people for work in structures which have yet to be built. Before the plans and instructions are given to Solomon, and before David and the princes offer their gold for the temple,[22] we get four chapters recording the jobs of the Levites. God always has His eye on His people. Not only their death is precious in His sight; their training is too. We tend to think, if only we had this building or that money, we could do so much for the Lord. But people are the great commodity—people called, trained, and organized by God—people who accept their callings and the discipline that goes with them. The chronicler spends more time on the Levites than on the temple, its gold, and its furnishings. Thus he shows us the mind of the Lord.

David made musical instruments for praising God. These instruments of praise were the very first things produced for the temple worship.[23] When Hezekiah restored the service of the Lord,

> he stationed the Levites in the house of the Lord with cymbals, with stringed instruments, and with harps, according to the commandment

> of David, of Gad the king's seer, and of Nathan the prophet; for thus *was* the commandment of the Lord by his prophets. (2 Chronicles 29:25)

The Lord's first preparation for His temple was to order His people and their instruments of praise. Maybe that old notion of heaven, with saints playing their harps, is sounder and more profound than we think.[24]

It is interesting to compare verse 3 with verses 27 and 28 in 1 Chronicles 23:

> Now the Levites were numbered from the age of *thirty* years and above; and the number of individual males was thirty-eight thousand. . . .
>
> For by the last words of David the Levites were numbered from *twenty* years old and above; because their duty was to help the sons of Aaron in the service of the house of the Lord. . . . 1 Chronicles 23:3, 27–28, emphasis added)

Scholars have different ideas about this change from thirty to twenty. I don't feel clear about it, but I like the suggestion of Dr. Otto Zöckler:

> It is conceivable, though not indicated by our author, that David may have established a distinction of classes, in such a way that he introduced the Levites of twenty years to the lower and easier duties, and those of thirty years to the higher and holier functions.
>
> At all events, any mode of harmonizing the two accounts appears more reasonable than . . . (the solutions of certain scholars who assume either the chronicler or his copyists were incompetent.)[25]

Whatever the true explanation of their ages may be, not all of these Levites were playing harps. Many of them were carrying ashes and firewood, cleaning courts and chambers, and washing holy vessels. Levites are appointed to serve every priest in his God-given duties—even if He is High Priest forever after the order of Melchizedek.[26]

I grew up about a mile from the old Bureau of Standards (which has since grown larger and moved to the suburbs). Keeping exact weights and measures, which in our culture is a function of the government, seems to have been under the Old Covenant a job for the Levites. Since they helped the sons of Aaron "with all kinds of measures and sizes" (1 Chronicles 23:29), there is reason to think that they were the ultimate authority on such things.[27] If, in fact, these standards were preserved in God's holy temple,[28] we may more fully understand His saying, "A false balance is an abomination to the Lord, But a just weight is His delight."[29]

The Twenty-Four Courses

In chapter 24, we come to the divisions of the priests. They were divided by lot into twenty-four groups, or courses (of a thousand men each),[30] who took turns doing the work of the temple. These divisions may seem like so much dead weight to God's people today, but it was not always so. A thousand years after these appointments were made, Luke referred to John the Baptist's father as "a certain priest named Zacharias, *of the division of Abijah*."[31] And Josephus, the first-century historian of the Jews, proudly remarked:

> The family from which I am derived is not an ignoble one, but hath descended all along from the priests; and as nobility among several people is of a different origin, so with us to be of the sacerdotal dignity, is an indication of the splendour of a family. Now, I am not only sprung from a sacerdotal family in general, but *from the first of the twenty-four courses*; and as among us there is not only a considerable difference between one family of each course and another, I am of the chief family of that first course also.[32]

Obviously, that was hot stuff in the first century. Yet each of us, if we are in Christ, has a social standing higher than the great historian's.[33] We are priests according to the order of Melchizedek, not the order of Levi. Our older brother Jesus has become High Priest forever of a better covenant than Aaron's. The least member of the new priesthood ranks above all the family of Josephus. Thus Tom Skinner, a former Harlem gang leader, could suggest that those thirsting for high society should rub shoulders with him, for he, like every Christian, has become a son of God.

The Rest of the Levites

The last twelve verses of chapter 24 tell us about "the rest of the sons of Levi." What is remarkable here is that none of Gershon's descendants are included. Levi had three sons, Gershon, Kohath, and Merari.[34] Descendants of all three sons are listed in 1 Chronicles 23, with the Gershonites appearing in verses 7–11.[35] Why then do we find only the descendants of Kohath and Merari in the end of chapter 24? Since the latter list follows the divisions of the priests, presumably it records those who assisted them in the temple, and Gershon's descendants may not have been called to that work. In 1 Chronicles 26:21–22, we find Gershonites supervising the temple treasuries, and they may have had other such duties. The truth is, these lists don't tell us everything we want to know, and I believe there's a good reason why.

Christians need to be content with partial knowledge. It's good to search the nooks of Scripture for useful bits of learning, but shouldn't we stop when we run out of nooks? There are some things God chooses not to tell us. I'd love to have more information about Jephthah's daughter or On the son of Peleth, but in this world I shall not obtain it. It's good for us to accept the limits God imposes,

> [For] knowledge is as food, and needs no less,
> Her temperance over appetite, to know
> In measure what the mind may well contain.[36]

Since we are limited in our knowledge of other people's callings, let's make the best of it. As churches and as individuals, let's be charitable in our judgments. Some people's callings and duties we understand; some we do not. Can't we leave their judgment to Him who has called them? If I trust the Gershonites were well employed, and I do, why not trust the Lord for others whose callings are beyond me? He who frets most about the vocation of others may well be deficient in fulfilling his own.

The musicians. Next we come to the musicians. We studied their genealogies in the begats; here in chapter 25 we see their twenty-four divisions. Have you observed that:

- David and the captains of the army chose the lead musicians? (v. 1)
- Asaph and Sons prophesied as the king commanded? (v. 2)
- Jeduthun and Sons prophesied with a harp to thank and praise the Lord? (v. 3)
- God gave Heman fourteen sons and three daughters? (v. 5)
- 288 men were instructed in the songs of the Lord?[37] (v. 7)
- Teachers and students cast lots equally for their duty? (v. 8)

In other words I don't have to scrape the bottom of this barrel to find something of interest.

I'm particularly intrigued by the generals choosing the musicians. Just envision, if you can, Generals Patton and Montgomery choosing the singers at Westminster Abbey, or Prussian field marshals helping Bach select his choir. The possibilities are endless. (So what if the sopranos shriek like mortars and the basses boom like twenty-four-pounders? *We* find it invigorating.) And, if I may sober up again, every Levite should understand the principle and tactics of unconditional surrender.

Some interesting results of Dr. Gill's intense study are summarized in his comment on verse 8.

> No regard was had to the age of a person, his being the first-born or a younger brother, or to his office and station, whether as a teacher or a learner in the science of singing; he was made the head of a course, as the lot came up; and it may easily be observed, by comparing the lots in the following verses with the sons of the chief singers, according to the order of them in ver. 2, 3, 4, that the younger are often preferred in the courses by lot to the elder, of which even the first lot is an instance.[38]

Get it? Joseph was the second son of Asaph, yet he obtained the first lot, while his older brother Zaccur came in third.[39] Notice that Asaph's four sons all landed in the top seven divisions. If Josephus is any indicator of how important these rankings were to the Jews, the children of Asaph had a lot to crow about.

Reader, have you received a high place by lot from the Lord? Are you, by your gifts or your station in life, prominent in your community? Remember, "A man's pride will bring him low, But the humble in spirit will retain honor (Proverbs 29:23)."

The gatekeepers. The first half of chapter 26 is devoted to the gatekeepers, or porters. These were the men "whose business it was to open and shut the doors of the temple, to keep all impure and improper persons from entering into it, or any of the vessels being carried out of it, and to prevent tumults and riots about it."[40]

I can relate to this description of the gatekeepers' duties. The church which I attend is located in a semi-industrial section of a small California city. Since our manner is informal and we are close to downtown, homeless and transient people come to our services with greater or less regularity. This makes being an usher more of an adventure than it is in some churches. Though we have had no tumults and riots in my time, I do see some familiar faces in the county jail when I visit the prisoners there. We need gatekeepers in the church, that all things may be done decently and in order.

There is a spiritual side to the work of these sons of Levi. Is it not the duty of New Covenant Levites to keep "impure and improper persons" out of the Church? I refer not to bodies dressed in tattered clothes, but to souls attired in the filthy rags of their own righteousness;[41] not to worshippers uncircumcised in flesh, but to those uncircumcised in heart.[42] Such spiritual gatekeepers are watchmen of the kind Ezekiel described.[43] The poor in spirit have nothing to fear from them.

Do you see Obed-Edom in 1 Chronicles 26:4? This name appears twenty times in Scripture. While there may have been more than one Obed-Edom,[44] I believe our gatekeeper is the man who once kept the ark of the covenant in his house, for he was blessed by God.[45] In verses 5–8, we discover the nature of this blessing: God gave the man eight sons. Moreover, his sons and grandsons were "able men with strength," men of "great ability." This tells us something about God's idea of blessing. Do you think He has changed His mind since Obed-Edom's time?

The Hebrew of verse 7 is difficult, but it is easy to understand that God wished to honor Elihu and Semachiah for their ability and service.

We don't know why Shimri's father (v. 10) made him the firstborn, but we know why the Lord switched the birthright among the sons of Jacob.[46]

The sons of Obed-Edom kept the storehouse of the temple.[47] (I'll bet it didn't look like my garage.)

The Rogues' Gallery

The last part of chapter 26 tells us about the treasurers and the men in charge of "the business of the Lord" (v. 30). The thing that strikes me in this section is the rogues' gallery.

> Some of the spoils won in battles they dedicated to maintain the house of the Lord. And all that Samuel the seer, Saul the son of Kish, Abner the son of Ner, and Joab the son of Zeruiah had dedicated, every dedicated thing, was under the hand of Shelomith and his brethren. (v. 28)

Poor Samuel! Look at the company he's in. Though Abner was not so bad as Joab or Saul, he was hardly a spiritual man.[48] I have no trouble with the things Samuel dedicated to God, but what shall we make of the others? Shall Joab build the Lord's house?

We must be able to distinguish men from their offices. (Saul was king of Israel; Abner and Joab were captains of the Lord's army.) In true positions of authority, as the leaders of God's people, fallible men take the spoils of God's enemies and devote them to His service. It is entirely right for them to do so. If later God casts them out for sin, that does not invalidate the actions they performed in His employ. It's a good thing, too.

What if the priest who baptized you renounces the faith? Would you then be a pagan? What if the pastor who married you runs off with the organist? Would you then be living in sin? What if the person who was instrumental in your conversion becomes a notorious sinner? Would you be contaminated? Not at all. Much as we may grieve over such things, we look not to the men, but to the Lord who made them His agents. You were converted by the Spirit, baptized into Christ, married in God's presence. You are the treasure which Joab brought to the house of the Lord, and treasure you shall remain. The sons of Shelomith shall see to it.

The Officers

At long last we come to the officers of the twelve tribes. The first half of chapter 27 is devoted to the commanders of the militia which David maintained in times of peace. These twelve leaders were not all from different tribes, but they are all found listed among David's mighty men.[49] Each of them commanded his group of twenty-four thousand men for one month of the year. Thus David had a quarter of a million trained men able to help out in an emergency, but free to follow their own business eleven months of the year. There is nothing new under the sun, especially the Army reserves.

Asahel

What touches me here is the mention in verse 7 of "Asahel the brother of Joab, and Zebadiah his son after him." Though he died before David became king of Israel, Asahel retained his place at the head of both lists of mighty men.[50] Here we encounter him as the leader of a militia which he probably never lived to see. (Scholars disagree about when this militia was first devised.) If he did function as one of its leaders, he could hardly have left a son ready to take his place. Allow me to explain.

Were it not for the begats in 1 Chronicles, we would have no way of knowing Asahel's relationship to David. There we discover that Zeruiah, the mother of Asahel, was David's sister (1 Chronicles 2:15–16). Even if we assume she was much older than David, we must admit that Asahel was Zeruiah's youngest son. While it is not too unusual for a firstborn son to be as old as his uncle, it is rare to find a youngest son much older than his uncle. Since we know that David was only thirty when he began to reign,[51] I conclude that either Asahel never led the militia, or that if he did, someone else took his place until Zebadiah was grown. Either way I see special honor being given to Asahel.

If Asahel never commanded the militia, why should he be mentioned here at all? If he did, why should his position have been saved for his son? (There is nothing to indicate that these positions were inherited. Would you leave your country's defense to the untried descendants of deceased heroes?) There was something special about Asahel. I believe that he, like Jabez, was more honorable than his brothers.

There is a considerable distance between Saint Francis of Assisi and Zeruiah's sons. Is it damning Asahel with faint praise, to call him the noblest of them? Joab was clearly a bad, if capable, man.[52] And though I love him for his boldness and his Shakespearean lines,[53] Abishai was hardly a man after God's own heart.[54] Lest he be judged no different from his brothers, Asahel was honored in the list of twelve commanders.

Joab was a commander who proved unworthy. Abishai was a valiant and capable fighter who, with David's help, did not as fully disgrace himself through sin. Asahel was brave and swift—and rash. Dying young at Abner's hands, he never received his command. Clearly he was impetuous; but had he been wicked, would we find him so celebrated a generation after his death? You know what I think. Either David or the Lord had a special place in his heart for this spirited nephew, and caused him to be remembered.

> Let four captains
> Bear Hamlet like a soldier to the stage;
> For he was likely, had he been put on,
> To have prov'd most royal.[55]

You could have a worse memorial.

Honor and Dishonor

In 1 Chronicles 27:16–22, we find the leaders of the tribes of Israel. No one knows why Gad and Asher are omitted from this list. At least the dishonor, if it is one, gets spread around a bit; Dan and Zebulun are here, who were not found in the begats.

Do you remember how David's oldest brother Eliab railed on him for coming down to see the battle?[56] Scholars agree that the Elihu of verse 18 is that same person. He was promoted to the headship of the tribe, either through David's kindness to him or by prevailing custom. I suppose that, as he went about his duties, he had plenty of time to meditate on (and repent of) his harshness to the youngest of his father's sons. Let him whose younger brother is now a reigning monarch cast the first stone at old Eliab.

Abner's son Jaasiel became the leader of Benjamin. I think David had a hand in Jaasiel's promotion, as he did in Zebadiah's. If you remember David's grief at the death of Abner,[57] I think you will agree. Nor will you be surprised to find among the leaders of Israel no son of Joab.

I can hardly bear to call the end of chapter 27 boring. If you can't read it for the content, as I do, get out the King James and read it for the sound:

> And over the vineyards was Shimei the Ramathite:
>
> (And) over the increases of the vineyards for the wine cellars was Zabdi the Shiphmite:
>
> And over the olive trees and the sycamore trees that were in the low plains was Baal-Hanan the Gederite:
>
> And over the cellars of oil was Joash. (1 Chronicles 27:27–28, KJV)

Didn't do much for you? My father tells me that as a young boy in Orthodox yeshiva, he and his classmates imitated the old Jews by rocking back and forth in their seats as they recited their lessons. (The public school teachers who taught them secular subjects in the afternoon recommended in vain that they read without motion.) Though I have never sat in yeshiva, I find that this passage can set me to rocking. Before you give up, you should say it again—this time with movement. (If you're still not satisfied, try it in Hebrew!)

Reading this list reminds me of some quite different poetry:

> The paving-man leans on his two-handed rammer,
> the reporter's lead flies swiftly over the note-book, the
> sign-painter is lettering with blue and gold,
> The canal boy trots on the tow-path, the book-keeper counts
> at his desk, the shoemaker waxes his thread,
> The conductor beats time for the band and all the performers
> follow him. . . .[58]

I am not one of those who feels the Word of God needs to be recommended as mere "literature." Far from it. But since we're enshrining self-singing Walt in our anthologies, shouldn't we give ear to the melodies of the boring parts?

Something So Unexpected

Believe me, I could spend more time in 1 Chronicles 27. (I haven't even got to the camels and donkeys yet!) However, we ought to look at the similar list in 1 Kings, chapter 4, which records the administrators of Solomon.

❧ ❧ ❧

I had planned to discuss the sons of David's friends who served under Solomon,[59] which I still think an interesting topic, but something so unexpected has come up, I shall concentrate on it alone.

❧ ❧ ❧

Take note of Ahimaaz in 1 Kings 4:15. We cannot be sure that he is the faithful messenger, the son of Zadok the high priest,[60] but there is good reason to think so. The other eleven officials with whom he is grouped are all called the son of so-and-so (or Ben-someone, which is equivalent).[61] Only Ahimaaz appears alone, without the name of his father. To me this indicates someone so well known as to need no introduction. If I have reasoned correctly, there could be no other candidate; the governor in Naphtali must be the high priest's son. Which would give us something else to puzzle about.

The first person on the list is Azariah the son of Zadok, the priest.[62] Elsewhere we learn that Azariah was really Zadok's grandson, but the son of Ahimaaz.[63] Why would Ahimaaz pass on the high priesthood to his son and become governor in Naphtali? I don't know. But the more I think about it, the more I think the boring parts are telling us something.

Do you remember Ahimaaz in "The Return of the Begats?" Looking back now, I discover that I wrote:

> The last man named is Ahimaaz the son of Zadok. The Scriptures show him to have been a famous runner and a man of great love and sensitivity. If you know the wonderful story of his service to his king, you will linger over his name when you find it in the boring parts. And should we not remember our glorious High Priest, who surpasses Ahimaaz in His power and His grace? (page 47)

Little did I dream what I was saying! Zadok's son is more a figure of Christ than I thought. Much more.

What first caught my attention was the fact that Ahimaaz was governor of Naphtali. The high priest in Galilee? Doesn't make any sense, does it? But in the fullness of time there would be another High Priest who would show a like fondness for that despised region.[64] Of Him we are told that the government would be upon His shoulder.[65] Furthermore, whom did Ahimaaz marry? The princess Basemath, whose father was Solomon. To make my analogy fit, this other Priest would have to marry a King's daughter. Not much chance of that, is there?[66]

Having come this far, I looked through new eyes at the story of Ahimaaz.

> Then Ahimaaz the son of Zadok said, "Let me run now and take the news to the king, how the Lord has avenged him of his enemies." And Joab said to him, "You shall not take the news this day, for you shall take the news another day. But today you shall take no news, because the king's son is dead." (2 Samuel 18:19–20)

I believe there is only one other time in the Bible when the King's Son dies even as the King is avenged of His enemies. We can understand that strange day better by examining the famous run of Ahimaaz (2 Samuel 18:19–33).

There is good news and bad news when Absalom dies. The good news is that the rebellious forces have been destroyed and the king's people are safe. The bad news is that the king's son is dead. Wicked Joab, who has killed the king's son, sends forth a dark messenger[67] with the gospel according to Joab in his mouth. Nevertheless, Ahimaaz, the son of righteousness,[68] whose primary motive is love, brings the good news to his lord. Setting out on his own, though hopelessly behind, he gets to David first. The good news outruns the bad.[69] There is only one prize in this race, and the son of righteousness claims it.

Here's how I apply the story. I consider Absalom as both a figure of Satan and a negative image of Christ. Like Satan he rebels against his Lord and brings destruction to his followers. Yet, like Christ, he is physically perfect and the king's beloved son. (Observe that he dies upon a tree, lifted up from the earth, pierced by three spears, encompassed by his enemies.) Thus we perceive in Absalom's death Messiah bruised and Satan crushed. Reminded of these momentous events, we have reason to sorrow and reason to rejoice. (Greatly we should grieve, as David did, mourning the Son whose death resulted from our sins! Greatly we should celebrate our new life in His death!) How shall we resolve the conflict? By looking to that other symbol of Christ, Ahimaaz. The High Priest runs to His Lord before anyone else can get there, and says to Him one word: *Shalom.*[70] Peace. Peace to You, for Your righteous wrath is satisfied. Peace to Your people, for they are delivered from sin. (Not a word about the price of these blessings.) Nothing but peace. The good Man brings good news (and nothing else). Why shouldn't we call it Good Friday?

13

THE RESTORATION

(Ezra and Nehemiah)

Ezra begins with the proclamation of Cyrus. The time, the set time, has come: God's people shall return to their land. Hallelujah! However, not everyone is interested in returning. Some of the chosen people are quite content in Babylon, and thus it shall ever be. The divine wisdom does not focus on them.[1] Rather, God delights in His pilgrims, in those who leave the security of this world (such as it is) to seek the things of the Spirit. He has proven it by recording and repeating their names in the boring parts.

Similar Lists

Both Ezra and Nehemiah give us similar lists of the captives who returned from Babylon.[2] Neither of them tells us the names of those who stayed. The Lord rejoices in the names of His servants and fills His Word with them, but He passes over thousands of others in silence. He could easily have recorded the leaders who sided with Korah, the cowards in David's army, or the tarriers in Babylon, but that would not be like Him. When it comes to naming names, He loves to emphasize the positive.[3] Go thou and do likewise.

The People Who Returned

Let's get a general idea of the people who returned; then we can examine the differences in the lists. The first thing to observe is that in this list the lay people come first. The Levites had priority in 1 Chronicles 23–27, but here they come after the other tribes. I do not know why this is so, but it could be related to the deplorable dearth of Levites among those who returned. The priests, who were just one family of the Levites, make up roughly a tenth of the whole group, while the other Levites comprise less than 1 percent.[4] If I were not acquainted with the boring parts, I would wonder what to make of this. Instead I think immediately of those passages where Ezekiel contrasts the Levites with the priests of the sons of Zadok.

> The sanctuary of the Lord shall be in the center. It shall be for the priests of the sons of Zadok, who are sanctified, who have kept My charge, who did not go astray when the children of Israel went astray, as the Levites went astray.[5]

If there was a great falling away of the Levites in Ezekiel's time, it might explain why so few of their children and grandchildren returned to Jerusalem with Ezra.[6]

The next thing that strikes me is that the number of Jews who returned is greater than the number who were carried away. Nebuchadnezzar took captive several groups of Israelites, but the total, as far as we know, appears to be well short of twenty thousand.[7] Both Ezra and Nehemiah say the whole congregation which returned numbered 42,360. As they multiplied in Egypt, the seed of Abraham multiplied in Babylon. The Church grows, and grows strong, under affliction.

Has disaster struck your family or church? Let the boring parts be your consolation. Are you a visionary, an idealist? Behold Ezekiel's vision of the restored worship—of a temple greater than Solomon's. Are you a practical, nuts-and-bolts kind of believer? Then read the double census of those who returned to prosper in Zion. Either way, the message is the same. Calamity is but the prelude to blessing, if we receive it as discipline from the hand of the Lord.[8]

Children of slaves. Speaking of bringing good out of evil, consider the Nethinim and Solomon's servants in Ezra 2:43–58 and Nehemiah 7:46–60. While we can't be certain about who they were, the Nethinim appear to have been "foreign slaves, mostly prisoners of war, who had from time to time been *given* to the temple by the kings and princes of the nation, and . . . assigned the lower menial duties of the house of God."[9]

Solomon's servants probably descended either from the Canaanites who built the first temple or from Gentile prisoners of war.[10] These formerly despised peoples here receive more attention than the priests and the Levites together, and their numbers are greater than the Levites'. How the mighty have fallen! How the poor have been raised up!

Cast your eye upon the names appearing in the lists of the servants. They are not the names of the individuals who returned, but the names of certain ancestors of theirs. Who were these ancestors, and when did they live? We do not know. Perhaps the Nethinim, like the priests and the Levites, were divided into courses in David's time.[11] In any event, the forefathers remembered here are known today to Bible readers the world over. Though they had been slaves or the children of slaves, in the fullness of time they received more honor from the Lord than His own appointed tribe. Think about it. If you are humbled now, take heart. If you are exalted now, beware. "Let him who thinks he stands take heed lest he fall" (1 Corinthians 10:12). Let him who is certain he's flat on his back put his trust in the Nethinim's God.

The sons of Barzillai. Matthew Henry has an interesting perspective on "the sons of Barzillai" in Ezra 2:61.

> One of their ancestors married a daughter of Barzillai, that great man whom we read of in David's time; he gloried in an alliance to that honourable family, and, preferring that before the dignity of his priesthood, would have his children called after Barzillai's family, and their pedigree preserved in the registers of that house, not of the house of Aaron, and so they lost it. In Babylon there was nothing to be got by the priesthood, and therefore they cared not for being akin to it. . . . Now that the priests had recovered their rights, and had the altar to live upon again, they would gladly be looked upon as priests. But they had sold their birthright for the honour of being gentlemen, and therefore were justly degraded, and forbidden to eat of the most holy things.[12]

Two things impress me here. One is, "They had sold their birthright for the honour of being gentlemen." God save us from that fate! The other, "In Babylon there was nothing to be got by the priesthood." (The priesthood and poetry have some things in common.) Ah, but in the Jerusalem which is above, which is the mother of us all, it's a different story.

The Variations

There is some variance between Ezra's numbers and Nehemiah's. The totals are the same, but many of the particulars are not. How shall we account for these differences? Many commentators think Ezra listed all the men who signed up in Babylon for the return to Israel, but some of them died or changed their minds before they got there. Then Nehemiah recorded those who actually arrived in Jerusalem, including some who joined up after Ezra finished his list. I'm not convinced that this answer is better than my favorite one ("We don't know"), but take your choice.[13]

There are only two categories in which we find no variations of name or number—the priests and the animals. Now here is an interesting problem! Why should the priests and the beasts be distinct from all others? My explanation is that the priests continued to be faithful in the decades after Ezekiel commended them.[14] They knew the opening indictment of Isaiah, and they heeded it.

> Hear, O heavens, and give ear, O earth!
> For the Lord has spoken:
> "I have nourished and brought up children,
> And they have rebelled against Me.
> The ox knows its owner
> And the donkey its master's crib;
> *But* Israel does not know
> My people do not consider"
>
> (Isaiah 1:2–3)

The priests so read, marked, learned, and inwardly digested this passage,[15] that in time it no longer applied to them. They were as faithful as the beasts of burden: not one of them changed his mind about the journey to Jerusalem. Mark Twain said, "Man is the only animal that blushes—or needs to."[16] In the census of Ezra and Nehemiah, neither the priests nor the animals have anything to blush about.

Rebuilding the Wall

I have heard only one memorable sermon taken wholly from the boring parts.[17] It was preached on the third chapter of Nehemiah. To me this chapter is so lively and fun, that it is hardly work to write about it. I could spend a dozen pages on the builders of the wall, but it's better for you to discover them for yourself. So I'll just mention those I can't bear to pass by.

I give first place to Baruch the son of Zabbai.[18] He is singled out from the crowd as one who diligently or earnestly repaired a section of the wall. Translated more literally, he "made hot to repair" or he "burned with zeal in repairing." (The slothful in Zion, I surmise, steered clear of Zabbai's son.) It is reasonable to suppose that Baruch had his faults. It's likely he didn't consider the lilies. He didn't write sonnets or patronize the arts. But were those the qualities Nehemiah needed in a man? With a single Hebrew word the Lord bestowed upon Baruch His seal of approval, and no man shall take it from him.

In the next verse, we encounter Meremoth, the son of Urijah, the son of Koz. Ezra tells us that Meremoth weighed and recorded "the silver and the gold and the articles" which the exiles brought from Babylon (Ezra 8:33–34). Though he had come to Jerusalem early and was clearly a person of some importance, he knew how to get his hands dirty. One section of wall was not enough for him. When he finished one portion he took on another (Nehemiah 3:4, 21). If you want to see a man diligent in his business, look on Meremoth, the son of Urijah.

There were others who built more than one piece of the wall. The men of Tekoa repaired two sections, which is the more remarkable since "their nobles did not put their shoulders to the work of their Lord."[19] What a strange place, this Tekoa! Having furnished a wise woman for Joab, a mighty man for David, and a prophet for the Lord, it now provides us the best and worst examples of sanctified labor. I know it's a contradiction to say so, but mediocrity must have been rare in the town of Tekoa.[20]

You could hardly expect me to overlook the daughters of Shallum in Nehemiah 3:12, the only females mentioned in the list. What is clear is that the Lord delighted to honor them. After that, it's every man for himself. Dr. Gill thought these ladies were "rich widows or heiresses, [who] employed men to build at their own expense."[21] I consider this an eighteenth-century English conceit. (It may be correct, but until I see the check stubs of the laborers, I'll hardly believe it.) I think these ladies had a hand in the work, and that God approved of it. Personally, I hope never to see my daughters driving cement trucks (unless they're involved in a cause like Nehemiah's). Yet at this particular barn-raising, if you want my opinion, the daughters of Shallum did more than cook for the men.

What more shall I say? For the time would fail me to tell of the goldsmiths, the perfumers, and the apothecaries, of the gates of Jerusalem and the pool of Siloah, of the son of Rechab and the sixth son of Zalaph. I only hope that you'll further explore this unique and informative chapter of the Bible.[22]

The Sons of Joab

I was going to say, "Skipping over some of the shorter boring parts, we pass on to Nehemiah 11 and 12." However, when I turned to the first of those shorter parts (to record it in a footnote), my eye lighted on the phrase, "the sons of Joab" (Ezra 8:9). The sons of Joab? Having just made some hard remarks about the gentleman in the previous chapter, I ought to consider the possibility that good things were found in his family.

The sons of Joab appear in Ezra 2:6, Ezra 8:9, and Nehemiah 7:11. I cannot gain from the commentators any certainty about whether or not they are the descendants of David's general or someone else. There is only one other Joab in the Bible, the father of the Valley of Craftsmen.[23] He is mentioned only once, while Joab's name recurs a hundred times. Looking at the other names in Ezra 8:1–14, we find some men unknown to us, some who lived before Joab, and some who lived after him. Therefore I proclaim this an area of Christian liberty. Free to follow my fancy, I incline toward the view that these were Joab's descendants, and that they provide some balance to the curse pronounced by David, "Let it rest on the head of Joab and on all his father's house; and let there never fail to be in the house of Joab one who has a discharge or is a leper, who leans on a staff or falls by the sword, or who lacks bread" (2 Samuel 3:29).

Wouldn't it be nice if that weren't the whole story?

The Covenant

Solemnity surrounds the men who pledge their lives, their fortunes, and their sacred honor to some high cause or calling. However you regard the signers of the Magna Charta, the Mayflower Compact, or the Declaration of Independence, you must admit their names have special power. Who can look without emotion upon the signatures of those documents? In this day of categorical denials and outright lies, of prenuptial agreements and broken promises, when a man's word seems no longer to be his bond, even the blotted flourishes of men who meant what they said can move our souls to wonder.

Have you read the stirring speech of the Levites in Nehemiah 9? It prepares us for the covenant of Nehemiah 10. There we are given the names of eighty-four leaders who set their seal to the document, *before* we see the covenant itself. This passage is remarkable for more than just the order of the text. I can think of no other biblical covenant with a like number of persons subscribed to it. Over and over again in Ezra and Nehemiah the Lord preserves the names of His servants. He has a special regard for each participant in the great Restoration. This should be an encouragement to us, who must strengthen the things that remain, who must repair the breaches in the house of the Lord. Though we are little among the thousands of Judah, if we are faithful in this work, we shall not be forgotten.

Some Came Freely

In Nehemiah 11 and 12 we find extensive lists of the dwellers at Jerusalem.[24] The striking thing here is that some were chosen by lot (i.e., compelled) and some came freely. It seems that most people were not eager to live in the holy city, presumably because it was the focus of pagan hostility. (Ours is not the first time Jerusalem has been a hot spot of the earth.) Consequently, "The people blessed all the men who willingly offered themselves to dwell at Jerusalem" (Nehemiah 11:2). I like to think that Nehemiah recorded the names of these volunteers, mostly as a monument to their faithfulness. Precious in the sight of the Lord are those who offer themselves for hazardous service.

Here's an anecdote I consider relevant to Nehemiah's list. The United States Marine Corps prides itself on being an elite group of volunteers. During the Vietnam War, however, a few of the men drafted for military service ended up in the Marines. I happened to know one of them. He was an affable, happy-go-lucky, and brilliant young man. I could not imagine him as a Marine. Assuming the drill sergeants at Paris Island were not fond of draftees, I cringed to think of what awaited him there. He was gone a long time. I still remember how he looked when I first saw him on leave. In his sandals and jeans, with a large peace symbol around his neck, except for the length of his hair, he seemed hardly to have changed. "How'd it go?" I anxiously enquired. In his modest way, he told me it wasn't so bad. Turns out he graduated third in a class of ninety-some men, was able to choose his own assignment, and had found himself a job far from where the bullets were flying. Which just goes to show, you never can tell (or else that fear is a great motivator).

Nehemiah was the leader of the Lord's Marines. Nothing, not even deceit or the threat of death, could induce him to desert his post.[25] Can you imagine him filling his list with the names of the draftees in Jerusalem? Even if, like my friend, they excelled at providing for the common (and their private) defense, I doubt that Nehemiah was overly impressed. He had a heart for the fight; he wanted to be where the action was. Thus, I imagine that most of the men in chapters 11 and 12 were like the valiant son of Hachaliah.[26]

I notice in Nehemiah 11:22 that the singers were "in charge of the service of the house of God." In David's time, as we have seen, the singers "were free from other duties."[27] Why the change? The tenuous position of the Jews, and the small number of Levites who returned, must have required it. Surrounded by enemies who resented their presence, and few in number themselves, the Jews' resources had to be devoted to survival.[28] When the builders on the wall must double as soldiers, the singers shall have other duties as well. What a blessing, what a privilege it is for the Church to have workers fully devoted to the arts! If only we could understand this! If only, when we were rich enough to employ architects and musicians, we would retain our zeal for the Lord, we should find ourselves clearing the ruins of Zion less often than we do.

It must have been strange for the men of Anathoth to return to their city. Their grandfathers had persecuted the prophet Jeremiah, and the Lord had rewarded them according to their evil intentions.[29] It was a field in Anathoth that the imprisoned and childless prophet had purchased shortly before the fall of Judah.[30] Imagine the descendants of his persecutors returning to their inheritance and seeing the field which belonged to Jeremiah. Do you think that they felt the fear of the Lord, that they finally stood in awe of His Word? Do you think they thought twice before scorning a prophet?

Priest and King

In Nehemiah 12, we find a genealogy of the high priests after the restoration (12:10–11, 22). The last man on the list is Jaddua,[31] about whom Josephus relates a fascinating story. When Alexander the Great marched upon Jerusalem, he had reason to be angry with the Jews.

> Jaddua the high priest . . . was in an agony, and under terror, as not knowing how he should meet the Macedonians, since the king was displeased at his foregoing disobedience. He therefore ordained that the people should make supplications, and should join with him in offering sacrifice to God, whom he besought to protect that nation . . . whereupon God warned him in a dream, which came upon him after he had offered sacrifice, that he should take courage, and adorn the city, and open the gates; that the rest should appear in white garments, but that he and the priests should meet the king in the habits proper to their order, without the dread of any ill consequences, which the providence of God would prevent. Upon which, when he rose from his sleep, he greatly rejoiced, and declared to all the warning he had received from God. According to which dream he acted entirely, and so waited for the coming of the king.

Imagine the scene. Alexander, soon to be lord of all the earth, comes with his army upon a band of unarmed people in robes of white. All alone, the young king approaches Jaddua, whose attire was "purple and scarlet clothing, with his mitre on his head, having the golden plate whereon the name of God was engraved." Then, to everyone's astonishment, Alexander greets the high priest with reverence. Since this is not what the army expects, they suppose their commander to be "disordered in his mind." It is Alexander's explanation which I find most interesting.

> I did not adore him, but that God who hath honoured him with his high priesthood; for I saw this very person in a dream, in this very habit, when I was at Dios in Macedonia, who, when I was considering with myself how I might obtain the dominion of Asia, exhorted me to make no delay, but boldly to pass over the sea thither, for that he would conduct my army, and would give me the dominion over the Persians; whence it is that, having seen no other person in that habit, and now seeing this person in it, and remembering that vision, and the exhortation which I had in my dream, I believe that I bring this army under the Divine conduct. . . .[32]

Alexander, though he little knew it, was preparing the way for the apostles of Christ. He made the crooked places straight for them, and the rough ways smooth. All his empire came to know the Greek language and customs; even the Jews translated their Scriptures into Greek. Thanks to Alexander and the Romans, Christ's ambassadors found throughout the known world new highways, a common language, and a common culture. The kingdoms of the earth were prepared for the gospel. Imagine Paul's task, had he encountered different customs, tongues, and authorities in every valley and every island of his travels. The spread of the good news, the publication of the New Testament, would certainly have proceeded more slowly. Thus we have reason to believe that Alexander's dream, as related by Josephus, was not an idle fantasy but a vision from the Lord.

If it were not for the boring parts of Nehemiah, we would have no way to correlate Josephus' story with the Scriptures. In their double mention of Jaddua's name, the sacred and secular histories intersect, causing the thoughtful reader to hesitate in wonder.

❧ ❧ ❧

We have finished our course. We have come to the last of the boring parts. Strange as it may seem, I hear the words of Edward Gibbon upon finishing his life's work.

> I will not dissemble the first emotions of joy on the recovery of my freedom, and, perhaps, the establishment of my fame. But my pride was soon humbled, and a sober melancholy was spread over my mind, by the idea that I had taken an everlasting leave of an old and agreeable companion, and that whatsoever might be the future date of my History, the life of the historian must be short and precarious.[33]

Though Gibbon's work is incomparable, and my life's work (God willing) is before me, nevertheless I too am "taking leave of an old and agreeable companion." I do so with reluctance. Though I cannot claim to know the boring parts, I may truly say I love them. They touch me in ways I cannot express. They open my mind to understand the Scriptures. This book, which started as an afterthought,[34] has become my friend and teacher. But authors, like parents, nearly always have an inordinate fondness for their first productions, however heedlessly begun. The real test of a book is the emotion it generates in the reader's heart at parting. To that jury of my peers, the lovers of Scripture who have continued with me through moments lucid and obscure, I leave this work for judgment. May it find favor in their sight, as its author has found grace in the eyes of his Redeemer. Remember me, O my God, for good!

The Last of the Boring Parts

The last of the boring parts is Ezra's list of those Jews who had married foreign wives.[35] Nehemiah ends his book on the same theme, but without mentioning the names of those who had sinned. The King James translators put Nehemiah's speech to the offenders in memorable language.

> Did not Solomon king of Israel sin by these things? Yet among many nations was there no king like him, who was beloved of his God, and God made him king over all Israel: nevertheless even him did outlandish women cause to sin. (Nehemiah 13:26)

References to outlandish women by scholars versed in Hebrew and Ugaritic are, if not noteworthy, certainly rare.[36] (The wives of the translators may well have had opinions on this subject too, but the results of their deliberations have not come down to us.) In any event, the meaning of the passage is clear. Believers must let nothing, no matter how lovely or stylish it seems, interfere with their heartfelt devotion to God.

Idolatry was the sin which had destroyed Israel. As Balaam had foreseen, and as Solomon had proven, strange women were the easy way into idolatry. Therefore, Israel's survival depended on her being cleansed of this sin. While putting away the foreign wives was doubtless a trial for all involved, it was a light thing compared to the destruction of Jerusalem. Ezra and Nehemiah understood that unless this thankless task were performed immediately,[37] the horrors of the captivity were likely to be repeated. Those who clearly see what sin must lead to will not shrink from hard measures for its eradication. Nor will they be surprised if near-sighted saints and hawk-eyed worldlings condemn them as severe.

Four men seem to have opposed Ezra in putting away the foreign wives of the Jews.[38] Their names are recorded in Ezra 10:15. Opposition to the Lord's work must come, but woe to the men by whom it comes! And double woe to those whose shame the Lord has not cloaked with anonymity.

A Deep Infection

Ezra lists four divisions of priests among those who returned from Babylon, the house of Jeshua, the sons of Immer, the sons of Pashhur, and the sons of Harim (2:36–39). All four of these groups are represented among those who had married foreign wives (10:18–22). How deeply the holy people were infected! How essential it was that someone take a stand against their unholy practices! God so blessed the efforts of Ezra and Nehemiah that outward idolatry no longer dominated the Jews after their captivity. They never fully returned to those external sins which had provoked the Lord to anger. (If only their hearts had remained as unsullied as their synagogues!)

While most of the families in Ezra's list are represented by a handful of members, twenty-seven of the sons of Bani had married foreign wives.[39] Since the people of Bani were not more numerous than others who returned from Babylon, we cannot explain why so many of them were addicted to this sin.[40] Every family has its particular vices, for the sins of our fathers are visited upon us.[41] Whether our ancestors committed obvious sins of the flesh or subtle sins of the spirit, we do well to know their failings and to guard ourselves against them. (We are not doomed to repeat our parents' transgressions, for visitors cannot force themselves upon us. The trouble is, we are so accustomed to or intimidated by familiar sins, we rarely understand that we can kick the critters out.) On Judgment Day, or sooner, the sins of every family shall be revealed. If our descendants are not prominent in that census of offenders, we shall be blessed indeed.

Shechaniah the son of Jehiel shows us, I think, how a son may resist the sin of his fathers. He is the one who suggests to Ezra a remedy for the people's sin. Notice how he expresses himself: "*We* have trespassed against our God, and have taken pagan wives from the peoples of the land; yet now there is hope in Israel in spite of this. Now, therefore, let *us* make a covenant with our God . . . " (Ezra 10:2–3, emphasis added).

You might think Shechaniah was one of the offenders, but his name does not occur in Ezra's list. However, the name of his father appears in verse 26 among the sons of Elam. If, in fact, Shechaniah's father and relatives had married foreign wives,[42] we can learn a lot from watching him deal with the problem. He does not distance himself from the sinners; rather, he identifies with them. Yet he refuses to condone their iniquity. (Honoring our parents does not mean denying they have sinned.)[43] As one of those "who tremble at the commandment of our God," Shechaniah refused to honor his father more than his Maker. He would neither condemn the sinner nor tolerate the sin. (These things were written for our instruction.)

Two Honored Saints

I have been much encouraged to discover in the boring parts so many obscure saints whom God has delighted to honor. Here in our last list I find some more of them. How is it an honor to be included in a list of sinners? First of all, the men in this list had repented. It seems that either they were represented in the promise and sacrifice of the priests in Ezra 10:19, or else they made promises and sacrifices of their own. They had sinned, but they acknowledged their guilt before God, and cooperated with His leaders in fulfilling their repentance. But that is not the end of the story for men like Kelaiah and Malchijah.

Of the 113 men named by Ezra, Kelaiah (the same as Kelita) is the only one for whom we have extra means of identification. Surely that is significant. It enables us to identify Kelaiah with the Kelita of Nehemiah who later helped the people to understand the Law.[44] He also signed the covenant in Nehemiah 10. Once again the Lord has gone out of His way to show us the good side of one of His servants. Why shouldn't He do the same thing for you?

I shall close with Malchijah the son of Harim found in Ezra 10:31. His past sins did not deter this worthy man from serving the Lord. Though he had married a pagan woman and then put her away, we later find him building the wall of Jerusalem under Nehemiah: "Malchijah the son of Harim and Hashub the son of Pahath-Moab repaired another section, as well as the Tower of the Ovens" (Nehemiah 3:11).

He seems to have done more than ordinary duty, repairing a section of wall and a tower. (He may also have placed his seal on the covenant document in Nehemiah 10:3.) If Malchijah went through any spiritual depression at the time of his divorce, he had certainly recovered from it when Nehemiah came to town.

The heart knows its own bitterness and the sins of its youth. The heart of a Christian knows the joy of God's forgiveness. Having put away many of the sins of my youth, and trusting the Lord to purge out the lump that remains, I press forward in His service. Forgetting those things which are behind, and reaching forth unto those things which are before, I intend to repair my portion of Jerusalem's wall. May the Lord give me strength for a tower as well!

Malchijah, you'll notice, did not work alone. I'd love to have your company on the battlements of Zion.

APPENDIX

SUGGESTIONS FOR FURTHER STUDY

There are many levels of Bible study. The deeper ones are beyond me, but I can give you some tips on excavating the first few levels. You may find it helpful to review the section on digging deep in chapter 2 before reading this appendix.

Level One

To get below the surface you need only two books, a reference Bible and a concordance.[1] A reference Bible has a system of references to guide you from one Scripture to another. This is its essential feature; all others are optional. When you read in the Gospels, "Then was fulfilled what was spoken by Jeremiah the prophet, saying, 'And they took the thirty pieces of silver, the value of Him who was priced, whom they of the children of Israel priced, and gave them for the potter's field, as the LORD directed me' " (Matthew 27:9–10), you could spend a long time looking for this passage in Jeremiah. That's because it's in Zechariah. But a reference Bible will steer you right to it. Or, if you want to trace the development of the first commandment with promise, you'll find a note at any of its three primary locations—Exodus 20:12; Deuteronomy 5:16; Ephesians 6:1–2—which will guide you to the other two. (In some Bibles you may have to look up the note at a second passage in order to find the third location, but you'll get there before long. In other Bibles you'll encounter more references than you need, but when you study a topic in depth you'll be glad they're there.) With a little practice, you'll find references make it easy to explore the Scriptures.

While some reference Bibles have a short concordance in the back, I recommend the purchase of a complete one. (I love the title of Strong's—*The Exhaustive Concordance of the Bible.*) These ponderous tomes enable you to find any passage of Scripture (or to begin the study of any topic) if only you can remember a couple of key words *in the version your concordance is geared to.* I remember the King James version best, so I use Strong's concordance to hunt up a passage. (Young's is just as good, though organized on different principles. Both these volumes give you preliminary access to the meaning of the original Greek and Hebrew words, which I find very helpful. Cruden's does not deal with the Hebrew and Greek, but it's good for finding passages or studying a topic.) There are many concordances available today, as well as computer Bibles that function like concordances. If you take the time to find one that's good for you, you'll be glad you did. (Where you have a choice, select a concordance that gives the Greek and Hebrew meanings and/or is keyed to Strong's numbering system. If you never bother with these features, you've only lost a few dollars. If you learn to use them, they will lead you to treasure.)

The blessing of first level tools is that they are inexpensive. The American Bible Society sells a hardback King James reference Bible for eleven dollars.[2] Reference Bibles and complete concordances range from about thirteen to twenty-five dollars (leather Bibles are more) from the major discounters.[3] For thirty dollars, you can have the two tools you really need for extensive studies in the Scriptures.

Level Two

Ah! but what if you're the kind of reader who wants to know *why* Matthew attributes Zechariah's prophecy to Jeremiah?[4] (I hope you are.) Then you need a commentary, the ticket for admission to Bible study, level two.

If you can handle eighteenth-century English, consider Matthew Henry's Commentary. It's tried and true, inexpensive, and very helpful on the boring parts. Henry specializes in drawing out the spiritual meaning of a passage, and he has a gift for distilling his wisdom into useful aphorisms.[5] However, if you like technical analysis and textual criticism, you may find some other commentary is best for you. (Matthew Henry died before he got to Paul's epistles: the last of his six volumes was written by his friends, and is lacking in places. There are also one-volume editions of Matthew Henry, but the abridged ones are not suitable for students of the boring parts. The complete version in one volume, published by Hendrickson, is okay.)

The best commentary on the boring parts is Dr. John Gill's.[6] (This work is currently in print.[7]) I had owned a six-volume edition for years, but used it only sparingly—until I started to write this book. Then the good doctor came into his own. He is a mine of all kinds of information. True, he sometimes tells you more about the rabbinical writings (or variant manuscripts, or eccentric authors) than you care to know. But he gives you all the commentary that's fit to print, a full portion for every boring part. The incredible thing about Gill is that he mastered not only the Talmuds, the translations (Greek, Syrian, Coptic, etc.), and the commentators, but he was also a student of the poets. He often refers to the works of Homer, Virgil, Milton, and other literary men.

Once I began to appreciate Dr. Gill, I started to feel inferior. How is it, I asked myself, that I have taken more than a year to write a book which is roughly one hundredth the length of Gill's *Commentary?* (And he wrote other volumes on the side!) I'm using a word processor, not a quill pen. I have one reference to medieval rabbis, where he has thousands. My knowledge of Arabic and Amharic is, shall we say, skimpy compared to the Doctor's. Yet his knowledge of the poets is extensive. It's true that I spend more time on the sound and humor of my prose, but I would need Methuselah's lifetime to equal Gill's output. Sebastiano del Piombo said that Tintoretto could paint as much in two days as he himself in two years,[8] and I felt almost as slow compared to the Doctor. The truth seemed unbearable. Then, when I could stand it no longer, the Lord gave me relief.

I found out Gill's secret. In the biography prefixed to his commentary, I discovered the crucial information. (Are you ready for this?) "He breakfasted constantly in his study, and always on chocolate."[9] Eureka! No doubt, I thought to myself, if I were to breakfast on chocolate, surrounded by leather-bound tomes in curious languages, I too should do great things. Take away the Doctor's chocolate, and he would be a mere mortal. (It's a good thing he wasn't exposed to modern theories of nutrition!) Where other men might have imitated Gill, and researched the composition of eighteenth-century chocolate, I was content with understanding. There was no need to imitate; it was enough to *know.*[10]

There is one aspect of Gill's *Commentary* from which I must publicly dissent. He often refers to the Roman Catholic church as "the Romish antichrist," "the mother of harlots," or something equally condemning. (I have not found any such passages in his comments on the boring parts.) His anti-Catholic bias is extreme. While some readers may consider this one of Dr. Gill's strengths, I do not.

I should mention two nineteenth-century commentaries from Germany. The *Commentary on the Old Testament* by C. F. Keil and Franz Delitzsch is available from the discounters for roughly a hundred dollars. This set combines the many books of the original into ten volumes, which offer in-depth commentary on all the Old Testament. The work is designed for those who can read Hebrew, but with a little patience (and sometimes a Hebrew dictionary) one can understand the vast majority of the authors' arguments. Keil and Delitzsch are prone to scholarly disputes with other commentators; but if you have followed my footnotes, you know how often I have found them helpful. Every addicted book-buyer has in mind his next acquisition. I haven't bought Keil and Delitzsch yet, but I sure have thought about it.

In seminary libraries you may find the multi-volume commentary on the whole Bible edited by John Lange in German and Philip Schaff in English. Though it has many authors, it is known as *Lange's Commentary.* It is certainly worth consulting if you have access to it.

❧ ❧ ❧

No doubt you have noticed my fondness for older commentaries.[11] There are several reasons for this. I find greater devotion and reverence in the older works. I prefer commentaries written by one man, whom I can get to know well, to those written by an assortment of little-known scholars with diverse views. Of course one must refer to the work of specialists in narrow fields of study, and I often do, but I rarely delight in them as I do in Calvin, Henry, or Gill. And here an important point needs to be borne in mind. The old-timers often exceed the modern specialists in length of commentary on a passage, especially in the boring parts. I don't prefer Gill for sentimental reasons. No, he tells me what I want to know. And in sheer words per dollar, you cannot beat Matthew Henry. His six volumes would surely become twenty if they were printed in the same format as more recent commentaries.

The main reason I am wary of most modern scholarly studies is their pernicious attitude toward the historic people of God. Modern scholars commonly assume that the saints who transmitted the Scriptures to us were incompetent. They are always saying that "scribal error" or "misunderstanding" on the part of the copyist has caused the text to become corrupt. (Henry and Gill will sometimes say this too, but it is hardly their constant refrain.) Naturally I prefer guides who have a respectful attitude toward the men and women who in ancient times, and sometimes at the cost of their lives, tended the torch of Truth. When you find a modern scholar who honors the ancient texts and the people who preserved them, you have found a good thing.

Reference Books

Somewhere in the first two levels of Bible study we must mention the hundreds of specialized reference books. These include Bible dictionaries, topical Bibles, historical atlases, encyclopedias, and a host of similar works. Everyone has his own favorites here. Having some of these books on hand will certainly enhance your study of the boring parts. Remember, however, that a few simple tools well used are of more help than a lot of costly machinery less skillfully applied.

I do want to mention one inexpensive tool which I have found very helpful. This is *The Treasury of Scripture Knowledge.*[12] It is mainly a set of references from one Scripture to another, like those found in reference Bibles, but more extensive. A typical entry for a verse (this one is for Leviticus 10:7) reads:

> 7 *ye shall.* ch. 21. 12 [i.e. Leviticus 21:12]. Mat. 8. 21, 22. Lu. 9. 60. *the anointing.* ch. 8. 12, 30. Ex. 28. 41; 30. 30; 40. 13–15. Ac. 10. 38. 2 Co. 1. 21.

Obviously this book is not for everyone! However, once you get used to it, the *Treasury* provides much food for thought. Its particular strength is in concepts. Concordances and dictionaries can help you follow persons, places, or things through the Bible, but what other short work will lead you from Leviticus 10:7 ("Ye shall not go out from the door of the tabernacle") to Matthew 8:21–22 ("Let the dead bury their dead")? None of my reference Bibles makes that connection. Take a look at those two passages in context, and perhaps you'll understand why I often refer to the *Treasury.* On the other hand, like every reference work, it has its weak points. In Leviticus 10:4 (and especially in Numbers 3:30) it hardly does justice to Elizaphan the son of Uzziel. But there are other ways to learn about him. Every tool has its limits; it's what a book does well that counts.

Level Three

The third level of Bible study leads us to the Hebrew and the Greek. Since I myself do not read these languages, I cannot offer guidance to those who study them. What I can do, however, is lead others in my benighted condition to books which are designed to help the uninitiated get at the meaning of the original Scriptures. "A little learning is a dangerous thing"[13]—a warning we do well to remember. A smattering of Greek and Hebrew will be a blessing, as long as we do not mistake it for real knowledge and exalt ourselves as the equals of the learned. C. S. Lewis was a great scholar who knew many languages, but he also knew his limitations. Speaking of Milton's opinion that Hebrew lyrics are better than Greek, Lewis tells us:

> I once had a pupil, innocent alike of the Greek and of the Hebrew tongue, who did not think himself thereby disqualified from pronouncing this judgement a proof of Milton's bad taste; *the rest of us, whose Greek is amateurish and who have no Hebrew,* must leave Milton to discuss the question with his peers.[14]

I believe Mr. Lewis is a better model for us than his student in judging the fine points of ancient languages. Let us leave Milton to discuss such matters with his peers, and confess our knowledge of the Scriptures to be rudimentary.

Practice What You Preach!

I shall be disappointed at this point if some of my readers do not exclaim, "Practice what you preach! You raked Hengstenberg and Zimmerli over the coals in chapter 9, and now you tell us to be mindful of our ignorance. You hypocrite, take the beam out of your own eye. . . ." Touché. Before sentence is passed, may I offer a few words in my defense? My criticisms of Messrs. H. and Z. were not entirely my own. I have read a number of books on textual criticism, and I have imbibed certain principles from scholars whose learning is established. Also, I was diffident enough to send my manuscript to a competent Hebrew scholar, who has published commentaries on the Old Testament, asking (and paying) for his critical review. (The hard part was when he corrected my English grammar!)

We must strive for balance. Of course it is foolish to proclaim ourselves experts as soon as we have gained a little knowledge. On the other hand, when God's people leave crucial questions entirely "to the experts," the consequences can be disastrous for all involved. How can God use "the foolish things of the world to put to shame the wise," if the foolish ones are overawed by the experts' credentials? The apostles were unlearned men. Do you wish they had listened to the Pharisees?

Breaking the Language Barrier

I became a Christian through reading the Scriptures. At the time, I did not know, and did not want to know, any Christians. When I emerged from my secluded state in the woods of upstate New York, I already had a strong desire for two different kinds of Bibles. One was a modernized King James; the other was an interlinear. In the next few years, I managed to find both of them, only to discover that they were produced by the same man. That really got my attention. After I had used his Bibles a while, I called him up. Thus I became acquainted with Jay P. Green, Sr., Bible translator, publisher, pioneer, and maverick in the world of Christian publishing. Mr. Green has since produced *The Break-Through-the-Language-Barrier Series*, a group of books so helpful to me that I must recommend them to you.

The Break-Through-the-Language-Barrier Series consists of a Bible and four reference works. (In all of them the Greek and Hebrew words of Scripture appear with the numbers assigned them in Strong's Concordance. This feature enables a person to use them with no knowledge of the original languages.) The Interlinear Bible[15] gives a literal interpretation (and a Strong's number) for every Greek or Hebrew word. It also has an English translation in the margin of each page. This arrangement brings us as close to the original as we can come without actually reading it. (While using an interlinear, one becomes familiar with the Greek and Hebrew letters and learns a little vocabulary.)

The four reference works[16] are dictionaries and concordances, one of each for the Hebrew and the Greek. I have come to value the concordances most. When I want to learn about a Greek or Hebrew word, the first place I turn is the appropriate concordance. It gives me the verse reference and the context (in English) for every occurrence in Scripture of the term I am studying. Some Hebrew and Greek words are translated by many different English words. In such cases it is very difficult to locate every use of the original word, even when using the most thorough English concordances (such as Strong's or Young's). With a Hebrew or Greek concordance, however, all occurrences of the original term are listed together in Scriptural order. Thus one sees how the word is used and what its different meanings are before one turns to a lexicon (dictionary). (In these concordances the English context for each use of a word is given in the King James version.)

It's easy to use a Greek or Hebrew concordance equipped with Strong's numbers (and contexts in English). It's not so easy to use a Greek or Hebrew dictionary. It has taken me a long time to feel comfortable with my *B-D-B* (the common nickname for Brown, Driver, and Briggs) and *Thayer's* lexicons. On first opening these (and similar volumes), the reader is greeted by a hodgepodge of Greek or Hebrew words, strange symbols, abbreviations, Scripture references, and English words. It's hard to find what your looking for, and easy to conclude that it can't be worth the trouble. Once you're acclimated, however, you can learn a lot. You can discover what scholars think was the particular meaning of a word in a given passage. You can find out what Greek word was used to translate a Hebrew word in the Septuagint. You can see how classical authors used New Testament words. But it takes some digging.[17]

If, after spying out the lexicons in the library, you decide that their secrets are walled up to heaven, that the scholars are intellectual giants and you are a grasshopper, there is an alternative approach. You may elect to purchase *Vine's Expository Dictionary of Old and New Testament Words, Wilson's Old Testament Word Studies,* or other similar books. These are not as informative as the scholarly lexicons, but being uncluttered with critical apparatus, they are easier to use. (They're also cheaper.)

Please understand that there are many other word study tools available to Bible students. I have simply recommended those which I have found useful. If you want to delve into Hebrew and Greek a little, these books are one of many ways to do it. I must admit that Mr. Green's *Break-Through-the-Language-Barrier Series* has its imperfections. Occasionally the Strong's number listed for a word is incorrect, and you may find other minor errors here and there. If you contemplate the labor involved in making the first complete interlinear Bible in the history of the world, you may take a charitable view of these flaws, which I have always found easy to work around. However, if perfection is your trademark, you may prefer some of the other books on the market which are coded to Strong's numbers. (Some of these seem to have been inspired by the success of Mr. Green's publications.)

I have a fondness for pioneers, and I'm quick to see their virtues. William Tyndale used the word *love* in 1 Corinthians 13. The King James translators changed it to "charity," which nearly everyone agrees was less than an improvement. In the same way, I find that Mr. Green's translations sometimes hit the nail on the head more squarely than the scholars'.[18] You may view the matter differently. But we should all be grateful for our trailblazers and the settlers who follow them.

Are you grateful for your choices among Bible study tools? As you seek what's best for you, remember that many Christians around the world have never seen even one of these books. "Everyone to whom much is given, from him much will be required; and to whom much has been committed, of him they will ask the more (Luke 12:48)."

NOTES

Introduction

1. See 2 Kings 2:23.
2. Gilead was famous for its balm (Genesis 37:25; Jeremiah 8:22).
3. "Do not say, 'Why were the former days better than these?' For you do not inquire wisely concerning this."
4. *Boring* was not even listed in Noah Webster's dictionary (1828). Its first usage, according to the Oxford English Dictionary, occurred in 1840. Tedious, tiresome, wearisome, and dull were the English words in use before that date, but they lack the power and the resonance of boring.
5. James Russell Lowell, "The Present Crisis," stanza 18. The hymn, taken from Lowell's poem, begins, "Once to every man and nation. . . ."

Chapter 1: Bread in the Desert

1. See, for example, Matthew 5:17–19; Luke 16:17; John 10:35.
2. Thomas Hobbes, *Leviathan,* chapter 13 (A.D. 1651).
3. Shakespeare, *Macbeth,* Act V. 5:26–28.
4. Lucretius, *On the Nature of the Universe,* Book Five, translated by R. E. Latham (Baltimore: Penguin, [1951] 1971), 177.
5. "How many times shall I make you swear that you tell me nothing but the truth in the name of the Lord?" (1 Kings 22:16).
6. We have, of course, another great desert in English-speaking lands, but not having had the pleasure of visiting Australia, I cannot speak of it.
7. See Numbers 14:39–45.
8. By most people's estimate, the longest portion of boring parts runs from the Ten Commandments to the death of Moses (Exodus 21–Deuteronomy 34, 117 chapters in all). At three chapters a day, it takes exactly thirty-nine days to read this section of the Bible. (How's that for a temptation in the wilderness?)
9. See Exodus 12:5; Leviticus 4:3, 23, 32; Leviticus 16:3, 5 compared with 4:3.
10. See Leviticus 22:17–25.
11. See Leviticus 21:23.
12. See Exodus 25–30 and 36–40; Leviticus 11–15; Leviticus 27–Numbers 4.

13. See 1 Chronicles 1–3, 6–9, and 23–27; Ezekiel 40–42 and 45–48.

Chapter 2: Finding Water in the Desert

1. See 1 Kings 3.
2. See Numbers 17 and Joshua 14–15.
3. 1 Chronicles 4:9–10 and 4:39–43.
4. Those who never do so are susceptible to Tedium Syndrome. The first sign of this debilitating condition is taking more than forty days to traverse the great desert of the boring parts. A more dire symptom is not being able and not even wanting to hold one's own in discussions about the end times. Pathologists agree that once the victim tries to interest others in the boring parts, the syndrome has become incurable. It is best to make him comfortable and let him pursue his studies, lest a worse thing come upon him.
5. See Numbers 21:16–18.
6. The cost of the tools can be a problem for advanced students of the boring parts, but the basic tools are cheap and readily available. See Appendix: Suggestions for Further Study.
7. 1 John 4:1, 6.
8. F. F. Bruce, *The English Bible* (New York: Oxford University Press, 1961), 29–36. William Tyndale, *Expositions and Notes on Sundry Portions of the Holy Scriptures* (Cambridge: The University Press, 1849), 226–236.
9. See Exodus 20:25.
10. See John 21:15–17. Christ used *agapao* the first two times, then *phileo.* Peter used only *phileo.*
11. For a detailed discussion of the colors in Numbers 4:5–15, see James B. Jordan, "From Glory to Glory: Degrees of Value in the Sanctuary," Biblical Horizons Occasional Paper No. 2 (Tyler, TX: Biblical Horizons, 1988), 11–15. Rev. Jordan examines the use, the symbolism, and the holiness of each item to account for the color of its covering. Scholars may well prefer his explanation. Poets and other garret-dwellers (see Samuel Johnson's essay on the garret, *The Rambler,* 117), should rest content with mine.
12. See Matthew 27:28; Mark 15:17; John 19:2.
13. Kregel's Bookstore (P.O. Box 2607, Grand Rapids, MI 49501) and Baker Book House (2768 E. Paris Ave. S.E., Grand Rapids, MI 49546) have large inventories of second-hand Christian books.
14. See Deuteronomy 8:4.
15. Not knowing any Christians when I came to know the Lord, how would I hear any evil reports? (The twelve spies whom Moses sent out were not pagans, but members of the chosen people. Numbers 13:1–16).
16. Be careful, though, to check it out by comparing relevant passages in the whole Bible and considering the historic teaching of the whole Church. We all need to be wary of twisting the Scriptures to our own destruction. See 2 Peter 3:16.

Chapter 3: Numbers 7

1. For the record, the leader of each tribe offered: "One silver platter, the weight of which was one hundred and thirty shekels, and one silver bowl of seventy shekels, according to the shekel of the sanctuary, both of them full of fine flour mixed with oil as a grain offering; one gold pan of ten shekels, full of incense; one young bull, one ram, one male lamb in its first year, as a burnt offering; one kid of the goats as a sin offering; and for the sacrifice of peace offerings: two oxen, five rams, five male goats, and five male lambs in their first year" (Numbers 7:13–17).

   Notice that the vast majority of the animals were for peace offerings, of which "the remainder was consumed by the worshiper and his friends at the meal which followed. . . . It was [the Lord's] table, in His own house, to which the worshiper and his household were called; and this feast at the Lord's table was the symbol and pledge of friendship and peace with Him" (John Brown Paton, "Offerings," *Classic Bible Dictionary* [Lafayette, IN: Sovereign Grace, 1988], 863). Should the God who prescribed this form of worship be styled the "God of wrath"?
2. The second half of Exodus contains three chapters of assorted laws; thirteen chapters about the tabernacle, its furnishings, the priests' garments, etc.; and only four chapters (24, 32–34) which might be called exciting by modern standards. Then comes Leviticus, which may safely be called the most boring book of the Bible. Of its twenty-seven chapters only three (9, 10, and 24) have exciting portions, while chapter 26 is a kind of sermon and prophecy about blessings and curses. The remaining twenty-three chapters we may designate as more or less dull for the uninitiated. Next comes Numbers. Its first four chapters are genuine boring parts. Chapters five and six (the law of jealousy and the law of the Nazarite) are more stimulating, but still not transparent to a modern reader.
3. See chapter 1, 9–10.
4. See Joshua 22:27. It is interesting to note that the first leader to offer, Nahshon (Numbers 7:12), is the only one who is *not* referred to as the head of his tribe. This deliberate omission may have been a reminder to him (and his successors in Judah) not to exalt themselves over their brothers. Or it may have been a hint that the true Prince of Judah had yet to make His greater offering at the altar.
5. I am aware that Matthew Henry, in his fine commentary on the Bible, says that the offering was for *both* altars. My reasons for differing with him are mainly two. First, the Scripture uses the singular word for altar. Second, Numbers 7:10 states that the princes offered their offering *before* the altar. I believe this could apply only to the altar of burnt offering in the courtyard, for the altar of incense in the tabernacle could be approached by no one but the priests.
6. See Leviticus 1:2–3, 10–11.
7. See Exodus 29:37 and 40:10.
8. The future tense is used in the New American Standard and the New King James Bibles, which also put Numbers 17:4 in the present tense,

providing further support for my argument. However, not all versions employ the same tenses in translating these passages.

9. "The report refers to one specific occasion, the *when* of the text meaning 'on a certain occasion' and not 'whenever,' for the tense used is not the imperfect" (The Interpreter's Bible, [New York: Abingdon, 1953], II, 180–81 [on Numbers 7:89]).
10. See Leviticus 16:15–16.
11. Many good commentators point out that the altar is a type (or symbol) of Christ. They are right, for only through Him can we make an offering acceptable to God. However, if we picture Christ as the Lamb of God, then the cross is the place of sacrifice and the equivalent of the altar.
12. See Exodus 16:23; Numbers 11:8.
13. "[Numbers 7] follows the Aaronic blessing (6:22–27). The priesthood and the altar belong together. The princes are thus portrayed as responding to the prevenient grace of God shown in the establishment of the tabernacle and priesthood. Their generosity leads in its turn to greater divine blessing, God's continued presence among them (v. 89). This pattern—divine blessing/believing human response/greater blessing—is basic to Old Testament theology" (Gordon J. Wenham, *Numbers* [Downers Grove, IL: Inter-Varsity, 1981], 92).
14. Compare Numbers 1:1 and 9:1–5.
15. Compare Exodus 40:17 and Numbers 7:1.
16. Alternatively, the day mentioned with each leader's offering could refer to the precise day of the month on which each of them offered. If so, they would have finished offering on the twelfth day, the Levites would have been sanctified on the thirteenth, and the Passover would have been celebrated that evening, the start of their next day.

Chapter 4: The Begats (Matthew 1; Luke 3; Genesis 5, 10, and 11)

1. Begats, as in "Abraham begat Isaac; and Isaac begat Jacob; and Jacob begat Judas and his brethren" (Matthew 1:2, KJV).
2. See Hebrews 6:20; 7:27. Yet in Hebrews 7:3, Melchizedek is said to be without genealogy. I believe this refers to the divine nature of Christ. Surely as God He has no genealogy. In the Middle Ages, Boccaccio wrote a lengthy Latin treatise, *Genealogy of the Gentile Gods,* delineating the ancestry of the gods of Greece and Rome. How blessed we are to have one God without genealogy!
3. See Isaiah 11:1–4; Jeremiah 23:5–6.
4. "Nothing is more common in the Jewish writings than for *the son of David* to stand alone for the Messiah; it would be endless to cite or refer to all the testimonies of this kind . . ." (John Gill, *An Exposition of the New Testament* [London: William Hill, 1854, and Grand Rapids: Baker Book House, 1980], 2).
5. See Luke 2:36 (Anna), Acts 4:36 (Barnabas), Romans 11:1 (Paul).
6. Eusebius, *Ecclesiastical History,* Book I, chapter VII (Grand Rapids: Guardian Press, 1976), 31–35.

7. Scholars have often doubted Luke's accuracy, only to discover later that he was right. For example: "It was formerly considered that it was a historical error on the part of Luke to mention Lysanias as ruling over Abilene. . . . Inscriptions have, however, been discovered which prove that while several years previously (about 36 B.C.) one Lysanias ruled over Abilene as king, another Lysanias later governed the same territory as tetrarch. . . . Today it is practically admitted by all that at that time (when John the Baptist began to preach) a younger and less famous Lysanias did rule over Abilene" (Norval Geldenhuys, *Commentary on the Gospel of Luke* [Grand Rapids: Wm. B. Eerdmans, 1983], 135, 142).
8. Assuming that Terah was 130 years old when Abraham was born. "From Genesis 11:32 we learn that Terah, Abram's father, died in Haran at the age of *205 years.* The following verse (Genesis 12:1) should be read as a continuation of this, and without the word 'had,' for which there is no warrant in the original. For it appears by the wording of the narrative, as well as by Stephen's words in Acts 7:4, that God gave *two distinct calls* to Abram. . . . From this it appears that Terah died at the age of 205, and that upon the death of Terah Abram departed out of Haran, being then 75 years old [Genesis 12:4]. If then Abram was 75 years old at the death of Terah, the latter was 130 years old when Abram was born" (Philip Mauro, *The Chronology of the Bible* [New York: George H. Doran, 1922], 29–30). This fine book, to which I am much indebted, is still available through GAM Publications (Sterling, VA 22170) under the title *The Wonders of Bible Chronology.*
9. What little we know of Enoch is found in Genesis 5:21–24; Hebrews 11:5; and Jude 14 and 15.
10. See Genesis 10:3. "Ashkenaz was originally a Hebrew name for an ancient kingdom in eastern Armenia. In medieval rabbinical usage, it became a name for Germany" (Arthur Naiman, *Every Goy's Guide to Common Jewish Expressions* [Boston: Houghton Mifflin, 1981], 8). "*Ashkenaz* is equivalent to Assyrian Ashkuz, the Scythians. . . . They were rude and unadvanced in civilization and periodically overran extensive territories, so that they came to signify barbarians [!]" (Merrill F. Unger, *Archaeology and the Old Testament* [Grand Rapids: Zondervan, [1954] 1960], 80).
11. John Gill, *An Exposition of the Old Testament* (London: William Hill, 1854, and Grand Rapids: Baker Book House, 1980), I, 56. Javan is the Hebrew word for Greece.
12. Werner Keller, *The Bible as History* (2nd revised edition. New York: William Morrow, 1981), 33.
13. "Now nearly all the names in this chapter [Genesis 10] may be elucidated by the archaeological discoveries of the past century" (Unger, 77).
14. See Genesis 36:6–7. (Contrast this perilous condition with Acts 2:42–47 and 4:32–35.)
15. Dr. Gill admits that "the commonly received opinion is that [the Amalekites] were descendants of Amalek, a grandson of Esau," though to him "it seems more probable that the Amalekites were of the posterity of Ham" (Gill, *Old Testament,* I, 83).

16. Before you descend into the nether world of modern criticism, be sure to imbibe the necessary antidote, "Modern Theology and Biblical Criticism," by C. S. Lewis, in his *Christian Reflections* (Grand Rapids: William B. Eerdmans, 1978). "The 'assured results of modern scholarship,' as to the way in which an old book was written, are 'assured,' we may conclude, only because the men who knew the facts are dead and can't blow the gaff," (161).

    Another useful antidote is: *The Hoax of Higher Criticism* by Dr. Gary North (Tyler, TX: Institute for Christian Economics, 1989) available from the I. C. E., P.O. Box 8000, Tyler, TX 75711.
17. The reference to Jacob's "sons' daughters" in 46:7 does not prove the existence of other granddaughters, since it could refer to his sons' daughters-in-law.
18. In Exodus 6:20 and Numbers 26:59 we learn that Jochebed, the mother of Moses and Aaron, was "the daughter of Levi, who was born to Levi in Egypt."
19. If you feel you are a super-Christian among mediocrities, I offer this advice: "In lowliness of mind, let each esteem others better than himself" (Philippians 2:3).

Chapter 5: The Return of the Begats (1 Chronicles 1–9)

1. See chapters 5, 10, 11, 36, and 46.
2. I. W. Slotki, *Chronicles* (London: Soncino Press, 1952), 2.
3. Dr. Gill, who is learned in such matters, prefers Huz the son of Nahor (Genesis 22:21) as the Uz of Job 1:1. John Gill, *Old Testament*, II, 601 (on Job 1:1).
4. Compare 1 Chronicles 2:6 with 1 Kings 4:31 and 1 Chronicles 2:6–7 with Joshua 7:17–18.
5. Shakespeare, *Julius Cæsar* III, ii, 81–82. "Interred" is pronounced in-ter'-red.
6. See 1 Chronicles 2:31, 34–36; 11:41. (Gill, *Old Testament*, II, 457).
7. See Ezra 2:2; 3:2, 8; 4:2, 3; 5:2. Nehemiah 7:7; 12:1, 47. Haggai 1:1, 12, 14; 2:2, 4, 21, 23. Zechariah 4:6, 7, 9, 10.
8. If we read 1 Chronicles 3:21 as six generations, the genealogy would be Zerubbabel, Hananiah, Jeshiah, Rephaiah, Arnan, Obadiah, Shechaniah, Shemaiah, Neariah, Elioenai, and Anani. For what it's worth, Anani means cloudy in Hebrew, and some old Jewish commentaries connect Anani with the Messiah "coming on the clouds of Heaven" (Daniel 7:13). Gill, *Old Testament*, II, 458–459.
9. Matthew Henry, *Commentary on the Whole Bible* (McLean, VA: MacDonald Publishing Company, n.d.), II, 845.
10. Ibid.
11. Jeremiah 35:19. The whole thirty-fifth chapter is devoted to the Rechabites.
12. See 1 Chronicles 4:14 (compare Nehemiah 11:35) and 4:23.
13. Except possibly its location at the end of the genealogy of Judah.
14. Most Bibles follow the chapter divisions found in the Septuagint, but The New American Bible (a Catholic study Bible, *not* to be confused with The

New American Standard Bible [NASB]), Jewish Bibles, and The Jerusalem Bible follow the chapter divisions of the Hebrew (Masoretic) text, which differ from the Septuagint's in a few places. In the present instance, the Hebrew text has forty-one verses in 1 Chronicles 5 and sixty-six verses in 1 Chronicles 6, while the Septuagint and most English Bibles have twenty-six and eighty-one verses, respectively.

15. Compare 1 Chronicles 6:33–34; 1 Samuel 8:1–3, and 1 Samuel 1:1. Hard choices must be made in reconciling 1 Samuel 1:1 with 1 Chronicles 6:33–34, 38. Was Samuel a descendant of Levi or Ephraim? I believe he was descended from Levi, and that the word translated "Ephrathite" (KJV) or "Ephraimite" in 1 Samuel 1:1 means that the prophet's ancestors were Levites who had long lived among the Ephraimites. "As Elkanah came from the Levitical family of Kohath, son of Levi, whose land lay in Ephraim, Dan, and Manasseh (Joshua 21:5, 21 sq.), and as the Levites generally were counted as citizens of the tribes in which their residence was, it is not strange that Elkanah is here designated as an Ephraimite according to his descent . . ." (John Peter Lange, ed., *Commentary on the Holy Scriptures* [Grand Rapids: Zondervan, (1877), n.d.] V, 45 [on 1 Samuel 1:1]). This seems more reasonable to me than denying that the Samuel of 1 Chronicles 6:28, 33 is Samuel the prophet. Why? Their genealogies match over seven generations (from Zuph to Joel, the prophet's son). See also Gill, *Old Testament*, II, 107–8 (on 1 Samuel 1:1).
16. See 1 Samuel 8:1–3.
17. See 2 Samuel 15:35–37; 17:15–22; 18:19–29. For more on Ahimaaz see chapter 12 of this book.
18. In 1 Samuel 6:19, the Hebrew reads "seventy men, fifty thousand men." If the writer was trying to say "50,070 men," he picked a most unusual way to do it, for in all other such numbers in the Hebrew text the larger number precedes the smaller (Gill, *Old Testament*, II, 135). Evidently seventy Bethshemites were killed, as Josephus says, and we do not know what the "50,000 men" refers to. (Some scholars think the passage means, "Seventy men, fifty of whom were elders over thousands" [see Exodus 25:18].) It is good to confess our ignorance of the Scriptures. Otherwise we resort to absurd conjectures in defense of the text, or fall into the opposite error of saying that the text is corrupt or that the writer made a mistake(!).
19. Most English Bibles make the passage seem easy, but the Hebrew is obscure.
20. H. G. M. Williamson, *1 and 2 Chronicles [New Century Bible Commentary]* (Grand Rapids: Wm. B. Eerdmans, 1982), 84.
21. There is a somewhat parallel list in Nehemiah 11. See chapter 13, note 24.
22. See Numbers 25:6–13. See also Psalm 106:30–31.
23. Compare Luke 1:5 with 1 Chronicles 24:1, 3, 10. See Gill's comment on Luke 1:5, *Old Testament* (V, 404–405.)
24. Herman Melville, *Moby Dick*, chapter 62, "The Dart."
25. See Judges 18:30–31; 1 Kings 12:28–30.

26. Thomas Gray, "Ode: On a Distant Prospect of Eton College" (A.D. 1742). While we're waxing poetic, here's another remedy for the higher criticism which detects so many errors in the Bible: "If this be high, what is it to be low?" (Tennyson, *Idylls of the King,* "Lancelot and Elaine," line 1077.)
27. Many scholars think these passages were written to honor Saul, the first king of Israel, but to me that doesn't make sense. Why would the chronicler honor Saul after God had rejected him? If Eli, the rejected priest, is not even mentioned in the begats, why should Saul receive so much notice? Moreover, neither genealogy ends with Saul. Both follow Jonathan's descendants through many generations.
28. See Numbers 20:7–12.
29. Deuteronomy 34:4–6.
30. 2 Samuel 9 and 1 Chronicles 8:40.
31. John Donne, "Ascention" (the seventh sonnet of "La Corona").
32. "Are you the teacher of Israel, and do not know these things?" (John 3:10).
33. Campbell and Lynn Loughmiller, *Texas Wildflowers* (Austin: University of Texas Press, 1984, and still in print in 1990).
34. Incest for Reuben, murder and robbery for Simeon and Levi (see Genesis 34:25–31; 35:22; 49:3–8).
35. See Genesis 38. Does it seem a small thing to you that a man with patriarchal power should spare a condemned woman, confessing publicly, "She has been more righteous than I . . . "? (38:26).
36. See Genesis 44:18–34.
37. See 1 Chronicles 2:19; 2:24; 2:50; 4:4. I do not count those places where the Hebrew words for Ephrath and Ephrathite seem to have other meanings (Judges 12:5; 1 Samuel 1:1; 1 Kings 11:26; and Psalm 132:6). Francis Brown, ed., *The New Brown, Driver, and Briggs Hebrew and English Lexicon* (Lafayette, IN: Associated Publishers and Authors, 1981), 68b.
38. Salma (1 Chronicles 2:51) and Hur (4:4) are both called "the father of Bethlehem." Conceivably Bethlehem was a person, whose name appears only in Chronicles; more probably the phrase indicates that Hur's and Salma's descendants became the chief inhabitants of the city.
39. See 1 Chronicles 2:3–19. Chelubai (2:9) and Caleb (2:19) are thought to be the same person.
40. Ephrath might have been named after Rachel's burying place, if she were a descendant of Rachel. However, we do not know the tribe of Ephrath's parents.
41. Jebus is not appropriate for this comparison, because it was the capital city of the Canaanite tribe of the Jebusites.
42. See Genesis 23:2, 28:19; Joshua 14:15; Judges 1:10, 23, and Nehemiah 11:25. Nehemiah's usage of the older name for Hebron may have been a reminder that Sarah died and was buried "in Kirjath Arba" (Genesis 23:1–2).

43. Ruth 1:2; 1 Samuel 17:12. That is, they lived in Ephratah, or they lived among Ephrath's descendants, for they were not descended from her. See next note.
44. Micah 5:2. Yet Ephrath was not an ancestor of Christ. The Messianic line passed through her husband's brother Ram (1 Chronicles 2:9, 18).
45. See Luke 1:48–49.
46. See Esther 2:21–23.
47. Esther 6:1–3. (The three commentators I have on Esther [Matthew Henry, John Gill, and Alexander Carson] agree that the king did *not* read the chronicles in order to fall back to sleep. In other words, this is not a biblical precedent for using the boring parts as a soporific!)
48. See Genesis 40:23; 41:9.
49. According to Philip Mauro's chronology, the Exodus occurred in 1533 B.C. and the Second Temple was begun in 456 B. C. (Mauro, *Chronology*, 48 and 100). I am well aware of the scholarly disputes over biblical chronology. I like Mauro's book because it is built on God's Word, not the speculations of man or the chronologies of the heathen.

Chapter 6: The Tabernacle (Exodus 25–40)

1. Matthew Henry, *Commentary*, I, 407 (on Exodus 37:1–10).
2. See Genesis 17:7.
3. The Interlinear Bible (Peabody, MA: Hendrickson, 1984), IV, 248.
4. 1 Chronicles 28:11 refers to the Holy of Holies as "the place of the mercy seat."
5. Christians have many opinions about what the cherubim represent. Angels, the Old and New Testaments, believers in Christ, and ministers of the word are among the things suggested. I shall not add to the list. Yet I confess the cherubim (awesome as they must have been) remind me of "God's Grandeur" by Gerard Manley Hopkins: "the Holy Ghost over the bent World broods with warm breast and with ah! bright wings."
6. "He shall bruise your head, And you shall bruise His heel" (Genesis 3:15).
7. John Gill, *Old Testament*, I, 384 (on Exodus 28:2).
8. If you think me horribly old-fashioned because I consider the Song of Solomon a celebration of heavenly love, see note 15.
9. John Donne, "A Valediction: Forbidding Mourning."
10. Of course there are other ways of interpreting the colors of the veil.
11. See Hebrews 10:20.
12. See Exodus 28:33–34; 39:24–26.
13. Gill, *Old Testament*, I, 390 (on Exodus 28:34).
14. An exception is James B. Jordan, "Thoughts on Jachin and Boaz," Biblical Horizons Occasional Paper No. 1 (Tyler, TX: Biblical Horizons [P.O. Box 132011, Tyler, TX 75713] 1988), which gives a detailed discussion of the pomegranates on the pillars. See especially 8–9, where, taking a hint from the high priest's garments, Rev. Jordan suggests "that the pomegranates

dangled from chains on the pillars, and caused a ringing sound striking the pillars in the wind."

15. Modern writers who disparage the traditional interpretation do not tell you the whole story. For twenty-five hundred years virtually all Jews and Christians thought Solomon's Song a love song between God and His Church or between God and the soul. The only significant exception was Theodore of Mopsuestia (A.D. 350–428), who "regarded the Canticles as a poem written by Solomon in answer to the complaints of his people about his Egyptian marriage. This was one of the heresies charged upon [Theodore] after his death, which led to his condemnation at the second council of Constantinople A.D. 553." (Theodore also rejected Chronicles, Ezra, Nehemiah, and James as inspired Scripture!) "Theodore's name was accordingly deleted from the list of orthodox writers." Consequently, his works were lost. *Encyclopedia Britannica,* 11th edition, 5:214; 26:766–7. See Gill, *Old Testament,* III, 671 (preface to Solomon's Song).
16. After I wrote this chapter, I discovered *Signs and Symbols in Christian Art,* by George Ferguson (New York: Oxford, 1961). "In Christian symbolism, the pomegranate as a rule alludes to the Church because of the inner unity of countless seeds in one and the same fruit" (p. 37).
17. *Encyclopedia Britannica,* 11th edition, 22:46–7 (emphasis added).
18. William Wilson, *Wilson's Old Testament Word Studies* (McLean, VA: MacDonald Publishing, n.d.), 317.
19. Matthew Henry, *Commentary,* I, 382–3 (on Exodus 25:9).
20. Note the additional references to the pattern in Exodus 25:40; 26:30; 27:8; Numbers 8:4; Acts 7:44; and Hebrews 8:5.
21. "Is it right for you to be angry?" (Jonah 4:4; 4:9).
22. See Exodus 31:1–11; 35:30–36:2.
23. See the beginnings of Books I, III, VII, and IX.
24. *Paradise Lost,* I, 26.
25. "The great destroyer of *good* works is the ambition to do *great* works." Charles Spurgeon, sermon on Psalm 131:2, in his *Treasury of the Bible* (Grand Rapids: Baker, 1981), III, 114a.
26. Gene Edward Veith, Jr., *The Gift of Art* (Downers Grove, IL: Inter-Varsity Press, 1983, out of print in 1990). Since Mr. Veith shows a rare and commendable regard for the boring parts, we can easily forgive his reference to "the golden pomegranates" on the high priest's robe (p. 19).
27. See Exodus 30:11–16, 38:25–28.
28. For a detailed discussion of this tax in Israel's history, see James B. Jordan, *The Law of the Covenant* (Tyler, TX: Institute for Christian Economics, 1984), 225–34. Rev. Jordan concludes about the Mosaic tax, "Its purpose was to cover men from the wrath of God when they drew especially close to Him in His Temple/War Camp. It seems to have been collected whenever Israel was mustered for battle, and on one occasion at least it was subscribed to raise money to rebuild the Temple. It had no other purpose than to pay for the building and maintenance of the house of God." Of the tax which Peter paid, he says, "One custom which devel-

oped was the payment of a half-shekel head tax to the Temple on an annual basis. As we have seen, this was not prescribed in the Old Covenant itself. . . . If the Temple Tax had indeed been part of the Mosaic order, Jesus would have been bound to pay it. This proves that the annual Temple Tax was not a proper understanding of Exodus 30."

29. Compare Exodus 38:8 with 38:29–31.
30. Cullen Clout, "Cosmetology."

Chapter 7: The Sacrifices (Leviticus 1–9)

1. Andrew Bonar, *A Commentary on the Book of Leviticus* (New York: Robert Carter, 1877), vii.
2. Because He looks on the heart, God allows exceptions to His own rules. See, for example, 2 Chronicles 30:18–20.
3. See Galatians 3:23–24.
4. 1 Corinthians 10:11–12. This passage warns against idolatry as well as immorality.
5. I have not overlooked "a male without blemish" and "of his own free will" in verse 3. "If we had world enough and time," I'd study them with pleasure.
6. I use the name loosely. The modern Webster's, however necessary it may be, is a far cry from Noah Webster's original (1828 ed.), available in reprint from Foundation for American Christian Education, 2946 25th Ave., San Francisco, CA 94132. Which Webster's, do you suppose, says under *Duty,* "Reverence, obedience, and prayer to God are indispensable *duties*"?
7. See, for example, Exodus 23:19; Deuteronomy 22:6–7; Proverbs 12:10.
8. David lived centuries after Moses, but since the Jews enjoyed cultural continuity throughout that period, I see no reason to think their love of animals was something new. Would brutish men preserve the tale of Balaam and his donkey?
9. Another difference is that their sacrifices were costly. Ours are not, unless we tithe to the church where we take the Lord's Supper.
10. Andrew Bonar, *A Commentary on the Book of Leviticus* (New York: Robert Carter, 1877) 29.
11. See Ezekiel 16:49.
12. See Esther 2:15–17. (The poor man's doves remind us of our Keeper, the Holy Spirit.)
13. The Lord will " . . . gather His wheat into the barn" (Matthew 3:12). Ornan was threshing wheat when David came to buy his threshing floor, which later became the site of Solomon's Temple (1 Chronicles 21:18–22:2). See also Amos 9:9 and Luke 22:31.
14. See Mark 8:15; 1 Corinthians 5:6–8. "The use of leaven was forbidden in all offerings made by fire to the Lord (Leviticus 2:11). But when the offering was to be consumed by man, leaven might be used (Leviticus 7:13; 23:17). The principal reason for the prohibition was that fermentation is incipient corruption, and was emblematic of corruption. . . . The word is used, however, in a good sense in the parable of the leaven . . . (Matthew

13:33)." Henry Snyder Gehman, *The New Westminster Dictionary of the Bible* (Philadelphia: Westminster, 1976), 554.

15. "Because it acts like a leaven, producing fermentation, honey might not be used in offerings made by fire to the Lord (Leviticus 2:11)." Ibid., 403. "Some think the chief reason why these two things, leaven and honey, were forbidden, was because the Gentiles used them very much in their sacrifices. . . . Some make this application of this double prohibition: leaven signifies grief and sadness of spirit (Psalm 73:21), *My heart was leavened*; honey signifies sensual pleasure and mirth. In our service of God both of these must be avoided, and a mean observed between those extremes; for the sorrow of the world worketh death, and a love to the delights of sense is a great enemy to holy love" [Matthew Henry, *Commentary,* I, 453 (on Leviticus 2:11)].
16. "Perhaps no passage in the New Testament has given more perplexity to commentators than this . . . " (Albert Barnes, *Barnes' Notes on the New Testament* [Grand Rapids: Kregel, 1986], 165 [on Mark 9:49]). How shall we interpret it without knowledge of Leviticus, chapter 2?
17. Robert Frost, "The Figure a Poem Makes," *Complete Poems of Robert Frost* (New York: Henry Holt and Company, Inc., 1967), vi-viii (emphasis added).
18. See chapter 2.
19. The Hebrew words for sweet aroma may be translated more literally as "soothing, tranquillizing odor or aroma of rest."
20. i.e., all the burnt offerings where the burning on the altar is specifically mentioned.
21. 2 Corinthians 2:14–16 is the only other place in the New Testament where both Greek words for sweet aroma are used, but there they are used separately, not together as in the two verses quoted above.
22. Andrew Bonar, *A Commentary on the Book of Leviticus* (New York: Robert Carter, 1877) 52.
23. See John 1:29, 36; Revelation 5:6, etc.
24. Leviticus 3 and 7:11–21, 28–34.
25. See 1 Corinthians 11:28–29. Those taking Communion in an unworthy manner are like unclean persons eating the sacrifices (Leviticus 7:20). Notice how severe the penalties are for this offense.
26. ". . . a heave offering from the children of Israel from the sacrifices of their peace offerings" (Exodus 29:28).
27. See 1 Kings 8:62–66.
28. Wordsworth, "The Sonnet," (part 2, line 14). If you read aloud other modern versions of Hebrews 13:14, you'll hear what I mean.
29. Leviticus 6:23 in The New American Bible and some other Bibles. See note 14, chapter 5.
30. See Exodus 29:14; Leviticus 4:12; 4:21; 16:27. The red heifer whose ashes produced the water of purification was burned outside the camp (Numbers 19:1–9), but its blood was not brought into the tabernacle. Evidently

"the blood of bulls and goats and the ashes of a heifer" in Hebrews 9:13 refers to these particular sacrifices.

31. Months after I wrote this, a friend's suggestion got me to thinking about it again. Somehow everything seemed clearer. These sin offerings, whose blood was brought into the tabernacle, were offered for the priests or for the whole people of God: either way the ministering priest belonged to the guilty party. He was not allowed to eat the offering which atoned for his own sin. He could eat of every sin offering which atoned for the sins of others, even if the offerer were the ruler of Israel (Leviticus 4:22–26). But his own sin was too great for him; he could not eat of the flesh which atoned for it. Jesus Christ, however, was sinless. Unlike Aaron, He needed no offering for Himself. Thus His body and blood, though they were brought into the Holy of Holies to atone for the sins of the people, are eaten by His attendants ("a holy priesthood," 1 Peter 2:5), who are the ministers of a better covenant.
32. Robert Browning, "Andrea del Sarto."
33. Shakespeare, *Hamlet*, V.i.57–58.
34. Matthew Henry, *Commentary*, I, 467 (on Leviticus 6:30).
35. See Luke 17:32. (Remember also the drunk who exclaimed "I've been thrown out of better joints than this one!")
36. Andrew Bonar, *A Commentary on the Book of Leviticus* (New York: Robert Carter, 1877), 108 (on Leviticus 5:17).
37. See Leviticus 11, especially verses 29–32.
38. See 1 Samuel 12:23; Malachi 1:8 and 3:8–12; 2 Corinthians 9:7.
39. Compare Leviticus 4:13–15 and 9:15.
40. Herman Melville, *Moby-Dick*, chapter 96, "The Try-Works."

Chapter 8: The Law of the Leper (Leviticus 13–14)

1. "The leprosy here spoken of seems not to be the same with . . . what we now call (leprosy) . . . (but) rather an uncleanness than a disease, and the business of a priest, and not a physician, to attend unto; and did not arise from natural causes, but was from the immediate hand of God, and was inflicted on men for their sins, as the cases of Miriam, Gehazi, and Uzziah show." John Gill, *Old Testament*, I, 478 (on Leviticus 13:2).

   "The laws for leprosy in man relate exclusively to the so-called white leprosy . . . which is still found in that part of the world." C. F. Keil and F. Delitzsch, *Biblical Commentary on the Old Testament* (Edinburgh: T. and T. Clark, 1864), II, 377–8 (on Leviticus 13 and 14).
2. See Genesis 50:2; Job 13:4.
3. Numbers 12:10–15 (emphasis added). I have quoted Aaron's words from The Interlinear Bible (Peabody, MA: Hendrickson, 1985) which I consider the most literal of all translations.
4. See 2 Kings 5:1–19. Perhaps we should mention the ten lepers in Luke 17:14, who obeyed Jesus' command to show themselves to the priests, for "as they went, they were cleansed."

5. See Matthew 3:6; Mark 1:5; Luke 3:3; John 10:40–42. Get the picture? (Hoping to avoid the briar patch of baptismal theology, I shamelessly confess that I know nothing about *how* Naaman washed himself. If that makes me a theological marshmallow, make the most of it.)
6. Or so it seems to most patients. As the son of two physicians, I know that common diseases can be difficult to diagnose.
7. Richard Baxter, *The Reformed Pastor* [A.D. 1656] (Carlisle, PA: Banner of Truth, 1979), 248.
8. Matthew Henry, *Commentary*, I, 492 (on Leviticus 13:1–17).
9. Leviticus 13:45–46. As leprosy represents sin, the judgment of uncleanness symbolizes death—a state of separation from God.
10. See 2 Chronicles 26:19–21.
11. See 2 Corinthians 6:14
12. Watchman Nee, *The Release of the Spirit* (Cloverdale, IN: Sure Foundation, 1965), 38.
13. Gill, *Old Testament*, I, 479 (on Leviticus 13:3).
14. Shakespeare, *The Merry Wives of Windsor*, III.v. 95–6. (Falstaff is recounting not his sins but his misadventures in a laundry basket.)
15. Andrew Bonar, *A Commentary on the Book of Leviticus* (New York: Robert Carter, 1877), 249–50.
16. Matthew Henry, *Commentary*, I, 492.
17. Andrew Bonar, *A Commentary on the Book of Leviticus*, 252.
18. John Calvin, *Commentaries on the Last Four Books of Moses* (Grand Rapids: Baker, 1979), II, 18 (on Leviticus 13:58).
19. Keil, *Old Testament*, II, 384 (on Leviticus 13:47–59).
20. See Isaiah 51:6 and Hebrews 1:10–12.
21. See Ephesians 5:26.
22. Isaiah 6:5. Possibly a reference to the leper who must "cover the upper lip; and he shall call out, Unclean! Unclean!" (Leviticus 13:45, The Interlinear Bible).
23. 2 Chronicles 29–31 and 2 Kings 23:4–24.
24. See Jeremiah 7:16; 11:14; 14:11.
25. Philip Doddridge (1702–1751), "O Happy Day," adapted by Edwin Hawkins.
26. If you live in Newfoundland, the Hebrides, or some other place where Afro-American choirs are hard to come by, comfort yourself with 2 Corinthians 8:12.
27. See Leviticus 16:7–10. The ritual of the two birds is repeated in Leviticus 14:48–53, to make atonement for a house previously infected by leprosy.
28. See Exodus 29:20 and Leviticus 8:23–24.
29. That is, I thought of the commentators as residents of Mount Olympus (home of the Greek gods), and not as modern Olympic athletes. (A distinction without meaning to those whose religion is athletics.)

30. No man, particularly one who does not read Hebrew, Greek, Latin, and German, should assume he is doing original research on the Bible.
31. Keil, *Old Testament,* II, 388 (on Leviticus 14:15–18). Of course I have not seen every commentary, even in English, but I've served my time in seminary libraries.
32. See Leviticus 14:17–18 and 14:28–29.
33. The anointing oil for the priest is described in Exodus 30:22–33. Note verses 30–32. This holy oil was poured on the priest's head (Exodus 29:7; Leviticus 8:12; Psalm 133:2) as ordinary oil was poured on the leper's. In terms of the symbolism presented here, the oil of sanctification (for the priest) is distinguished from the oil of regeneration (for the leper).
34. While little is said about the clothes of the leper, Exodus 28 and 39 describe the priestly robes.
35. Perhaps we should say that the High Priest represents Christ, and the sons of Aaron represent those who minister under Christ's authority.
36. The ear, thumb, and toe are, so to speak, the horns of the human altar. Compare Leviticus 8:15 (Exodus 29:12).
37. See Hebrews 9:22 and Romans 8:9.
38. Before he is anointed with blood and oil, the healed leper may come into the camp, but not into his own tent (Leviticus 14:3, 8).
39. If you think poetic license a prime ingredient in this explanation, I will not deny it. Remember, however, that when Naaman was healed, "his flesh was restored like the flesh of a little child" (2 Kings 5:14. See also Job 33:23–26).
40. Andrew Bonar, *A Commentary on the Book of Leviticus,* 278–9.
41. See Genesis 38:24 and 1 Samuel 14:43–44. At least Judah had the humility to reverse himself: "She has been more righteous than I" (38:26).
42. Leviticus 14:36. This was the Lord's mercy to the homeowner, that he might not lose all his possessions if his house were condemned.
43. See Daniel 1:1–6; Ezekiel 1:1–3; Esther 2:5–6; Jeremiah 39:11–18; 45:5.
44. Eusebius, *Ecclesiastical History,* Book III, chapter V (Grand Rapids: Guardian Press, 1976), 86.
45. Josephus, *The Wars of the Jews,* VI.9.3.
46. Albert Barnes, *Barnes' Notes on the New Testament* (Grand Rapids: Kregel, 1962), 114 (on Matthew 24:18).
47. Acts 5:40–41.
48. J. Duncan M. Derrett, "No Stone upon Another: Leprosy and the Temple," *Journal for the Study of the New Testament,* 30 (June, 1987) 3–20.
49. Would you believe six footnotes in the first sentence?
50. See Leviticus 14:36, 39, 43–45. (Notice that Nebuchadnezzar destroyed the temple on his third visit to Jerusalem [2 Kings 24:1, 11–16; 25:1, 8–11]).
51. See John 2:14–17; Mark 11:15–19.

Chapter 9: Ezekiel's Temple (Ezekiel 40–48)

1. See Haggai 2:9.

2. "This and the eight following chapters contain a vision of a city and temple . . . and are thought to be the most difficult part of the whole Bible." John Gill, *Old Testament,* IV, 437 (on Ezekiel 40).
3. According to Philip Mauro's chronology, Ezekiel's vision occurred thirty-three years after the beginning of the Babylonian captivity and thirty-seven years before the emancipation proclamation of Cyrus. Mauro, *Chronology,* 88, 99, and 100.
4. See Ezekiel 40:4; 43:10–11.
5. Those who study the Revelation of John would do well to remember this.
6. Exodus 25:8; 29:45, and 1 Kings 6:11–14.
7. Many people can't receive the blessings God would give them, simply because they're focused on their earthly father's failings. Those who honor their parents, emphasizing their good points and believing the best about them, more easily accept the promises of God.
8. See Jeremiah 43:10–13 and Daniel 4:28–37.
9. Mauro, *Chronology,* 88–9. (Compare Daniel 1:1–4 with 2 Chronicles 36:5, 11, and 19.)
10. Adapted from Matthew Henry, *Commentary,* V, 13 (on Matthew 2:9–10), and III, 40 (on Job 6:15–20).
11. "[Ezekiel's temple] is not a picture first and foremost of the New Testament, but of the spiritual realities present in the Restoration. This is indicated by . . . the fact that the river in chapter 47 only flows in one direction, not four, and only to the edge of the Holy Land, not into the wider world. . . .

    In the world of the Restoration . . . the bronze ocean is tipped over. *There is no laver or ocean in Ezekiel's Temple.* It has finally become a river, flowing out. . . . For the first time, the Jews would begin to move out from Palestine as missionaries, so that by New Testament times there would be synagogues and Gentile converts in all the world" (James B. Jordan, *Through New Eyes* [Brentwood, TN: Wolgemuth and Hyatt, 1988], 246, 249 [emphasis added]).
12. And vice versa. For example, if you should take the vision literally, without finding its fulfillment in the second temple, then you would expect Ezekiel's temple to be built sometime in the future. But if you can't figure out when that might happen, or who would build it, you will probably assent to a symbolic interpretation. (If you don't worry about being consistent, or if you don't require some master plan for interpreting the Bible, then it's likely you won't care.)
13. I am referring, of course, to the heady years when the nation's capital had its own baseball team. The Lord has most properly cast down the mighty from their box (or bleacher) seats. Now that they must go to "Balmer" to see major league baseball, few natives of Washington can afford the prejudice which I absorbed.
14. I speak of restaurant lasagnes. Home cooking is a world apart, with which no restaurant competes. (Lest you think this "nonpareil syndrome" affects me only with pasta: I have it also with the Archiv [DGG]

recording of Bach's *Magnificat,* the RCA [Jascha Heifetz] recording of Beethoven's Violin Concerto in D, and the Sam Cooke [original] version of "Wonderful World.")

15. Most authorities agree that in this passage a cubit is about 1'9'' and a rod about 10'6''.
16. The Berkeley and Living Bibles use feet, while the Good News Bible uses meters, but all three are clearly based on a reading of "five hundred cubits" to a side.
17. Notice that the Jerusalem Bible translators stand out from the crowd in the cubit camp. They interpret Ezekiel 42:20 literally, giving no unit of measurement, as do six of the translations that utilize rods.
18. One potential complication occurs in the Hebrew of verse 16. There it says literally "five cubits rods," but the traditional Hebrew (Masoretic) text includes a marginal note instructing us to read "hundred" for "cubits." (If you reverse the first two consonants of the Hebrew word for "cubits," you get the Hebrew word for "hundred," and, of course, vice versa.) Thus we get "five hundred rods" from the Hebrew of verse 16, matching the text in verses 17–19. Since all the translators and nearly all the commentators accept this emendation, reading "five hundred rods" for "five cubits rods," this does little to explain their choice of rods or cubits. (The exceptions I have run across are Mr. Hengstenberg and Mr. Zimmerli, who make much of these peculiar "cubits rods." We shall discuss their views a little further on.)
19. According to an old tradition.
20. I am more sympathetic to, though no more convinced by, arguments from the Hebrew, which I shall discuss shortly.
21. As George Orwell might put it, all theologians are liable to distort the facts, but some are more liable than others.
22. See Proverbs 16:28.
23. The "other Realtor in town" is The Interlinear Bible, which reads "rods" in both of its translations. (See appendix).
24. E. W. Hengstenberg, *The Prophecies of the Prophet Ezekiel Elucidated* (Edinburgh: T. and T. Clark, 1869), 410–13. Walther Zimmerli, *Ezekiel* 2 (Philadelphia: Fortress Press, 1983), 402–3.
25. See note 18.
26. E. W. Hengstenberg, *The Prophecies of the Prophet Ezekiel Elucidated* (Edinburgh: T. and T. Clark, 1869), 410 (emphasis added).
27. F. W. J. Schröder, who acts like a moderator on this issue, calls Hengstenberg's *hundred cubits* "difficult to conceive and hard to accept." John Peter Lange, *Commentary on the Holy Scriptures* (New York: Charles Scribner's Sons, 1879), XIII, 403–4 (on Ezekiel 42:16). (Schröder authored the volume on Ezekiel in Lange's series.)
28. Mark Twain, *The Adventures of Huckleberry Finn,* chapter 1. ". . . mostly a true book, with some stretchers, as I said before."
29. Primitives long ago perfected this technique with statues of wood and stone. But to apply it to the Word of God requires sophistication.

30. Zimmerli means, I believe, that Ezekiel's previous measurements add up to 500 cubits on a side. But Ezekiel never says so directly, and Zimmerli's assumption is contradicted by Patrick Fairbairn on the grounds that 500 cubits leaves no room for the walls and stairs mentioned by the prophet. See Patrick Fairbairn, *An Exposition of Ezekiel* (Lafayette, IN: AP&A, n.d.), 228–9. Keil, *Biblical Commentary on the Prophecies of Ezekiel* (Grand Rapids: Eerdmans, n.d.), II, 268–73. It is common for modern scholars to take no notice of earlier commentators who do not share their assumptions. (Fairbairn's work was published in 1851.)
31. Walther Zimmerli, *Ezekiel* 2 (Philadelphia: Fortress Press, 1983), 402.
32. Where the critics present hard evidence, such as manuscripts in the original language, we need to consider it. However, we must separate the evidence from the assumptions in which they tend to wrap it. (Once it's out of the package, a child can distinguish beef from baloney.)
33. I continue to recommend the use of antidotes for those who read much textual criticism. See chapter 4, note 16.
34. E. W. Hengstenberg, *The Prophecies of the Prophet Ezekiel Elucidated,* 352. I cannot say whether we have the author or his translators to thank for this diversion.
35. See chapter 7, note 6.
36. For examples of how *apagogical* has been used, consult the *Oxford English Dictionary.* Students who are wise will employ the word only with teachers whose character and learning they truly respect.
37. Gill, *Old Testament,* IV, 449 (on Ezekiel 41:12).
38. See Ezekiel 40:46; 43:19; 44:15; and 48:11.
39. See 1 Samuel 2:30–36; 1 Kings 2:26–27, 35.

Chapter 10: Census and Itinerary (Numbers 1–3, 26, and 33)

1. The leaders of the twelve tribes in the wilderness are listed four times in Numbers, in chapters 1, 2, 7, and 10. (The exiles who returned from Babylon are listed in Ezra 2, Nehemiah 7, and the apocryphal book of First Esdras, chapter 5. The lists of those who returned are similar, but not identical.)
2. Every Christian who repents may say with Hezekiah, "You have cast all my sins behind Your back" (Isaiah 38:17).
3. Chicago: Moody Press, 1987.
4. Studies in Food and Faith, available from Biblical Horizons, P.O. Box 132011, Tyler, TX 75713–2011. (Since Rev. Jordan is no shrinking violet when it comes to deep discussion, less scholarly readers should start with his two-page summary of the project, which briefly describes each of the thirteen papers. I highly recommend these papers for seminary libraries.)
5. The first count was taken before the tabernacle was made, for it determined the amount of ransom money used in the sockets of that structure. The second count was taken a month after the tabernacle was erected. Compare Exodus 38:25–28; 40:2, and Numbers 1:1.
6. Compare Exodus 38:25–28 and Numbers 1:45–46.

7. See Exodus 30:11–16 and pages 65–66 of this book.
8. Henry W. Soltau, *An Exposition of the Tabernacle* (London: Morgan and Chase, n.d.), 96. Mr. Soltau knew, of course, that Christians do not pay for their own redemption. I regret that I must omit his excellent but lengthy comment on "the eternal preciousness of His (Christ's) blood . . . the solid foundation on which God's everlasting tabernacle rests," 99.
9. See Daniel 12:1; Malachi 3:16.
10. "We must try to imagine what the Old Testament would have been, if it had not been kept distinct from the Talmud; or the New Testament, if it had been mixed up not only with the spurious gospels, but with the records of the wranglings of the early Councils, if we wish to understand, to some extent at least, the wild confusion of sublime truth with vulgar stupidity that meets us in the pages of the Veda, the Avesta, and the Tripitaka" (Max Müller, preface to *The Sacred Books of the East* [Oxford, 1879], I, xv-xvi).
11. *The Bhagavad Gita* (New York: Penguin, 1979), 95–96 (11. 54. and 12. 2.).
12. For example, "Sanskrit literature is a great literature. . . . There are, however, two great branches of literature not found in Sanskrit. There is no history and there is no tragedy." Juan Mascaró, introduction to *The Bhagavad Gita,* (New York: Penguin, 1979), 9–10.
13. For example, "Let us pause to wonder at . . . this expectation of being a blessing to all mankind (Genesis 12:1–3). . . . Search the literature of other ancient nations . . . for something approaching such an expectation. What had the ancient Sumerians, Babylonians, Assyrians, Egyptians, Greeks, Romans, Hindus, Chinese, Japanese, in all of their extensive literature, or any other people that ever existed, to say about world-wide blessing to come through themselves? You will seek in vain. Then compare this with the magnificent confirmation of history, in the activities of the Christian Church, and if this be not proof of divine prophecy, it is difficult to see how such a thing could possibly be proved" (Albertus Pieters, *The Seed of Abraham* [Grand Rapids: Wm. B. Eerdmans, 1950], 12–13). (Dr. Pieters was eighty years old when he wrote this. He had behind him thirty years as a missionary to Japan and twenty-five more years as a seminary professor and author. In other words he was more qualified than most of us to make this sweeping statement. [Galatians 3:8 provides striking confirmation of Dr. Pieters' words.])
14. Even Joseph, that model of upright behavior, swore "by the life of Pharaoh" (Genesis 42:15–16). Matthew Henry and Calvin, among others, considered this a sin. Perhaps Daniel comes closest to a clean record in Scripture.
15. See Joshua 13–21.
16. See Numbers 26:63–65.
17. Compare Numbers 1:46 and Numbers 26:51. See also Numbers 14:3.
18. See 1 Corinthians 1:27.
19. From Numbers 16:26–33. (But notice the titles of Psalms 42–49 and 84–88.)

20. For a detailed defense of Samuel's (and Heman's) descent from Korah, see note 15, chapter 5. [In the New American Bible, the Scriptures in question are 1 Chronicles 6:18 and 6:22.]
21. See Exodus 6:16, 18, 22.
22. See Exodus 6:22; Leviticus 10:4; Numbers 3:30; 1 Chronicles 15:8; 2 Chronicles 29:13. (Since he is from the tribe of Zebulun, the Elizaphan of Numbers 34:25 must be another person.)
23. See Exodus 6:16.
24. See 1 Chronicles 25:1–6.
25. See Numbers 4:1–15.
26. See 1 Samuel 17:28–9.
27. Rev. M. Rosenbaum [!] and Dr. A. M. Silbermann, eds., *Pentateuch . . . with Rashi's Commentary* (London: Shapiro, Vallentine and Co., 1946), II, 77b (of Numbers). See Exodus 6:18–22 for the genealogy of Korah and Elizaphan. See also John Gill, *Old Testament,* I, 625 (on Numbers 16:3). (Gill refers to Rashi as "Jarchi.")
28. See 1 Chronicles 15:3–10.
29. See Numbers 26:33; 27:1; 36:11; Joshua 17:3. The daughters are also mentioned in 1 Chronicles 7:15, but not by name.
30. That our three children are all girls has, of course, no bearing whatsoever on my objectivity as an author. (While this chapter was in progress, my wife called to tell me that she's pregnant with our fourth [Matthew Philip, born September 5, 1990.])
31. Matthew Henry, *Commentary,* I, 694–5 (on Numbers 27:4).
32. John Peter Lange, D.D., *A Commentary on the Holy Scriptures* (New York: Charles Scribner's Sons, 1879), III, 154 (on Numbers 27:1–11).
33. ("Vatever dat may mean!")
34. See Numbers 36:10–12.
35. O Christian adventurers and archaeologists, where are the remains of Pharaoh's army? Why are they not exhibited for all to see? With Numbers 33 in one hand and modern technology in the other, and with many prayers to God in our hearts, is it not time to search for those historic relics? We have Moses' itinerary and all the latest gadgets. What more do we need?
36. "Affecting or moving the passions, particularly pity, sorrow, grief or other tender emotion." (Noah Webster, 1828).
37. See Numbers 20:1, 7–13, 22–24; 33:36–38.
38. See Deuteronomy 3:23–27.

Chapter 11: The Division of the Land (Joshua 12–21)

1. Philip Mauro reckons the time to be 986 years, from 1493 to 507 B.C. *The Chronology of the Bible* (New York: George H. Doran, 1922), 52 and 99.
2. Mr. Bob Cox, head of customer service at the G. P. O., informs me that they publish some 50,000 titles (!) a year. That comes to 192 new publications for each business day, plus daily issues of *The Congressional Record,*

The Federal Register, and *The Commerce Business Daily*. (Anyone still complaining about the length of the boring parts is hereby sentenced to read one complete issue of *The Federal Register*.)

3. (The ultimate proof of divine benevolence is that children require more sleep than their parents.)
4. I recognize that these two propositions are not mutually exclusive.
5. See Numbers 21:21–35 and Deuteronomy 2:24–3:17.
6. "Filicidal, concerned with the slaughter of sons and daughters." *Oxford English Dictionary*.
7. For a detailed argument that Jephthah dedicated his daughter to the Lord (and did not kill her), see James B. Jordan, *Judges: God's War Against Humanism* (Tyler, TX: Geneva Ministries, 1985), 191–214. (This fine commentary is available from Biblical Horizons, P.O. Box 132011, Tyler, TX 75713–2011.)
8. Romans 8:17. Notice the condition, "if indeed we suffer with Him . . ."
9. See Joshua 7:4.
10. See Deuteronomy 3:11.
11. See Joshua 12:15; 1 Samuel 22:1; 1 Chronicles 11:15–19; Micah 1:15.
12. Joshua 12:24; Song of Solomon 6:4–5.
13. Matthew Henry, *Commentary*, II, 70 (on Joshua 12:7–8).
14. However, in Acts 13:19 Paul tells us that God "destroyed seven nations in the land of Canaan." Note that the Greek verb for "destroyed" in this passage means "to take down," and has both non-violent (Acts 13:29; Mark 15:46; Luke 23:53, etc.) and violent (Luke 12:18; 2 Corinthians 10:5) usage in the New Testament.
15. See Numbers 16:12 and 16:23–33.
16. See page 10.
17. See 1 Samuel 27:5–7 and 30:1–6; Numbers 14:39–45.
18. Matthew Henry, *Commentary*, I, 875 (on Deuteronomy 33:6–8).
19. See Joshua 19:1 and 19:9.
20. "In the case of Levi, this curse was turned into a blessing, as they became the priests of Israel and dwelt in the Levitical cities; but to this point (Judges 1:3), no salvation has come for Simeon. . . . By identifying themselves with the royal tribe, however, Simeon finds salvation. The blessings that come to the tribe of Judah will come to Simeon as well. . . . Later in history, Simeon will be part of the southern kingdom of Judah, and thus will be spared the Assyrian captivity" (Jordan, *Judges: God's War Against Humanism* [Tyler, Texas: Geneva Ministries, 1985], 3).
21. Ezekiel 48:24; Revelation 7:7.
22. See 1 Chronicles 4:24–43, where you will discover most of Simeon's seventeen cities listed again.
23. See 2 Peter 2:15 and Jude 11.
24. See Numbers 31:16; Revelation 2:14.
25. See Deuteronomy 18:10, 14. I think it interesting that Moses' clearest prophecy of Christ follows this passage. Immediately after warning us

about counterfeits like Balaam, he delivers his great promise of the true Prophet of God.

26. 1 Samuel 15:23 (emphasis added). Actually the word used here is a close derivative of the word for diviner in Joshua 13:22.
27. 1 Samuel 28:8 (emphasis added). In this passage a literal translation of Saul's request would be, "Divine, I beg you, for me by the familiar spirit, and bring up for me . . ." The Interlinear Bible (Peabody, MA: Hendrickson, 1985, 2d ed.) 792.
28. Matthew 7:21–23. Not by their prophecies, but by their fruits, shall we know the false prophets: Matthew 7:15–20. (It takes time for a tree to produce its fruit.)
29. J. M. W. Turner (1775–1851).
30. Perhaps I got this notion from Joshua 11:22, failing to balance it with 13:2–3 and 15:45–47.
31. Joshua 15:45–47. The other two cities were probably included in Judah's inheritance, for we find in Judges 1:18 that Judah conquered Ashkelon as well. The only mention of Gath in the early boring parts is in Joshua 11:22. However, the "Gittites" of Joshua 13:3 were presumably inhabitants of Gath. See 2 Samuel 15:18.
32. Anyone applying these statements to current events is extending them on his own. I make no such implication.
33. See 1 Chronicles 1:8–16.
34. "A Mighty Fortress Is Our God," Martin Luther (hymn).
35. Gill, *Old Testament,* I, 902 (on Joshua 19:43). However, Dr. Gill's assertion must be qualified by Joshua 21:43–45 and Judges 1:18. (Apparently the Jews took Ekron, but lost it soon after to the Philistines.) There is also a statement in the apocryphal book of 1 Maccabees, "He [Alexander Balas, ruler of Syria] gave him [Jonathan Maccabeus] also Ekron with the borders thereof in possession" (10:89, KJV).
36. See 2 Samuel 15:30–37; 16:16–19; 17:5–14.
37. Hushai used four similes and one hyperbole in his speech to Absalom, 2 Samuel 17:5–14. The result? "Absalom and all the men of Israel said, 'The counsel of Hushai the Archite is better than the counsel of Ahithophel.'" Notice that Ahithophel used no figures of speech (16:20–17:4). [Card-carrying Fan Club members bristle at the notion that Hushai's deception was a sin. "Ain't Rahab in the Hall of Fame?," they retort. (For a better answer, see Proverbs 22:11.) Prudent readers will either join up, or, heeding Proverbs 26:17, give Fan Club meetings a wide berth.]
38. See 1 Chronicles 27:33. Presumably, Hushai was David's adviser. The biblical concept of friendship includes "telling all" (John 15:15). Compare also James 2:23 (2 Chronicles 20:7) and Genesis 18:17–21.
39. See Numbers 27:1–11.
40. See Judges 1:19.
41. See Exodus 23:30. Charles Haddon Spurgeon (1834–1892) "English Nonconformist divine," as the 1911 *Britannica* calls him, was styled the

"prince of preachers" by his admirers. I take the text from an eight-volume collection of his sermons, *The Treasury of the Bible* (Grand Rapids: Baker, 1981), I, 530–536.

42. One must always be wary. I still struggle with my sin from time to time, but when I do, the outcome is no longer a foregone conclusion. I have a fighting chance now (indeed I am often victorious), which is all one can ask for in this life.
43. Notice that this woman, unlike many whom Christ touched, did not come to Him for healing. She happened to be in the synagogue where He was teaching, when He noticed her and called her.
44. Beaumont and Fletcher, *Scornful Lady,* Act V, Scene 3. Spiritual beggars must be careful to confess their sins to an appropriate person. Secret sin is like a steam engine with no safety valve. Sooner or later it will explode, injuring many an innocent bystander.
45. Though the ark may have been moved on special occasions (to Shechem, Joshua 24:1, 26; to Bethel, Judges 20:26–28), it now had a permanent home in Shiloh (Judges 18:31; 1 Samuel 1:3, 9; 3:3; 4:3).
46. "Shiloh, A Requiem (April, 1862)," one of Herman Melville's *Battle Pieces.*
47. See 1 Samuel 3 and 4.
48. See also Jeremiah 26:4–9 and Psalm 78:59–61.
49. See chapter 9 on Ezekiel 42:16–20.
50. "Allon" is simply a transliteration of the Hebrew word in question.
51. In the division of the land this Hebrew word (and its derivative) are applied nowhere else to the cities of the Jews. In Joshua 14:12 Caleb says that the cities of the Anakim "were great and fortified." In 19:29 the border of Asher extends "to the fortified city of Tyre."

    Naphtali was the northernmost tribe in Israel, so the "fortified" cities may have been built for border protection. But if so, why is there no mention of fortified cities along the other borders?
52. For example, Joshua 19:38 sums up our current list, ". . . nineteen cities with their villages," but we find only sixteen names in verses 35–38. (Possibly three of the names in verses 32–34 were counted as cities belonging to Naphtali, and thus included in the total.)
53. At the time I was using *The Treasury of Scripture Knowledge* (McLean, VA: MacDonald, 1982), 163. See appendix for more on this valuable (and inexpensive) tool.
54. See Joshua 19:10, 13, 16.
55. After I wrote this section on Jonah, I noticed that most modern Bibles use a different tense of the verb employed by the Pharisees. With the NASB ("No prophet arises out of Galilee") and the NIV ("A prophet does not come out of Galilee"), they emphasize present and future considerations. On the other hand, the NKJV ("No prophet has arisen out of Galilee"), which I have followed, and The Interlinear Bible ("A prophet has not been raised out of Galilee") emphasize the past. The point is, the Pharisees appear less foolish in the NIV and NASB. They are saying only, "No prophet can arise from Galilee," not "No prophet has ever arisen from

Galilee." My remarks in the text do not apply to the present-oriented translations.

If you should ask, "Why do the translations differ?"—the answer is complex. A handful of very early Greek manuscripts (of Egyptian origin) use a present-oriented form of the Greek verb, and most modern Bibles follow them. Nearly a thousand less ancient manuscripts use a verb form which emphasizes the past: the NKJV and the Interlinear Bible reflect this traditional text, long used by the Orthodox churches. (My use of the NKJV indicates my preference for the traditional Greek text of the New Testament. But I shall spare you my three sonnets on the dubious character of the oldest Greek manuscripts in existence.)

56. See Matthew 12:38–41. Though Jesus reached the Gentiles mostly through His deeds and His apostles, occasionally He taught them in His own words. See John 4:6–26, 39–42.
57. Especially since we often reserve this tactic for other groups of believers.
58. See Romans 2:17–24.
59. See 2 Peter 1:5.
60. Joshua 20:6. Note the additional clause, "who was anointed with the holy oil," in the parallel verse, Numbers 35:25.
61. It seems significant that the death of the first high priest precedes the first conquest of Canaanites (Numbers 20:29–30:1), and that the death of the second high priest completes the book of the conquest of Canaan (Joshua 24:33).
62. Matthew Henry, *Commentary*, II, 95 (on Joshua 20:1–6).
63. See Numbers 35:7; Joshua 21:41.

Chapter 12: The Officers of the Kingdom (1 Chronicles 23–27)

1. Though we hear rumors (and reports of sightings) of persons who are bored by poetry, no reader of this book, I trust, is still in that benighted condition.
2. "Judge none blessed before his death: for a man shall be known in his children" (Ecclesiasticus 11:28 [Apocrypha, KJV]).
3. From the fact that the Hebrew word we translate "and with him" contains in correct order the letters which mean "high" or "above." Two 16th-century scholars, Junius and Tremellius, advocated this reading before Dr. Gill did.
4. John Gill, *Old Testament*, II, 311 (on 2 Samuel 23:39). The "37" of this verse may be counted thus: the first three (v. 17), the second three (v. 18, possibly including Asahel, for thirty names follow Asahel's), the thirty (vv. 23–4), and Joab the chief.
5. See 2 Samuel 23:25. "Eliam the son of Ahithophel the Gilonite" (2 Samuel 23:34) also appears in the first list of mighty men, but not in the second. However, several older commentators think "Ahijah the Pelonite" (1 Chronicles 11:36) is another name for Eliam. (Presumably this Eliam was the father of Bathsheba, 2 Samuel 11:3.)
6. See Acts 1:23–26.
7. See 2 Samuel 2:18–23.

8. See Exodus 28:1; Numbers 18:7.
9. 1 Chronicles 12:23.
10. *Dictionary of American Biography* (New York: Scribner's, 1943) XIII, 312. (When Muhlenberg's brigade attacked the British at Yorktown, the lead officer was a colonel named Alexander Hamilton.)
11. It is possible to contest this statement. For those of you who love the raging controversies of the boring parts, Dr. Gill states, "I have called Benaiah a priest in the note on 1 Kings 2:32; yet I am now rather of opinion that he was not one, for though priests might bear arms on some occasions, yet it is not likely that one should be in a constant military office, and especially general of an army; and besides, this man was of Kabzeel, a city in the tribe of Judah, which is not mentioned among the Levitical cities, see 2 Samuel 23:20, Joshua 15:21." Gill, *Old Testament*, II, 485 (on 1 Chronicles 27:5–6). Dr. Gill and some others say the word "priest" in 1 Chronicles 27:5 should be read "officer," thus making Benaiah the son of some other Jehoiada. To which I answer, first, that my Hebrew dictionary (Brown, Driver, Briggs, 464) does not countenance this "officer" reading and, second, that many good scholars accept Jehoiada as a priest. What Jehoiada was doing in Kabzeel remains a question to be asked. Since it was on the southern frontier of Judah, it seems just the place for a family whose idea of recreation was slaying lions and Egyptian giants (1 Chronicles 11:22–23). [N. B. Without the boring parts of Joshua (15:21), we would never know where Kabzeel was.]
12. See 1 Kings 1 and 2.
13. Compare 1 Chronicles 26:20–28 with 27:25.
14. See Hebrews 9, where the things of the temple are called "copies of the things in the heavens" (v. 23).
15. See Numbers 3:40–51.
16. See Numbers 4:1–33.
17. From the Latin *vocatus*, a calling or invitation.
18. Denis de Rougemont, *The Christian Opportunity* (New York: Holt, Rinehart and Winston, 1963), 37. Elsewhere he said, "To follow one's vocation, contrary to what is generally believed, is not to follow one's inclination (even uphill), but to be swept in spite of oneself toward goals and into an action to which nothing whatever inclines us. *I am the man least suited for this!* groans the individual. . . ." Denis de Rougemont, "John Calvin: An 'Engaged' Writer," in *Dramatic Personages* (New York: Holt, Rinehart and Winston, 1964), 116. Strange as it may seem, in my experience de Rougemont and Perkins (see below) are both correct. A chief part of accepting one's call is the willingness to fall in love with the work one is called to.
19. William Perkins, "A Treatise of the Vocations or Callings of Men," in *The Work of William Perkins*, edited by Ian Breward (Appleford, Abingdon, Berkshire, England: The Sutton Courtenay Press, n.d.), 446–476.
20. What kind of work, do you suppose, came out of the carpenter's shop in Nazareth?

21. 1 Chronicles 23:25–26.
22. See 1 Chronicles 28:11–13; 29:1–9.
23. See 1 Chronicles 23:5. Solomon built new furnishings for the house of God (1 Kings 7:48–51; 2 Chronicles 4:1). Thus, except for the ark and the mercy seat (and perhaps the priests' garments), David's instruments were the first holy things made for the temple.
24. See Revelation 5:8 and 14:1–2.
25. Dr. Otto Zöckler, *The Books of the Chronicles,* Volume VII of: John Peter Lange, *Commentary on the Holy Scriptures* (New York: Charles Scribner's Sons, 1877), 144 (on 1 Chronicles 23:27).
26. See Psalm 110:4; Hebrews 6:20.
27. The Hebrew words for "sizes" and "measures" in 1 Chronicles 23:29 appear together only there and in Leviticus 19:35: "You shall do no injustice in judgment, in *measurement* of length, weight, or *volume.*" The word for "measures" is used in only one other biblical passage (Ezekiel 4:11, 16).
28. "A just weight and balance are the Lord's; all the weights in the bag are His work" (Proverbs 16:11).
29. Proverbs 11:1; see also 20:10 and 20:23.
30. See 1 Chronicles 23:4.
31. Luke 1:5 (emphasis added). Abijah received the eighth division, 1 Chronicles 24:10.
32. Josephus, "The Life of Flavius Josephus," section 1, in *The Life and Works of Josephus* (New York: Holt, Rinehart and Winston, n.d.), 1 (emphasis added). Josephus, then, was a relative of the famous Maccabees, for they also were priests belonging to the first division, the sons of Jehoiarib (1 Chronicles 24:7; 1 Maccabees 2:1 [Apocrypha]).
33. Not by our own merits, of course, but by our relation to the great High Priest. Yet we should balance this knowledge with Charles Spurgeon's remark, "We all trace our line up to a gardener, who lost his place through stealing his Master's fruit." *The Treasury of the Bible* (Grand Rapids: Baker, 1981), III, 113 (sermon on Psalm 131:2).
34. See the genealogy of Levi in Exodus 6:16–25.
35. In 1 Chronicles 23:15–16 we encounter another Gershon, the son of Moses.
36. John Milton, *Paradise Lost,* VII, 126–128.
37. Divided into twenty-four groups, there were twelve song-leaders available at a time. The rest of the 4,000 musicians (23:5) were probably under their direction.
38. Gill, *Old Testament,* II, 482 (on 1 Chronicles 25:8).
39. Compare 1 Chronicles 25:2 with 25:9–10.
40. Gill, *Old Testament,* II, 482 (on 1 Chronicles 26:1).
41. See Isaiah 64:6.
42. See Romans 2:28–29; Colossians 2:11.
43. See Ezekiel 3:16–21.

44. See 1 Chronicles 15:18, 21, 24 and also 1 Chronicles 16:38 (where the Hebrew is obscure). [If there was only one Obed-Edom, he was very talented. How many bouncers do you know who worship the Lord with harps in their spare time?] See also, C. F. Keil, *Commentary on the Chronicles* (Edinburgh: T. and T. Clark, 1878) 206, 219 (on the passages cited).
45. Compare 2 Samuel 6:11–12 with 1 Chronicles 26:5. (The title "Gittite" in 2 Samuel could mean that Obed-Edom was a "man of Gath," i.e., a Philistine [Joshua 13:3; 2 Samuel 15:18–19] and therefore not our gatekeeper. However, it could also mean that he was from Gath-Rimmon, a city of the Levites [Joshua 21:24], or that he was a Jew who once had lived at Gath. See Gill, *Old Testament*, II, 250 [on 2 Samuel 6:10]. If you were David, the man after God's own heart, would you have left His ark with a Levite or with a Philistine?)
46. See 1 Chronicles 5:1–2.
47. See 1 Chronicles 26:15.
48. See 2 Samuel 3:7–10. (Before he was insulted about his concubine, Abner knew the will of God but would not do it.)
49. Two were Zarhites (from the tribe of Judah) vv. 11, 13; two were from "the children of Ephraim," vv. 10, 14. Jashobeam and Asahel were also from Judah, vv. 3, 7. See 1 Chronicles 11:11, 12, 22, 26–31.
50. 2 Samuel 2:18–23; 23:24; 1 Chronicles 11:26.
51. 2 Samuel 5:3–5. Asahel appears to have died soon, perhaps two years, after David was anointed king of Judah. (Compare 2 Samuel 2, vv. 4, 10–12, and 18–23.) Notice the "long war" mentioned in 2 Samuel 3:1, which intervened between Asahel's death and David's becoming king of Israel at age 37 or 38.
52. 1 Kings 2:31–32.
53. 2 Samuel 21:15–17 and 23:18. "Why should this dead dog curse my lord the king? Let me go over, I pray thee, And take off his head." (2 Samuel 16:9, KJV).
54. 1 Samuel 26:8–9; 2 Samuel 16:9–10. We are specifically told in 2 Samuel 3:30 that "Joab and Abishai his brother killed Abner . . ." Josephus says Abishai was present at the murder, *Antiquities*, VII, I, 5.
55. Shakespeare, *Hamlet*, V.2.398–401.
56. 1 Samuel 17:28.
57. See 2 Samuel 3:28–39.
58. Walt Whitman, "Song of Myself," 15.
59. Particularly Nathan's sons, 1 Kings 4:5, and the son of Hushai, 1 Kings 4:16. (If I pass up an opportunity to talk about Hushai, you know something momentous must have distracted me.)
60. See 2 Samuel 15:35–36; 18:19–32; 1 Chronicles 6:49–53.
61. 1 Kings 4:7–19.
62. 1 Kings 4:2. I shall not trouble you with all the scholarly debates as to whether the Azariah and Zadok in verse 2, and the Ahimaaz in verse 15, are the ones familiar to us from other parts of Scripture. Suffice it to say

that the commentators are not agreed on this. I am presenting my own interpretation of the available facts, hoping that it shall prove to be both comprehensive and plausible.

63. 1 Chronicles 6:8–9; (1 Chronicles 5:34–35 in The New American Bible.)
64. See Isaiah 9:1; 1 Kings 9:11–13; John 1:46.
65. Isaiah 9:6. (This Hebrew word for "government" is not related to the word for "governors" in 1 Kings 4:7. Yet in foretelling Christ's government, Isaiah linked Galilee and Naphtali. See Isaiah 9:1.)
66. I've heard the Gentleman's engaged; but if the rumors of the Bride's scandalous background are verified (and the press is looking into it), I'll certainly have made a fool of myself. Won't I?
67. "Cushite," from Cush the son of Ham, is here a synonym for Ethiopian (or possibly for Arabian). If you feel uncomfortable with the symbolism I detect in this story (dark-skinned messenger—messenger of darkness), consider how Scripture presents the other Ethiopians of the Bible. The Lord went out of His way to defend the Cushite wife whom Moses had married (Numbers 12). Ebed-melech (his name means "servant of the King") the Ethiopian is portrayed as one of the few good men in Jeremiah's time (Jeremiah 38:7–13; 39:15–18). The Ethiopian whom Philip met (Acts 8:26–40 [most Greek manuscripts omit verse 37]) was one of the first converts to Christ. All of them (except Joab's servant) were blessed with special grace.
68. Zadok is the Hebrew word for "righteous."
69. "The light shines in the darkness, and the darkness did not overtake it." John 1:5, The Interlinear Bible.
70. However your Bible translates 2 Samuel 18:28, in the original text Ahimaaz cries, "Shalom!"

Chapter 13: The Restoration (Ezra and Nehemiah)

1. While we cannot say that it was a sin to remain in Babylon, there are many Scriptures which emphasize that God's remnant would return to Israel. (See Jeremiah 23:3; Ezekiel 11:17–20; 20:41–42; 28:25–26; 34:11–16; 36:24–28; 37:21–22.) In the face of such overwhelming evidence, it seems reasonable to suppose that all the Jews ought to have returned to the Promised Land, except those who were called to remain in Babylon. Instead, only "those who spirits God had moved arose to go up and build the house of the Lord which *is* in Jerusalem" (Ezra 1:5). "Those who were around them encouraged them with articles of silver and gold, with goods and livestock, and with precious things . . . (Ezra 1:6)," which was certainly a good work, but not as good as joining the remnant of faithful pilgrims. In any event, the book of Esther makes it clear that God extended His love and protection to His people who stayed in Persia.
2. See Ezra 2 and Nehemiah 7:6–69. A third list may be found in First Esdras, the only Old Testament apocryphal book which contains lengthy boring parts. However, since neither Catholics nor Protestants recognize First Esdras as canonical or divinely-inspired (and since the Orthodox churches allow it only secondary status), I shall not examine it here.

3. I can't think of a list in the Bible which violates this principle. The list of the twelve spies (Numbers 13:1–16) introduces them as men worthy of honor. The conquered kings of Canaan (Joshua 12) were never the people of God. Those who married foreign wives (Ezra 10) had repented of that sin. Paul's lists at the end of his letters (Romans 16, Colossians 4) mention many more saints than hypocrites. How dreadful then to be named as one unfaithful!
4. See Ezra 2:36–42, 64; Nehemiah 7:39–45, 66; (1 Esdras [Apocrypha] 5:24–28, 41).
5. Ezekiel 48:10–11. See also Ezekiel 44:10–16.
6. Philip Mauro figures that Ezekiel's vision was given thirty-seven years before the proclamation of Cyrus. *The Chronology of the Bible* (New York: George H. Doran, 1922), 99–100.
7. Compare 2 Kings 24:14; Jeremiah 52:28–30; Daniel 1:1–3.
8. For a model of how to do this, see Daniel 9.
9. John A. Lees, "Nethinim," *The Classic Bible Dictionary* (Lafayette, IN: Sovereign Grace, 1988), 842. ("Nethinim" means "given" in Hebrew.)
10. Who says you can't have fun in the boring parts? *In the same volume* of Lange's Commentary, I find these two comments:

    The children of the servants of Solomon . . . were *certainly not* the descendants of those Amorites, Hethites, etc., whom Solomon . . . had made tributary and bondsmen, but apparently prisoners of war from tribes that were not Canaanites. (F. W. Schultz on Ezra 2:55).

    Solomon's servants were *doubtless* those whom Solomon enslaved of the Canaanites. (Rev. Howard Crosby on Nehemiah 7:57–60.)

    (It's the "certainly" and the "doubtless" that get me. Ah, scholarship! Ah, humanity!) John Peter Lange, *Commentary on the Holy Scriptures* (New York: Scribner's, 1877) VII, 32 of Ezra, 32 of Nehemiah (emphasis added).
11. Three of the priests named here appear in the courses established by David. (Compare Ezra 2:36–39 with 1 Chronicles 24:7–8, 14.) However, the gatekeepers named here are not found among David's gatekeepers in 1 Chronicles 26. (Some of their names do appear in 1 Chronicles 9, where the word "Nethinim" is first used in the Bible, 1 Chronicles 9:2. Compare Ezra 2:42 with 1 Chronicles 9:17.)
12. Matthew Henry, *Commentary,* II, 1034.
13. Needless to say, other commentators, even good ones, prefer another solution. "These differences are *undoubtedly* owing to mere clerical errors, and attempts to reconcile them in other ways cannot be justified." Keil, *Old Testament,* III, iii, 45 (on Ezra 2:64–67) (emphasis added). Would *you* assert something "undoubtedly"—about a census taken 2,400 years ago?
14. There is a wonderful Latin expression, *cum grano salis,* "with a grain of salt; with reserve or precaution." You may sprinkle it liberally on this "explanation."
15. "Blessed Lord, which hast caused all Holy Scriptures to be written for our learning: Grant us that we may in such wise hear them, *read, mark, learn, and inwardly digest them,* that by patience and comfort of thy holy

Word, we may embrace and ever hold fast the blessed hope of everlasting life, which thou hast given us in our Savior Jesus Christ." (*The Book of Common Prayer* [Anglican, 1559] Collect for the Second Sunday of Advent [emphasis added].)

16. *Pudd'nhead Wilson's Calendar.* But compare: "The man that blushes is not quite a brute." Edward Young, *Night Thoughts,* VII, 496.
17. To give credit where credit is due, the sermon was preached by the Reverend Mike Wilkins of the Cayucos Community Church, Cayucos, CA, in April, 1982. Dr. Wilkins in now professor of New Testament, Talbot School of Theology, La Mirada, CA.
18. See Nehemiah 3:20. "There is no evidence for or against the assumption that the Baruch of Nehemiah 10:6 is the man of Nehemiah 3:20." Elmer Smick, "Baruch," *Classic Bible Dictionary,* 185.
19. Nehemiah 3:5, 27. As Dr. Gill points out, "This is observed to their disgrace, when the common people of their city were ready to work, and did" (Gill, *Old Testament,* II, 557).
20. See 2 Samuel 14:2 and 23:26; Amos 1:1. To me it's intriguing that Jabez comes just after the men of Tekoa in 1 Chronicles 4:5–10. Could they be the brothers whom he excelled in honor?
21. Gill, *Old Testament,* II, 557. Matthew Henry agrees with Dr. Gill.
22. "This description of the walls of Jerusalem . . . forms the chief authority for the topography of ancient Jerusalem (before the captivity), and has been frequently discussed and explained" (Keil, *Old Testament,* III, iii, 173).
23. See 1 Chronicles 4:14.
24. There is significant correspondence between Nehemiah 11 and 12 and 1 Chronicles 9, but scholars are not agreed about their relationship, if any. The key to the debate, I think, is whether in 1 Chronicles 9:2 we render the Hebrew as "the first inhabitants" or as "the former inhabitants." "First" would mean the first to return from Babylon, implying kinship with Nehemiah's list. "Former" would refer to those who lived in Jerusalem before the captivity, indicating two entirely different lists with some coincidental names. Most English translators have used "first," which seems reasonable when we consider that "Shemaiah the son of Hasshub, the son of Azrikam, the son of Hashabiah" appears in both lists (1 Chronicles 9:14; Nehemiah 11:15). (How many guys by that name do *you* know?) For the "former" position, see Keil, *Old Testament,* III, ii, 152–162 (on 1 Chronicles 9:1–17). I think both lists date from the lifetime of "Shemaiah the son of Hasshub . . . ," but that either they were made some years apart or, as Dr. Gill suggests, they recorded different segments of the same population.
25. See Nehemiah 6:1–13.
26. "Nehemiah the son of Hachaliah" (Nehemiah 1:1; 10:1).
27. 1 Chronicles 9:33. See page 51.
28. Perhaps this also explains why the temple tax was only one-third shekel per man. Nehemiah 10:32.

29. See Nehemiah 11:32 and Jeremiah 11:21–23. Evidently, "there shall be no remnant of them" meant that none of them would remain in their inheritance, for we find 128 "men of Anathoth" returning from the captivity (Ezra 2:23; Nehemiah 7:27).
30. Jeremiah 32:6–15, 25, 43–44.
31. "The mention of Jaddua as a high-priest, in chapter 12:11, 22, has occasioned much perplexity. This Jaddua appears to have been in office in 332 B C., when Alexander the Great came to Jerusalem (Josephus, *Antiquities* xi. 8): how then could he be named by Nehemiah? The common, and perhaps the fairest, escape from this difficulty, is to regard the naming of Jaddua as an addition by a later hand. Yet it is just credible that Nehemiah wrote it, if we bear in mind that he lived to be an old man, so as possibly to see the year 370 B.C.; and if we further suppose that Jaddua had at that time entered on his office, so that he filled it for about forty years, i.e., till 332 B.C.." Benjamin Davies, "Nehemiah, Book of," *Classic Bible Dictionary* (Lafayette, IN: Sovereign Grace, 1988), 841.
32. Josephus, *Antiquities,* XI, viii, 4–5. (See Book XI, chapter vii, for the genealogy of Jaddua).
33. Edward Gibbon, *Memoirs of My Life and Writings,* as quoted in *The Oxford Book of English Prose,* (Oxford University Press).
34. In the spring of 1989, having realized that I must write a book on another subject, I decided to attend the Mount Hermon Writer's Conference (Mt. Hermon, CA 95041). Since this involved two things which I hate, paying tuition and going to class, I cast about in my mind for ways to make the best of it. One of these was to submit the maximum number of manuscripts allowed (three) to the editors in attendance. The first was the more serious work I had (and still have) in mind. Since miracles can happen, I thought to myself, why not make the second manuscript my *Holy Week Sonnets?* But what to do for the third? Having twice taught a Bible study on the boring parts of the Bible, I wrote up a proposal, an outline, and a sample chapter (on Numbers 7) and submitted it with the others. Needless to say, it was the boring parts that most intrigued the editors. (As it turned out, the editors who encouraged me to write the book were unable to convince their publishing houses that it would sell. "Children have come to birth, but there is no strength to bring them forth" [Isaiah 37:3]. But the Lord provides.)
35. See Ezra 10:18–44. Though all of Nehemiah's lists were probably written later than Ezra's, I have chosen to treat this one last, because both authors made foreign wives their final subject.

    I wish I could remember who said, "John Calvin has been accused of many things, but never of being disorganized." I too have been accused of many things, but never of being organized.
36. Though the same Hebrew word occurs dozens of times in the Old Testament, here alone the translators changed it to "outlandish." (It is usually rendered "strange" in the King James).
37. If you are married to an unbelieving spouse, remember 1 Corinthians 7:13–16.

38. The Geneva and King James translators, followed by Noah Webster, thought that these four men were in charge of the work of putting away foreign wives. However, today most commentators and translators read the Hebrew as expressing their opposition to the work.
39. See Ezra 10:34–42. Another group by the same name is found in verse 29.
40. See Ezra 2:10.
41. See Exodus 20:5.
42. Commentators are not agreed as to whether the Jehiels of Ezra 10:2 and 10:26 are the same person. Henry and Gill think they are; Keil and Lange (Schultz) think not. Since none of them presents conclusive evidence, may we not consider this an area of Christian liberty? I believe the two Jehiels are one and the same, since both are descended from Elam, and because his father's involvement seems compatible with the language of Shechaniah.
43. It does mean that we should be slow to believe the worst about them. Our parents should be innocent in our eyes until their guilt is clearly established. (Guilt is established by evidence or by confession, *not* by slander).
44. See Ezra 10:23 and Nehemiah 8:7.

Appendix: Suggestions for Further Study

1. Spurgeon thought much of concordances and little of reference Bibles: "I make but small account of most *reference Bibles*; they would be very useful if they were good for anything; but it is extremely easy to bring out a reference Bible which has verbal and apparent references, and nothing more. . . . The useful reference cuts the diamond with a diamond, comparing spiritual things with spiritual; it is a thought-reference, and not a word-reference. If you meet with a really valuable reference Bible, it will be to you what I once heard a country man call 'a reverence Bible,' for it will lead you to prize more and more the sacred volume. The best reference Bible is a thoroughly good concordance. Get the best, keep it always on the table, use it hourly, and you will have found your best companion." Charles Spurgeon, *Commenting and Commentaries* (Grand Rapids: Baker, [1876] 1981), 26.
2. Item No. 100008, eleven dollars plus one dollar handling (in 1990), American Bible Society, P.O. Box 5656, Grand Central Station, New York, NY 10164–0851.
3. Discounters of Christian books advertise in many popular Christian magazines. The two I have used (and can therefore recommend) are Christian Book Distributors (Box 3687, Peabody, MA 01961–3687) and Great Christian Books (Box 8000, Elkton, MD 21921–8000). (Membership is optional at C. B. D., while G. C. B. charges a five dollars per year [eight dollars Canada] membership fee.) If you live near your discounter, request shipping via UPS. It's faster. If you live more than a few hundred miles from your discounter, consider shipping via the Post Office. It's cheaper, because the Post Office rate is the same anywhere in the U.S., while the

UPS rate increases with the distance travelled. (Addicts needing a "quick fix" should ship by Federal Express.)

4. Where many commentators assume that Matthew or his copyists made a mistake, Dr. Gill suggests another solution: " . . . the sacred writings were divided, by the Jews, into three parts: the first was called the law, which contains the five books of Moses; the second, the prophets, which contains the former and the latter prophets; the former prophets began at Joshua, and the latter at Jeremy [Jeremiah]; the third was called Cetubim, or the Hagiographa, the holy writings, which began with the book of Psalms: now, as this whole third and last part is called the Psalms, Luke 24:44, because it began with the book; so all that part which contained the latter prophets, for the same reason, beginning at Jeremy, might be called by his name; hence a passage, standing in the prophecy of Zechariah, who was one of the latter prophets, might be justly cited under the name of Jeremy. . . . It is to be observed, that the Jew [R. Isaac Chizzuk Emuna] who objects to every thing he could in the Evangelist . . . and even objects to the application of (this) prophecy, yet finds no fault with him for putting Jeremy for Zechariah" (Gill, *New Testament,* V, 286 [on Matthew 27:9]).

   Who besides Gill would tell us that a learned Jew objected to the application, but not to the attribution, of this prophecy? When the most knowledgeable of adverse critics accepts a statement in the Gospel, why should the friends of Jesus doubt it?

5. Consider these fine Henryisms: "The fear of God is the best antidote against the fear of man" (on Jeremiah 1:17). "Many who have no idols in their sanctuary have idols in their hearts . . . " (on Ezekiel 14:3–7).

6. John Gill (1697–1771) was a Baptist pastor in London for more than fifty years.

7. Gill's commentary (with verse-by-verse comments on the whole Bible) is available in a nine-volume edition from: Baptist Standard Bearer, Inc., 1 Iron Oaks Dr., Paris, AR 72855 (Phone: 501–963–3831). The retail price (1990) is $320, but the price to members is $225. This work may also be purchased from Great Christian Books (see note 3).

8. William Michael Rossetti, "Tintoretto," *Encyclopedia Britannica* (New York: Britannica, 1911 [11th ed.]), XXVI, 1003.

9. Gill's *Commentary* (Grand Rapids: Baker, 1980) I, xxxi.

10. Though I own a copy of the ultimate book on the subject (*Chocolate: The Consuming Passion,* "written, illustrated, and overresearched by Sandra Boynton" [New York: Workman, 1982]) I cannot tell what form of chocolate the Doctor consumed. Hot chocolate? Chocolate bars? Count Chocula? (Looking for a term paper topic?)

11. I cannot refrain from recommending to you Charles Spurgeon's *Commenting and Commentaries* (Grand Rapids: Kregel's, 1990). This delightful book, still in print after a century, provides an entertaining overview of the world of older Protestant expositors. (The new Kregel's edition [$9] tells you which of their works are still available, and from which publishers.) Whatever your theology, you are likely to enjoy Spurgeon's wit and

his advice on the judicious use of commentaries and other reference works.

12. *Treasury of Scripture Knowledge* (McLean, VA: MacDonald Publishers, 1982), clearly a reprint of an older edition. The Christian Book Distributors catalog lists this book (at $9.95) as the work of R. A. Torrey, an evangelist associated with D. L. Moody. My copy has no compiler's name. (I believe Torrey wrote only the preface.)
13. "A little Learning is a dang'rous thing;
Drink deep, or taste not the Pierian spring:
There shallow draughts intoxicate the brain,
And drinking largely sobers us again."
(Alexander Pope, "Essay on Criticism")
14. C. S. Lewis, *A Preface to Paradise Lost* (New York: Oxford, 1961), 4–5 (emphasis added). Lewis continues: "But if any man will read aloud on alternate mornings for a single month a page of Pindar and a page of the Psalms in any translation he chooses, I think I can guess which he will first grow tired of."
15. The Interlinear Bible is available in either one-or four-volume hardback editions from Hendrickson. Since I do not carry mine about, I prefer the four-volume set, which has larger type. However, the one-volume Interlinear Bible is portable, cheaper, and still legible. The four-volume set costs roughly sixty dollars through the major discounters; the one-volume price is thirty-five dollars. There is also a paperback edition published by Baker Books ($35 in 1990). It consists of four smaller paperbacks and uses the same size print as the one-volume hardback from Hendrickson.
16. 1. *The New Englishman's Hebrew/Aramaic Concordance to the Old Testament* (George Wigram's work enhanced by Green). 2. *The New Brown, Driver, and Briggs Hebrew and English Lexicon of the Old Testament.* 3. *The New Englishman's Greek Concordance of the New Testament* (Wigram's work enhanced by Green). 4. *The New Thayer's Greek-English Lexicon of the New Testament.* All these works are printed by Hendrickson Publishers (Peabody, MA) and may be ordered from Christian Book Distributors or Great Christian Books (see note 3). A 1990 C. B. D. catalog offered the four reference works for a total price of $78.80 plus shipping.
17. There are some books which make it easier to use certain Hebrew and Greek lexicons. Bruce Einspahr has compiled an *Index to Brown, Driver & Briggs Hebrew Lexicon* (Chicago: Moody Press, 1976) which guides you directly to the relevant section of that work. This is an expensive paperback, but it can save a lot of time. There is a similar work for the New Testament (John R. Alsop, *An Index to the Revised Bauer-Arndt-Gingrich Greek Lexicon* [Grand Rapids: Zondervan, 1981]), but I have used neither the index nor the lexicon enough to recommend them (1 Samuel 17:39).
18. Recognizing that pioneers have their limitations, I purchased John Kohlenberger's NIV Interlinear Hebrew-English Old Testament, which I use to supplement my studies in The Interlinear Bible. I also have Berry's interlinear New Testament. (If I could own only one interlinear, however, I would go with Mr. Green's).

SUBJECT INDEX

O

P

R

S

T

Scripture Index

About the Author

Philip Brown Rosenbaum was born and raised in Washington, D.C. Though he was an atheist in his youth, he earned a scholarship to St. Albans School by singing as a choirboy at the Washington Cathedral (Episcopal).

He attended a well-known New England university (which was a good Christian school in the seventeenth century), graduating with a B.A. in English. During and after college, he worked in residential programs for troubled boys, mostly in wilderness settings. He became a Christian in his mid-twenties. Since then he has taught Bible studies, preached occasionally, and done some biblical counseling.

He married Jeanne Chrissos in 1979. They have four children.

Since writing his first poem when he was thirty-four, he has published sonnets in a variety of Christian magazines. This is his first book.

The typeface for the text of this book is *Palatino*. This type—best known as a contemporary *italic* typeface—was a post-World War II design crafted by the talented young German calligrapher Hermann Zapf. For inspiration, Zapf drew upon the writing legacy of a group of Italian Renaissance writing masters, in which the typeface's namesake, Giovanni Battista Palatino, was numbered. Giovanni Palatino's *Libro nuovo d'imparare a scrivera* was published in Rome in 1540 and became one of the most used, wide-ranging writing manuals of the sixteenth century. Zapf was an apt student of the European masters, and contemporary *Palatino* is one of his contributions to modern typography.

Substantive Editing:
Michael S. Hyatt

Copy Editing:
Peggy Moon

Cover Design:
Steve Diggs & Friends
Nashville, Tennessee

Page Composition:
Xerox Ventura Publisher
Printware 720 IQ Laser Printer

Printing and Binding:
Maple-Vail Book Manufacturing Group
York, Pennsylvania

Cover Printing:
Strine Printing Company
York, Pennsylvania